Learning for Economic Self-Sufficiency

Constructing Pedagogies of Hope among Low-Income, Low-Literate Adults

A volume in
Adult Education Special Topics: Theory, Research and Practice in Lifelong Learning
Kathleen P. King, *Series Editor*

Learning for Economic Self-Sufficiency

Constructing Pedagogies of Hope among Low-Income, Low-Literate Adults

Edited by

Mary V. Alfred

Texas A&M University

IAP

INFORMATION AGE PUBLISHING, INC.
Charlotte, NC • www.infoagepub.com

Library of Congress Cataloging-in-Publication Data

Learning for economic self-sufficiency constructing pedagogies of hope among low-income, low-literate adults / edited by Mary V. Alfred.
p. cm. – (Adult education special topics)
Includes bibliographical references.
ISBN 978-1-61735-110-5 (pbk.) – ISBN 978-1-61735-111-2 (hardcover) – ISBN 978-1-61735-112-9 (e-book)
1. Higher education and state–United States. 2. Economics–Social aspects–United States. 3. United States–Social conditions–1980- I. Alfred, Mary Vianna, 1951-
LC173.L43 2010
378.1'9826942–dc22

2010027128

Printed in the United States of America

CONTENTS

INTRODUCTION AND CONTEXT

Mary V. Alfred and Noelle R. Eason
Texas A&M University

The National Education Goals Panel (1994) noted, "Every adult American will be literate and will possess the knowledge and skills necessary to compete in a global economy and exercise the rights and responsibilities of citizenship" (p. 10). Two of the objectives of the learning and lifelong goal were (1) that every major American business will be involved in strengthening the connection between education and work, and (2) that all workers will have the opportunity to acquire the knowledge and skills, from basic to highly technical, needed to adapt to emerging new technologies, work methods, and markets through public and private educational, vocational, technical, workplace, or other programs. While Americans remained hopeful that such objectives would be realized, a review of the 1993 National Adult Literacy Survey (NALS) created much doubt among adult education researchers that such a goal would be accomplished.

The NALS report revealed about 95% of Americans have at least a fourth-grade literacy rate but nearly half scored in the lowest two-thirds of the literacy levels the National Education Goals Panel (1994) deemed necessary for successful labor force participation. Although these findings were shocking 16 years ago, "research showed that it was possible, even likely, that Americans would continue to fail to achieve a fully literate society" (Wagner

Learning for Economic Self-Sufficiency, pages vii–xv

& Venezky, 1999, p. 21). The gravity of this statement is supported by the following additional data from the NALS report: Nearly 25% of America's adults with an average of 10 years of formal schooling had fourth-grade literacy skills or lower; among many of the ethnic minority groups, nearly 50% of the children complete 10 of the 12 years of compulsory education; low achievement in schools, early dropout from schools, and a continuous flow of low-literate immigrants exacerbate the low literacy rate among today's working adults (Wagner & Venezky, 1999).

In a more recent survey of The National Assessment of Adult Literacy (NAAL) (National Center for Adult Statistics, 2003), it was reported that 50% of American adults aged 16–65 function below the level necessary for success in the labor market; about one-third of prison inmates function at the lowest tier of the literacy ladder, and re-arrest rates of correctional education participants were lower than those of non-participants; and about 27% of patients with inadequate health literacy did not know how to accurately take their daily medication. Moreover, further analyses of NAAL found that salaries increased with each increase in literacy level and that income differences between whites and other minority groups tend to disappear when both literacy and education factors are statistically controlled (NCES, 2003). Moreover, the NAAL (2003) survey of 1,200 incarcerated adults found that almost no percentage of prisoners surveyed was found proficient when assessed in the areas of prose literacy, document literacy, and quantitative literacy. In the area of prose literacy, for example, only 4% of prison men and 1% of prison women demonstrated proficiency compared to 13% of household men and 14% of household women (Alfred & Chlup, 2009).

These data suggest a direct link between literacy and economic well-being (Berryman, 1994; The National Center for Adult Statistics, 1993, 2003; Wagner, 1992), indicating that more attention must be paid to the barriers to participation in education and employment training programs and the potential solutions or strategies to overcome these barriers. As Berryman (1994) noted, lack of education and training is the single-most distinguishing characteristic of the poor. Lacking preparation for the workplace, they are less likely to earn a living wage or to be trained by their employers, and they are more likely to be unemployed, be dependent on the welfare state, have chronic health problems, and have encounters with the criminal justice system.

THE MANY FACES OF LOW LITERACY AND POVERTY

Learning for Economic Self-Sufficiency: Constructing Pedagogies of Hope Among Low-Income, Low-Literate Adults explores learning, work, and other life conditions among low-literate, low-income and unemployed adults within various contexts. Noting that literacy is the first step to economic, mental, and physical health as well as responsible citizenship, each chapter provides case examples and recommendations for creating learning programs and environments that would facilitate the development of a more literate and economically stable population. The contributing authors examine how the compounding effects of these characteristics can trap adult learners in a downward spiral, despite good intentions of the learners themselves, other individuals, education institutions, community organizations, and governmental agencies. The book makes visible the many sectors of our society that are challenged to survive with low literacy and with limited economic resources. As one reads the chapters, it is important to note that while there are differences in context among those who have low literacy and low economic power, each group is not isolated or totally unique from the others, and that the issues intersect to present a portrait of a segment of society whose education and economic situation call for us to create and offer pedagogies of hope.

This book is organized into 13 chapters, beginning with a generalized look at low-literate and low-income adults within the environment of formal education, and, in later chapters, moves towards more contextually specific environments. In "Promises and Challenges for Institutions of Higher Education in Educating Low-Income Adult Learners," Catherine Hansman highlights the challenges low-income learners experience in their attempts to gain access to public institutions of higher education. She examines the growing trends and current policies and practices in higher education in the U.S. that narrow educational opportunities for poor and working-class adult learners. She then highlights certain university and community college programs that have been successful, and concludes with a discussion of actions that adult educators, institutional leaders, and policy makers can take to support low-income adult students' participation in higher education. Hansman concludes that adult educators should advocate for all adult learners while seeking to reform current policies that favor traditional-aged college students and lack attention to returning adult learners.

In "Riches from the Poor: Teaching Humanities in the Margins," Janet Groen and Tara Hyland-Russell confront the many misperceptions of low-literate and low-income adults learners who occupy spaces in the higher education classroom. The authors taught and researched in a free university-level humanities program in Canada, offering courses for people living in poverty. In working to build learning communities at the margins of dominant learning institutions and discourses, Groen and Hyland-Russell are constantly reminded of the need to reassess personal assumptions—as researchers, theorists, and teachers—because they note that they are often surprised and delighted by the zest and joy for learning demonstrated by the learners in these humanities programs.

We then turn the discussion to what is being done to specifically address low-literate and low-income adult learners' needs in "The Role of the Community College in Redirecting Careers of Low-Literate, Low-Income, and Low-Skilled Citizens" by Liliana Mina, Deryl Davis-Fulmer, and Regina Smith. Community colleges in the United States are the first site of entry for a majority of adult learners seeking to develop their academic and employment skills. As a result, the authors concur that these institutions attempt to respond to the needs of their communities by anticipating employment trends and offer education and training services for emerging and established businesses and organizations. They agree that even within the current economic crisis, community colleges are providing essential services for low-literate, low-income, and low-skilled citizens with specific focus on displaced homemakers, displaced workers, the homeless, prisoners (pre- and post-incarceration), and urban and rural citizens. Mina, Davis-Fulmer, and Smith end the chapter with recommendations for purposeful and structured interventions for those hard-to-reach adults, namely, those low-literate, low-income citizens who are residing in shelters, receiving services from churches and religious-based organizations, and living in rural and urban communities. No one entity, the authors argue, should be expected to solve these challenges of building economic health among those who have been excluded from education and employment that pays a living wage.

In "Using Technology to Improve Pedagogy and Empowerment with Low-Literacy Adults," Kathleen King notes that adult literacy students who have not mastered media literacies, technology literacies, and information literacies are often excluded from many economically viable opportunities. King proposes that adult literacy educational orientation, instruction, and programs should more completely incorporate the vital technology and related literacies so that adult learners develop proficiency. King contends that building experiences of exposure, learning, understanding, and meaningful dialogue around these technology uses for everyday life and work in the literacy classroom is indispensable in helping adult learners to develop greater economic viability. In this chapter, King recommends strategies to plan and deliver 21st century learning, which will leverage literacy practices for greater earning power for adult learners.

One of the underlying assumptions is that adult education is not only the process of acquiring new knowledge, but of adult learners' applying the new knowledge in a significant way that would lead to a host of benefits. By comprehensively assessing the current state of adult literacy education and the structures within which learning takes place, we can transition toward a better framework to meet learners' educational needs and thus support their economic self-empowerment. Without such deliberate interventions, low-literate, low-income adults will continue to experience a lower quality of life in terms of education, employment, economics, and healthcare, to name a few.

In the next chapter, Lilian H. Hill explores the serious personal health risks of low literacy in "The Connection Between Health Literacy and Adult Literacy in Developing Economic Self-Sufficiency." Hill notes that low literacy has been linked with not only poverty but also poor health outcomes, delayed/ incorrect diagnosis, compromised disease management skills, and higher health care costs. Nearly half of the U.S. population, according to statistics stated by Hill, ranks in the low health literacy range. The various implications include limited access to personal health care information including compromised understanding of disease-related information and even incorrect self-health assessment. Furthermore, Hill reports that low health literacy has been found to be prevalent among those with lower socioeconomic status, racial/ethnic minorities, and those living in rural communities, thus supporting Mina, Davis-Fulmer, and Smith's call for a more aggressive approach to educating these segments of the population.

Noting the interconnection between English and mathematics literacy and financial literacy, Larry Martin, in "Adult Learners in Urban Communities: Challenges and Opportunities for Economic Independence," discusses the meaning of financial self-sufficiency in American society. He highlights the challenges to low-income urban residents' economic independence and explores the resources, knowledge, and skills required for financial independence. Martin notes, for example, that government financial assistance programs such as welfare and state-supported healthcare were not chiefly designed as anti-poverty programs to assist individuals and their families toward becoming self-sufficient and financially independent. To achieve that next level of success often requires not only employment that pays family-supporting wages but also a different mindset, Martin asserts. He argues that individuals and their families must often change how they think about money, employment and careers, financial transactions, savings, and asset development. Martin closes his chapter by presenting several approaches adult educators and continuing educators can employ to assist low-income urban residents to develop and grow their economic assets via the provision of financial literacy education and training programs.

We expand the focus to examine low-literate, low-income adults in the workplace and the cultures, structures, policies, and practices that serve as barriers to their economic development. In "No Worker Left Behind: Providing Low-Wage Workers Equitable Access to Workplace Learning," Laura Bierema examines workplace learning to determine the extent to which learning and educational opportunities are available for workers in low-status, low-wage, and low-skill jobs. In this chapter she highlights the marginalized group of low-wage workers and critically assesses approaches to and investment in their workplace learning. Bierema found that much of the workplace learning literature and rhetoric does not apply to these adult learners. She found that while the number of low-wage jobs has grown in the U.S., the nature of these jobs implies that workers can expect few opportunities for training or advancement. Low-wage workers, Bierema reports, are predominantly women and the consequence of low-paying employment is often living near the poverty level. The author notes that workplace learning holds the potential to help low-wage workers improve their income and advancement prospects, but organizations must ensure equal access to workplace learning and provide meaningful development that leads to stable employment and advancement opportunities.

Educational institutions are not the only significant role players empowering adult learners for the workplace. E. Paulette Isaac explores the significant contribution of the church in "The Role of the Black Church in Developing Congregants for the Workplace." She makes the case that in the United States, there is a shrinking pool of qualified applicants, particularly qualified minorities, to fill job vacancies. To address the gap between vacancies and qualified employees, many employers have relied on colleges, universities, or proprietary schools to train individuals to meet the workforce needs, according to Isaac-Savage. For those willing and able to participate, post-secondary formal educational settings provide a viable option for employment training and the development of workplace skills. However, Isaac reminds us that low-literate adults sometimes are unable, embarrassed, or without the desire to participate in such public settings. Thus, she makes the case that the church offers another conduit for learning and that the Black church has contributed to the education and employment skills training of its congregants. Further, it presents a unique opportunity for adult educators, colleges, and universities as well as businesses to partner with the church to promote economic development among community members.

The next few chapters provide insights to the lives of adult learners in highly specific working, learning, and living contexts. "Learning on the Move: Migrant Workers in Adult Education" by Aida A. Nevárez-La Torre examines the educational struggles within migrant education for both participants and institutions alike. Nevárez-La Torre explores the compounding issues of providing quality education for migrant workers, including a lack of appropriate language services and the conflicts of learning on the move. She asserts that educating highly mobile adult students demands creative alternatives to obtain an education and break the cycle of travel and poverty. The author closes the chapter by offering innovative strategies towards achieving this goal and discusses key areas of need, including the development of a cohesive system for information gathering and sharing, a relevant curriculum, and the restructuring of programs to make adult migrants visible.

All too often in popular discourse, low-income, low-literate adult learners are only considered from a deficit perspective, according to Jennifer A. Sandlin in "Consumption, Gendered Stereotypes, and the Struggle for Respect: Controlling Images of Poor Women as Consumers in Popular, Political, and Adult Education Discourses." Sandlin examines dominant discourses about poor women as consumers in public culture and how these stereotypes have infiltrated adult basic education programs, with curricula that present a deficit perspective that blames poor, low-literate women for their economic situations. Adult literacy learners, she found, are often taught using texts that assume they make poor decisions; are wasteful overspenders, impulsive, disorganized; and have absent value systems. Sandlin uses what she terms "critical description" to examine the racism, classism, and sexism in these discourses. Negative discourses circulating within adult education programs about poor women as consumers, contends Sandlin, create yet another barrier women must fight against in their struggle for economic self-sufficiency.

As an immigrant society, Canada has had success with certain innovative educational programs aimed at adult learners. In the chapter "Learning for Self-Sufficiency Among Immigrants in Canada: The Role of Community-Based Adult Education," Shibao Guo highlights programmatic approaches by the Canadian government and community groups to empower immigrants to Canada. Similar to the plight of migrant workers in the U.S., Guo notes that new immigrants to Canada face a number of barriers, including language and cultural barriers, integrating into the labor force, lack of social networks, devaluation of their prior learning and work experience, racism, and other systemic barriers. Guo highlights that with the erosion of the welfare state and the subsequent downsizing of its settlement programs, community organizations took on greater responsibility for the development of programs to assist immigrants with their settlement and in achieving self-sufficiency. He draws from case study research to examine the role of community-based organizations in helping immigrants achieve self-sufficiency. In this chapter Guo illustrates the role of grassroots organizations as important sites for emancipatory learning and social action.

Dominique T. Chlup and Irene C. Baird bring to focus another marginalized group of adults with a high percentage of low literacy and underpreparation for the workplace—adults who experience the criminal justice system. In "Literacies from the Inside: Learning From and Within a Culture of Corrections," the authors provide illustrations of literacy education programs established in adult correctional facilities and explain how writing and literacy education practices are connected to the pursuit of economic self-sufficiency among low-literate and low-income prisoners. They discuss the constraints of working in a culture of corrections and provide case examples that demonstrate "pockets of hope," and make recommendations on how to create programs and environments that facilitate the development of literate and potentially economically stable inmates equipped to re-enter the civilian community.

The overall objective of the book is to explore economic self-sufficiency among low-income and low-literate adults from various contexts and the role of adult, higher, and community education as well as the workplace in developing learners for greater economic independence. Developing adults for economic well-being is a complex, multi-layered undertaking that must include the personal as well as the structural dimensions of development. In the concluding chapter, Mary Alfred provides some insights on the role of social capital—along with elements of the structural dimensions to include the philosophies and ideologies of government, the workplace, education, and other institutions for a more comprehensive approach to human development.

TARGET AUDIENCE

Learning for Economic Self-Sufficiency: Constructing Pedagogies of Hope Among Low-Income, Low-Literate Adults is an important literary contribution as it highlights the problems and issues that low-literate adults encounter in various environments, and it presents strategies for addressing the chronic low literacy among low-income workers. While many of the issues that are addressed in the book have been identified individually and under separate publications, the power of this book is that the reader will have a more holistic view of the complexities of educating a population of low-literate learners from various life conditions.

Learning for Economic Self-Sufficiency: Constructing Pedagogies of Hope Among Low-Income, Low-Literate Adults will have wide appeal among adult education researchers and practitioners alike. Because it addresses literacy and economic self-sufficiency among various population groups, those interested in one or more of these groups will find value in the book as it will highlight challenges and provide suggested approaches to addressing the problems within that context. Additionally, the book will be an excellent source for a foundation course in adult literacy—one that is offered in many university adult education programs. It will also be an excellent textbook for a course in sociology that addresses contemporary social issues in education and society. Finally, this book can serve as a reference book for practitioners who are interested in improving the practice of adult education in one or more of the various contexts identified.

REFERENCES

Alfred, M. V., & Chlup, D. T. (2009). Neoliberalism, illiteracy, and poverty: Framing the rise in black women's incarceration. *The Western Journal of Black Studies, 33*(4), 240–249.

Berryman, S. E. (1994). *The role of literacy in the wealth of individuals and nations.* NCAL Technical Report TR94-13. Philadelphia: University of Pennsylvania, National Center for Adult Literacy.

National Center for Education Statistics. (1993). *National adult literacy survey.* Washington, DC: Author.

National Center for Education Statistics. (2003). *National assessment of adult literacy.* Washington, DC: Author.

National Education Goals Panel. (1994). *Building a nation of learners.* Washington, DC: U.S. Government Printing Office.

Wagner, D. A. (1992). World literacy: Research and policy in the EFA decade. *The Annals of the American Academy of Political and Social Science, 20*(1), 15–26.

Wagner, D. A., & Venezky, R. L. (1999). Adult learning: The next generation. *Educational Researcher, 28,* 21–29.

CHAPTER 1

PROMISES AND CHALLENGES FOR INSTITUTIONS OF HIGHER EDUCATION IN EDUCATING LOW-INCOME ADULT LEARNERS

Catherine A. Hansman
Cleveland State University

INTRODUCTION AND STORY

Rita was a "second chance" student at the urban university campus—an adult who, because of a myriad of economic and personal challenges, was entering higher education for the first time at the age of 33. She was also a first-generation college student—no one in her family had previously graduated or even attended college. Rita, a single parent, was determined to earn her degree in nursing and get out of the trap of the low-income jobs in which she had worked since she was 15. Although the urban campus where she was planning on enrolling served a large population of adult learners, Rita was surprised to learn that there was no special office for "returning second-chance" adults to which she could turn with questions. She

Learning for Economic Self-Sufficiency, pages 1–13

attended an "adult student orientation" a few weeks before the semester began and after 15 minutes with an advisor, signed up for classes. Once she was registered for classes, she made arrangements with a neighbor to take care of her three children while she was attending classes. She thought she was ready to embark on her college career.

From the beginning of her first classes, however, Rita encountered difficulties. She did not understand how to apply for financial aid or even know what a FASFA (Free Application for Federal Student Aid) form was. By the time she went to the campus financial aid office and filled one out she was too late to receive anything but minimal loans, even though she would have qualified for Pell grants if only she had applied earlier. No one in Rita's circle of friends and family had previously attended an institution of higher education, so she did not know that she would have to pay for parking and buy books, all expenses she hadn't counted on when she first figured out her school budget. Even though many of the students in her classes on campus were also "second chance" students, the university had no central office or gathering place for older students that might have provided some support and guidance for her. As the semester wore on, although she attended her classes regularly, she fell behind in some the work for her classes and the tutoring center did not have evening hours for students. Finally, her babysitter quit unexpectedly, Rita's car broke down, and, frustrated, she quit going to classes, thinking she would return in another semester once she solved her child-care issues and her other problems.

Two semesters later, Rita had found solutions to the child-care issues and returned to campus to register for classes, but she ran into new barriers. Because she had not understood that she needed to formally withdraw from the classes she had started previously, she had simply quit going, and she had received failing grades for all those classes. Because of her failing grades, and because she had not attended school long enough, financial aid had not covered her previous classes and she realized that she owed the university for the prior semester. She would have to pay this debt before she could even register for new classes. To make matters worse, a new university policy required the university registrar to turn her name in to a collection agency to try to recover the tuition. Rita, needless to say, felt defeated and rejected by the very institution she had hoped would help her attain a better life.

As this story illustrates, low-income adult learners' access to higher education is many times stifled and blocked by the very systems that purport to help them. Added to this failure is adult learners' lack of knowledge about higher education systems and how to enter and successfully exit with a college degree. A variety of interlocking barriers limit access to higher education for low-income adults; among these are restrictive welfare to work policies that focus on participants obtaining low-paying jobs rather than assisting them with educational opportunities that might permit them to better provide for their families and to participate more fully in a knowledge-based society (Carnevale & Desrochers, 2004; Cook & King, 2004; Hansman, 2006). Other barriers include governmental and institutional policies that favor traditional-aged college students, limited financial aid for adult students, a lack of support for adults by higher education institutions, and the continuing cycle of poverty itself. The purpose of this chapter is to examine the growing trends and current policies and practices in higher education in the United States that narrow educational opportunities for poor and working-class adult learners, examine some university and community college programs that have been successful, and conclude with a discussion of actions that adult educators, institutional leaders, and policy makers must take to support low-income adult students' participation in higher education.

POVERTY AND LOW-INCOME ADULT LEARNERS

In 2007, 12.5% of the United States population or 37.5 million people lived in poverty (DeNavas-Walt, Proctor, & Smith, 2008). Further examination of poverty ratings reveals that women and minorities are disproportionately represented: Women make up 69% of low-income workers, and African Americans and Hispanics make up 50% of those in poverty (Hansman, 2006). Contributing to poverty rates are the numbers of adults who have not continued their education beyond their high school diplomas or General Education Development (GED) certificates and are therefore disqualified from higher paying employment. Approximately 54 million people in the labor force have not completed a college degree and 34 million have never attended any higher educational institutions (Pusser et al., 2007). "Over 60 percent of the US population between the ages of 25 and 64 had no postsecondary educational credential in 2004... demographic shifts are expected to worsen the gap between qualifications and job demands, creating a shortage of 9 million qualified workers by 2014" (Kazis et al., 2007, p. 1).

A large number of low-income adults age 16 or older are unemployed, and of those classified as in poverty, 70% work part-time and 34% work in service positions with no hope of advancement or benefits (Cook & King, 2004). Seven out of ten adults categorized as the working poor have a high school education or less, and 10 million Americans have not earned beyond an associate degree (Hansman, 2006). Poor adults find themselves trapped in low-wage jobs with little expectation of leaving poverty behind.

LOW-INCOME ADULTS IN HIGHER EDUCATION

Having the ability to participate in higher education is essential for low-income adult learners to achieve self-sufficiency, greater economic independence, a higher quality of life, and further, participation in a democratic society. Previous generations were able to negotiate a high school diploma or a GED diploma into a living-wage job, but "the knowledge economy and global industrial production have necessitated postsecondary education—individually and nationally" (Pusser et al., 2007, p. 1). Postsecondary credentials will become increasingly essential for future employment. According to Kazis et al. (2007), "15 of the 20 occupations predicted to grow the fastest (in terms of percentage growth in new and vacant positions) require some form of postsecondary education, while nine require a Bachelor's degree or better." (p. 4) In addition, 2003 census data showed that the median earnings of a person with only a high school diploma were 38% less than that of someone who had earned a bachelor's degree (Kazis et al., 2007).

The decline in educational attainment by adults is happening concurrently with the rise of a knowledge-based economy that requires higher levels of education by its workers. As well-educated baby boomers retire, the younger generation entering the workforce who are replacing them are more racially and ethnically diverse (The National Center for Public Policy and Higher Education, 2005) and have historically been less well-served by educational systems. This leads to a workforce that may not be educationally prepared for current and future jobs. The National Center for Public Policy and Higher Education (2005) contend, "The racial/ethnic groups that are the least educated are the fastest growing. If current population trends continue and states do not improve the education of all racial/ethnic groups, the skills of the workforce and the incomes of U.S. residents are projected to decline over the next two decades" (p. 1).

Race and class issues shape who will participate in the future workforce and who will be able to gain access to higher education in the future. According to The National Center for Public Policy and Higher Education (2005), the gap between White Americans with a bachelor's degree or higher and African Americans and Hispanics/Latinos with this degree has widened and continues to grow. The 2000 census data show that White Americans are twice as likely as African Americans and three times as likely as Hispanics/Latinos to earn bachelor's degrees (Kazis et al., 2007). Groups historically marginalized by race or class continue to struggle to engage in educational opportunities and encounter many barriers to participation, especially financial barriers. Although the need for education and training is essential for individuals in order to obtain a living-wage job, educational participation patterns still show that what has been true in the past remains true (Merriam, Caffarella, & Baumgartner, 2007; Hansman & Mott, in press): Those who are already educated continue to participate in educational activities to improve their quality of life, while low-income adult learners, for many reasons, struggle to enter and successfully exit higher education institutions.

THE DOOR TO HIGHER EDUCATION: HALF OPEN FOR LOW-INCOME ADULTS

Adult learners in higher education may have several characteristics that can be viewed as risk factors to their persistence and success. These characteristics are particularly relevant to low-income adults and include (1) delayed enrollment in postsecondary education beyond the first year after high school graduation, (2) part-time attendance, (3) financial independence from parents, (4) full-time work, (5) having dependents (other than a spouse), (6) being a single parent, and (7) no high school diploma or GED (Kazis et al., 2007, pp. 8–9).

Low-income adult learners may face additional personal, structural, and institutional barriers to participating in higher education and becoming economically self-sufficient, including "health crisis, inadequate and unstable housing, mental health problems, alcohol and drug dependence, domestic violence, poor access to day care and lack of transportation" (Alfred, 2006, p. 109). According to Sander (2008), 60% of adult students are from single-income households.

Cook and King (2004) compiled the following challenges cited by low-income adult learners: (1) competing demands of work, family, education, and the need for a social life; (2) difficulties financing higher education; (3) receiving inadequate advising and counseling from higher education institutions; and (4) self-esteem issues. Additional institutional and policy barriers are (1) restrictive Welfare Reform Act and Work First Policies, (2) lack of higher education programs and policies that address the needs of adult learners in general and low-income adults in particular, (3) the rising cost of higher education, and (4) financial aid policies that do not meet the expenses of college students. Most institutions of higher education are ill-equipped to handle these issues and to assist adult learners to find the help they need in order to participate in higher education.

Welfare Reform and Work-First Policies

Work First Policies were crafted in the booming economy of the 1990s and, therefore, they have not translated well to the current economy, which requires more educational achievement to participate in the workforce

(Alfred, Butterwick, Hansman, & Sandlin, 2007; Hansman, 2006). Work First Policies essentially move people from public dependency to working in low-skill and low-wage jobs, still in poverty with no way out. Wilkerson (1996) described the cycle of policies, rules, and structures that prevent low-income adults from participating in educational opportunities as trying to "punish them out of being poor" (Wilkerson, 1996, p. 373).

University Programs and Policies that Favor "Traditional" College Students

Despite the growing number of adult learners or "non-traditional" students on four-year college campuses, adult learners on university campuses are "punished" in favor of policies, curriculum, programming, and missions that favor traditional-age students (Sissel, Hansman, & Kasworm, 2001). As money for higher education dries up at state and national levels, traditional-age students, aged 18–24, with middle-class or upper-class parents who are willing to pay for their education, are favored on college campuses. "First chance" systems and programs are tailored to benefit traditional-aged students and focus on their needs in higher education, while many adult learners, particularly those in Work First Programs, are relegated to "second chance" educational systems, which typically consist of short-term, job-specific training events outside of universities or four-year educational institutions that teach non-transferable skills, making the employability of these adults vulnerable to technology changes and competition in the workforce (Carnevale & Desrochers, 2004; Hansman, 2006). While vocational retraining programs, contract education, and non-credit bearing programs can provide short-term job skills and employment for low-income adults (Pusser et al., 2007), they also need access to degree programs that will help them become and remain competitive now and into the future.

Particularly if they are the first generation in their family to attend institutions of higher education, low-income adults face a confusing and difficult array of choices as they enter higher education. Even with the rising numbers of adult learners on university campuses, many universities continue to disregard the needs of adult learners. Key offices, such as the office of the registrar, advising services and financial aid, are not kept open into the evening so that working adults may take advantage of their services. Although some universities do provide services for adult learners, many others still focus recruiting and retention efforts on traditional-aged students (Hansman, 2006).

Finally, since many low-income adult students are also first-generation college students, they must negotiate the confusing application and financial aid process frequently with little help from the university at which they are applying (Alfred, Butterwick, Hansman & Sandlin, 2007; Hansman, 2006). Hegemonic structures keep low-income adult learners marginalized regarding higher education, resulting in this group of marginalized adults becoming disenfranchised from the educational opportunities that could help them gain self-sufficiency.

Costs, Financial Aid, and Funding

States are slashing funding for higher education across the nation, resulting in steep tuition hikes, which further affect adult learners. In Ohio, the average yearly tuition per pupil at state universities rose from $4816 in 2001 to $6843 in 2004 (Koff & Gonzales, 2004). Between 2002 and 2003, 16 states increased tuition and fees by more than 10%, and10 states increased the same for community colleges (Hansman, 2006). Despite tuition increases, state funding of grants to students decreased overall. Between 2002 and 2003, Massachusetts' tuition and fees rose 24% while at the same time financial aid to students decreased 24% (Heather, 2003). Most are facing tuition hikes, and because most states have decreased the amount of funding for public higher educational institutions, students are paying a higher percentage of the total cost (Delta Project, 2009). In most states, students at public research institutions pay 51% of the total costs of their education. Due to lack of state funding, "students at public research institutions in Ohio now are charged for fully 65% of the cost of their education—an increase of 10 percentage points between 2002 and 2006" (Yantek, 2009, p. A7).

Because of the rising cost of tuition, access to financial aid for all students, particularly for low-income adults, is essential. Most financial aid/scholarships, however, focus on the 18–22-year-old population. Many low-income adult learners are part-time students and unfortunately, most financial aid that is available favors full-time students. Many students may turn to private bank loans—an option usually not open to low-income adult learners.

PROPPING THE DOOR OPEN: SUPPORTIVE PROGRAMS AND POLICIES

According to Alfred (2006), "the purpose of education should be to situate the individual in a stronger position to compete for better employment opportunities while promoting equity and justice for a more tolerant society" (p. 114). Despite the obstacles and barriers that impede low-income adults from fully participating in higher education, some states and institutions are responsive to adult learners. Various programs have proved helpful in attracting and retaining learners. The following are several examples of programs and initiatives that are currently in place to assist adult learners.

Kentucky

Many states realize that their workers will need higher education to compete in the changing workforce. Kentucky would like to double the number of adults they have in the workforce, but in order to do this, they must assist almost half of a million of their adult citizens who obtained some college credits but never completed a degree. Kentucky plans to devise ways to make the state's higher education system more user-friendly for their adult students through focusing on financial aid and student support services. All of the public universities in the state, as well as the community and technical colleges, are part of this arrangement. Another key element of this plan is to provide professional development to faculty members who work with adult students to further their understanding of adult learners. As part of their marketing of this program to adult learners, Kentucky administrators have designed a website that promises "exclusive incentives" to returning adult students, such as priority enrollment, financial assistance, individual advising, and a free application process. Morehouse State University has created a scholarship fund that can provide from $600 to $2640 to each adult student who cannot qualify for federal financial aid because they are only attending classes on a part-time basis (Sander, 2008). Because the Kentucky plan is so new, it is too early to accurately measure its success at helping adult learners complete degree programs and also how many low-income adults will participate. Kentucky will need continual support from its governor and legislative body to help financially support the programs.

Ohio

Kent State University and Ohio University in Ohio are attempting to address the 1.5 million adults in Ohio who have obtained some college credit but have not earned a degree. Jointly, they have 14 campuses that serve more than 60,000 students. Through their partnership, they will share a total of 12 existing degree programs and will mutually develop other market-driven programs. The advantage to this program is that it will provide access for adults pursuing degree programs at universities within driving distance, giving them more options for careers. Classes and programs will also be offered through convenient formats, such as online classes and distance learning venues, which will allow flexibility for students who may not be able to drive to campus to attend classes (Edler, 2006). These formats can be particularly helpful to low-income adults who may have transportation issues.

New Mexico

The University of New Mexico Graduation Project enables adult learners who dropped out of the university to return to finish their degrees. The mission of the Graduation Project is to “facilitate the graduation for students who left the university for one reason or another, provide timely support and act as a ‘home base’ for students returning to the university through the project” (University of New Mexico, 2009, n.p.). Through research, program planners identified three main reasons adult learners had not completed their degrees: the financial inability to afford tuition, lack of access to advisors, and the inability to enroll into the specific classes they needed for graduation. The university addressed these needs through giving tuition awards from the Board of Regents, creating advising centers focused on adult learners, and helping students get into closed classes so they can complete their degrees.

Utah

The University of Utah has begun a program entitled *Returning to the U* to attract adult learners who have some college credits but who never completed a degree. To help these students, the university received private funds that allowed it to make $50,000 in scholarships available to students. To be eligible, however, the student must have already completed at least 90 credit hours (Sander, 2008).

Western Interstate Commission for Higher Education

The Western Interstate Commission for Higher Education created the program *Non-traditional No More: Policy Solutions for Adult Learners* from a grant from the Lumina Foundation. The program is a two-year project that increases access and promotes success for the adult learner population in postsecondary education. Arkansas, Colorado, Nevada, New Jersey, and South Dakota are currently participating in the program. The project employs two strategies: (1) *Identifying Ready Adults*, a process of locating adults who are close to completing a degree but have not yet returned to college, and (2) *Building a Path to College Success*, a comprehensive focus on academic policies, financial aid/financing, student support services, and communications marketing and information strategies designed to reach out to the ready adult population (Western Interstate Commission for Higher Education, 2009).

Nellie Mae Education Foundation New England ABE-to-College Transition Project

This project operates in 25 adult education programs in New England that partner with more than 40 postsecondary institutions in the region, preparing adults who have earned a GED certificate or External Diploma Program (EDP) certificate to enter higher education and succeed. The ABE-College-Transition Project "helps students prepare academically, but also helps them navigate the culture of higher education, from securing student aid to choosing courses" (Donahue, 2008, p. 22). The project has been so successful thus far that the Maine Legislature has adopted ideas from the program for their own adult college transition program.

Center for Women and Returning Adults

Indiana University–Purdue University Ft. Wayne provides a continuum of services to adult learners who are either new or returning to higher education. Among these services are academic, financial, and personal guidance; Adult Student Orientation at the beginning of each semester; Freshman Success Classes specifically geared to adult learners; scholarship resources for women and adult learners; and "Students with Families" programs that encourage students to involve their families in their school life (Center for Women and Returning Adults, 2009; Rapport, 2006). The center is particularly helpful to students who are first generation to higher education.

HOLDING THE DOOR OPEN: ADULT EDUCATORS AS ADVOCATES

While Kentucky, Ohio, New Mexico, Utah and the other states and programs discussed above are making attempts to reach adult learners, these programs will only help low-income adult learners who have already been successful in completing some college. States should develop similar programs that assist adults with no or little higher education to navigate the path into higher education, including one-stop centers for advising, registration, and expanded financial aid options. In addition, as the Nellie Mae Education Foundation New England ABE-to-College Transition Project illustrates, literacy programs should partner with institutions of higher education in structuring the most effective programs to assist these low-income adult students into higher education.

There are still many areas that need to be addressed to help low-income adults have greater access to and success in higher education. Chief among these issues is the spiraling cost of college tuition combined with shrinking financial support options from states for higher education. There may be some hope on the horizon to accelerate increase in funding for Pell grants for low-income students in the Obama administration's economic stimulus package. Currently, the bill would accelerate Pell grant funding to a new annual level of $5,231 per eligible student (National Association of Student Financial Aid Administrators, 2009). As welcome as this increase in funding would be, low-income adult learners need much more aid made available to them in order to be able to attend institutions of higher education. In the absence of state or federal funding, universities should increase partnerships with private non-profit and for-profit businesses that may be able to help pay tuition and fees or provide other benefits for this group of learners. In Dubuque, Iowa, in an effort to increase the domestic workforce in a region of the country with high unemployment rates, IBM is opening a remote computer services center that will employ up to 1,300 people. The city of Dubuque is providing $52 million in financial support and tax breaks, and Kirkwood Community College has developed a two-year degree program for IBM employees that will provide them with a broad background in computing (Borg, 2009). Although employees will be trained in a technical degree to fit the needs of IBM, they will still earn an associate's degree that will qualify them for work not only at IBM but for other employers in the future. Graduates should also be able to continue at a four-year institution if they so choose. These kinds of partnerships, although quite expensive and difficult to negotiate, particularly in the dismal economic times we are currently experiencing, should serve as a blueprint for other communities and higher educational institutions.

It is essential that adult educators be proactive on their campuses regarding procedures and policies that can assist low-income adult learners to become successful students and graduates. Adult educators should advocate for all adult learners while seeking to reform policies that favor traditional-aged college students and "punish" returning adult learners. Adult educators can partner with other university staff and faculty to develop and sponsor on-campus mentoring, tutoring, and advising programs and centers that support and sustain low-income adult learners and their families. In addition, adult educators can provide much-needed staff development workshops to university faculty and administrators who may not have much experience working with adult learners. Adult educators as researchers should focus their efforts on not only studying adult learners who are on campuses but also devising studies that can further the development of supportive and caring programs for low-income adults that will help them access and successfully navigate the culture of higher education. Finally, adult educators must be activists and advocates for low-income adult learners and represent the voices of these learners who are frequently missing from the discourse of higher education policies. As educators, our purpose should include empowering learners to become competitive in the job market and critical thinkers in a democratic society. Through listening to and representing the missing voices, perhaps learners like Rita will have opportunities to participate and succeed in our society.

REFERENCES

Alfred, M. (2006). Race, politics and economic self-sufficiency in a culture of welfare reform. In S. M. Merriam, B. C. Courteney, & R. Cervero (Eds.), *Global issues and adult education: Perspectives from Latin America, Southern Africa and the United States* (pp. 106–117). San Francisco: Jossey-Bass.

Alfred, M., Butterwick, S., Hansman, C. & Sandlin, J. (2007). Neoliberal welfare reform, poverty, and adult education: Identifying the problem and engaging in resistance. In L. Savage & T. Fenwick (Eds.), *Learning in community: Proceedings of the Joint International Conference of the Adult Education Research Conference (AERC) and the Canadian Association for the Study of Adult Education (CASAE),* (pp. 669–676). Halifax, Nova Scotia: Canada.

Borg, D. (2009, February 2). *IBM To Open Center, Bring New Jobs To Dubuque: Morning Edition* [Radio broadcast]. Washington, DC: National Public Radio.

Carnevale, A. P., & Desrochers, D. M. (2004). Guest essay. In B. Cook & J. E. King (Eds.), *Low-income adults in profile: Improving lives through higher education* (pp. 33–43). Washington, DC: American Council on Education Center for Policy Analysis. Retrieved April 5, 2004, from http://www.acenet.edu

Cook, B., & King, J. E. (2004). *Low-income adults in profile: Improving lives through higher education.* Washington, DC: American Council on Education Center for Policy Analysis. Retrieved April 5, 2004, from http://www.acenet.edu

Delta Project on Postsecondary Education Costs, Productivity, & Accountability. (2009). *Trends in college spending: Where does the money come from? Where does it go?* Retrieved January 28, 2009, from http://deltacostsproject.org

DeNavas-Walt, C., Proctor, B. D., & Smith, J. C. (2008). *U. S. Census Bureau, current population reports: Income, poverty, and health insurance coverage in the United States: 2007.* Washington, DC: U.S. Government Printing Office.

Donahue, N. C. (2008). Adult education: From terminal degree to lifelong learning. *New England Board of Higher Education, 22*(4), 22–23.

Edler, M. (2006, Fall). *Complete to compete: Kent State, Ohio University join forces to help working adults finish degrees.* Retrieved December 31, 2008, from http://www.kent.edu/Magazine/Fall2006/CompleteToCompete.cfm

Hansman, C. A. (2006). Low-income adult learners in higher education: Politics, policies, and praxis. In S. M. Merriam, B. C. Courteney, & R. Cervero (Eds.),

Global issues and adult education: Perspectives from Latin America, Southern Africa and the United States (pp. 399–411). San Francisco: Jossey-Bass.

Hansman, C. A., & Mott, V. W. (2010). Who are adult learners? Definitions, demographics, and related discussions. In A. Rose, J. Ross-Gordon, & C. Kasworm (Eds.), *Handbook on adult and continuing education* (pp. 13–23). Thousand Oaks, CA: Sage.

Heather, J. (2003). *Public college tuition soars, higher education appropriations plummet—College affordability in jeopardy.* San Jose, CA: National Center for Public Policy and Higher Education. Retrieved February 9, 2005, from http://www.highereducation.org

Kazis, R., Callahan, A., Davidson, C., McLeod, A., Bosworth, B., Choitz, V., et al. (2007). *Adult learners in higher education: Employment and training administration occasional paper 2007–03.* Washington, DC: U.S. Department of Labor, Employment and Training Administration, Office of Policy Development and Research by Jobs for the Future.

Koff, S., & Gonzalez, J. (2004, April 16). Kerry blames Bush for tuition spike. *Cleveland Plain Dealer*, p. A2.

Merriam, S., Caffarella, R., & Baumgartner, L. (2007). *Learning in adulthood: A comprehensive guide (3rd edition).* San Francisco: Jossey-Bass.

National Association of Student Financial Aid Administrators. (2009). *Plan for second economic stimulus package could include pell increase, education tax credit.* Retrieved January 28, 2009, from http://www.nasfaa.org/publications/2009/gstimulusdraft011409.html

National Center for Public Policy and Higher Education (2005). *Policy alert: Income of U.S. workforce to decline if education doesn't improve.* Retrieved December 20, 2008, from http://www.highereducation.org

Pusser, B., Breneman, D. W., Gansneder, B. M., Kohl, K. J., Levin, J. S., Milam, J. H., & Turner, S.E. (2007). *Returning to learning: Adults' success in college is key to America's future.* Indianapolis: Lumina Foundation for Education New Agenda Series.

Rapport. (2006). *Center for Women and Returning Adults.* Retrieved January 4, 2009, from http://www.ipfw.edu/cwra/Newsletter/PDFs/RapportNewsletter-FALL06.pdf

Sander, L. (2008, February 15). Colleges woo adults who have some credits but no degree. *Chronicle of Higher Education, 54*(23), p. A 29.

Sissel, P., Hansman, C. A., & Kasworm, C. (2001). The politics of neglect: Adult learners in higher education. In C. A. Hansman & P. Sissel (Eds.), *Understanding and negotiating the political landscape of adult education* (pp. 17–27). New Directions for Adult and Continuing Education, no. 91. San Francisco: Jossey-Bass.

University of New Mexico. (2009). *The Graduation Project.* Retrieved January 15, 2009, from http://www.wiche.edu/policy/readyAdults/meetings/co-08Oct/Handout-TheGradProject.pdf

Western Interstate Commission for Higher Education (2009). Home page. Retrieved January 15, 2009, from http://www2.wiche.edu/index.php?q=ntnm

Wilkerson, D. (1996). Punishing people out of poverty: Jobs, welfare, and community concern. In D. Dujon & A. Withorn (Eds.), *For crying out loud: Women's poverty in the United States* (pp. 369–377). Boston: South End Press.

Yantek, T. (2009, January 31). Why are Ohioans paying a higher cost for higher education? *Cleveland Plain Dealer*, pg. A7.

CHAPTER 2

THE ROLE OF THE COMMUNITY COLLEGE IN REDIRECTING CAREERS OF LOW-LITERATE, LOW-INCOME, AND LOW-SKILLED CITIZENS

Liliana Mina
University of Wisconsin–Milwaukee

Deryl Davis Fulmer
Madison Area Technical College

Regina O. Smith
University of Wisconsin–Milwaukee

INTRODUCTION

Two of the major roles community colleges play in the United States are to promptly respond to the needs of their communities by anticipating employment trends and to proactively offer education and training services for

Learning for Economic Self-Sufficiency, pages 15–28

emerging and established businesses and organizations. Besides addressing issues affecting their districts, community colleges also offer entry-level training programs for low-literate, low-income, and low-skilled citizens. At this time, however, delivery of these services is particularly challenging to produce due to the dire circumstances of the U.S. economy and the world financial crisis (Adela & Stinson, 2008). We begin the first segment of the chapter with a snapshot of the current economic crisis and its impact on American citizens in general. We then briefly identify ways community colleges provide services to their constituents for greater inclusion in our society. The second segment of the chapter highlights essential services community colleges are providing for low-literate, low-income, and low-skilled citizens by presenting three case studies within a family unit. We intertwine their experiences as low-literate, low-income, and low-skilled citizens and simultaneously focus on the following populations: (1) displaced homemakers, (2) displaced workers, (3) the homeless, (4) prisoners (pre- and post-incarceration), and (5) urban and rural citizens. Included in this segment are exemplary community college practices that are positively redirecting their socioeconomic status; accordingly, they can take full advantage of the resources that lead to achievement and increasing upward mobility. The third segment of the chapter provides salient information useful to community college administrators and practitioners as they deal with meeting the needs of these groups of learners. We conclude the chapter with implications for practice.

The subsequent terms are defined in the context in which they are used in the chapter:

- *Low-literate*: Low-literate or limited literacy is the inability to use printed and written information. Individuals who are low-literate usually cannot complete a job application, follow written directions, or solve issues that are needed in order to function in U.S. society.
- *Low-income*: According to the U.S. Department of Health and Human Services Federal Poverty Guidelines as of January 23, 2008, a family or household of four is considered poor if their total income is $21,200 per year except for Hawaii and Alaska, where the guidelines are slightly higher.
- *Low-skilled*: Refers to individuals with limited education as well as work experience. Individuals in this category are also referred to as at-risk workers.

The Current Financial Crisis

A great deal of attention is paid to the dramatic incidents surrounding the financial crash of the years 2008 and 2009. Consumer confidence is at an all-time low. Banks are often unable or unwilling to give credit, home mortgages are collapsing, and massive layoffs continue to escalate.

In their first effort to survive and avoid bankruptcy, General Motors and Chrysler downsized by cutting their labor force and attempting to renegotiate contracts with the United Auto Worker (Hyde & Spangler, 2008). Unfortunately, those initial efforts contributed to massive layoffs and loss of jobs in other manufacturing industries. In February, 2009, for example, Michigan's unemployment rate reached 12.1% and was predicted to worsen, due in large part to the collapse of the auto industry (Pepitone, 2009). In Vandalia, Ohio, Dephi Corporation, which manufactures seat belts and airbags, planned to lay off over 140 workers (Ivcic, 2009). Interestingly enough, in an attempt to avoid and survive the economic crunch, many individuals who are employed, unemployed, and those who are laid off are upgrading their skills by returning to school, particularly at community colleges, with the hope of gaining security in their current jobs or switching careers that are more stable and lucrative (American Association of Community Colleges, 2009; Greenhouse, 2009).

As the financial markets across the globe experience chaotic swings, a number of community colleges are solidifying their efforts to meet the needs of low-income, low-skilled, and low-literate citizens. These institutions are cultivating unique partnerships by proactively connecting businesses with the purpose of the Workforce Investment Act (WIA), a set of federal programs designed to support adults who are seeking jobs or improve their skills as a path to better employment, sustainable wages, and upward mobility among other comprehensive workforce services. Moreover, institutions like Lansing Community College (LCC), Wayne County Community College (WCCC), and Florida's Miami Dade Community College (MDCC) are offering unique employment training opportunities for low-literate, low-income, and low-skilled citizens. Concomitantly, in certain regions of the country, the harsh realities of a failing economy are impacting the capability of some community colleges to offer programs in emerging areas such as environmental preservation, renewable energy technology, and green chemistry because of poor infrastructures and insufficient higher education state appropriations. For instance, San Diego Community College has many courses that are not being offered because California's educational allocations are not sufficient to pay their faculty even with an increase in demand (Dembicki, 2009).

Aspects of the American Community College

Community colleges significantly contribute to ongoing economic development by providing and often customizing comprehensive, rigorous programs of study that prepare their students to compete in the global, technology-driven economy. A case in point, certain employers are requiring machinists to complete programs in Computer Numerical Control (CNC) in order to run high-tech equipment such as manufacturing and processing machinery, laser cutting machines, and other precision machine components. These individuals are trained to program, control, and maintain highly sophisticated and expensive equipment. Subsequently, low-income, low-skilled, and low-literate citizens are often left out of these employment opportunities because they do not have the required preparation.

Community colleges offer remediation in developmental reading, writing, and mathematics, often in conjunction with other programs such as Adult Basic Education (ABE), General Education Development (GED), and High School Equivalency Diploma (HSED). More often than not, for these students such offerings and access to basic skill enhancement can also act as gateways to success in technical and occupational careers.

FAMILY STORIES

In this next segment of the chapter, we present three case studies within a family unit describing their individual quests for attaining a living wage. Following their stories, we identify issues low-literate, low-income, and low-skilled citizens face by highlighting community college partnerships with businesses and social service agencies that situated potential students to earn a living wage and further career opportunities. After that, we discuss programs for prisoners, pre- and post-incarceration, as well as programs for urban and rural citizens. We describe a number of programs and identify best practices. Subsequently, we identify gaps in services that need to be addressed in order to spur greater and more effective measures. We conclude with practical recommendations that are specifically important to their success.

A Mother's Story

Karan, a single mother of four children, is trying desperately to move out of her house-cleaning job and into a position that can make owning a home a reality. Karan constantly worries about her four children's safety and the negative influences that are part of living in a drug-infested neighborhood. Before moving to Lansing, Michigan, Karan's husband paid all the utility bills and signed permission slips for their children's school activities. He also made sure that each child was given the appropriate medication and dosage while still managing to work two jobs for less than adequate wages. Because of a felony conviction ten years ago, he was unable to find a stable job. Karan's husband recently died, and life has never been the same for the family.

Karan and her husband George shared a little secret: Karan can neither read nor write. She has not finished high school and is too scared to try to obtain her GED. She is also convinced that it is a waste of her time to participate in a local job club assistance program since she believes that all they have to offer are positions at fast food restaurants. Karan does not want to be like some of her friends and neighbors. She does not want to waste her time. Nevertheless, Karan knows that she lacks the employability skills needed to enter the workforce and earn a decent wage to support her family.

A Husband's Story

George and Karan married right out of high school. A year later, George landed in jail for possession of controlled substances. For the next four years, he was in and out of jail. Eventually, he was given a seven-year prison sentence for breaking and entering. By the time George entered prison, he was the father of four children and married to a woman who desperately needed him. While incarcerated, George participated in activities that would prepare him for work after completing his sentence. He attended workshops on time management, communication skills, anger management, and teamwork.

A Sister's Story

Angela, who is Karan's younger sister, always talked about having a resume. She learned about resumes at one of the job club orientation sessions sponsored by Advent House, a local social services non-profit agency in Lansing that serves homeless and chronically poor individuals and their families. For Angela, having a resume is something to be proud of, although her short list is of positions in the food services industry. Angela knows that her resume is not much. She has an address and a cell phone paid by Advent House as well as bus tickets to travel back and forth for the purpose of looking for employment and employment support.

For citizens like Karan and Angela, the future can appear very bleak. Karan and Angela and their families have lived for many years without good, solid, and sustainable jobs. They are now facing dwindling job opportunities, competition from skilled workers who have lost their jobs, and the outsourcing of jobs to other nations. The harsh reality is that there is a major change in the demand for employment skills. Fortunately, many American community colleges are attuned to this plight and are diligently and fiercely responding to these unique needs, even under constrained financial resources.

SPECIFIC POPULATIONS

Displaced Homemakers

The definition of a displaced homemaker often varies by state. In Illinois, The Displaced Homemakers Assistance Act (2006) uses the term to refer to an individual who has not worked outside the home and needs support and assistance with job searches due to circumstances such as divorce, separation, abandonment, illness, or the death of a spouse. In another example, Seminole Community College, under the auspices of New Directions Programs for Displaced Homemakers, defines eligibility and requires proof that the homemaker is at least 35 years of age, is no longer supported by their spouse or other family member, is underemployed, and has a history of federal assistance dependency (Seminole Community College, n.d.). In Michigan, for example,

> Local Michigan Works! Agencies (MWAs) operate the Displaced Homemaker Program. Displaced homemakers' employment and training needs are assessed on an individual basis and services are tailored to meet each participant's individual needs. The employment and training services must include core, intensive and training services. Core services include, but are not limited to, outreach, intake, and orientation to other services; initial assessment, job search, and placement assistance. Intensive services include comprehensive and specialized assessment, group counseling, and short-term pre vocational services. Training services include on-the-job training, skill-upgrading, and occupational skills training. (Displaced Homemaker Program, n.d., para. 2)

Hence, the delivery of services to displaced homemakers is often linked with social service agencies and community colleges.

Programs for the Homeless

Current reports forewarn that more individuals and families will be classified as chronically poor as unemployment increases nationwide. For those suffering in poverty, coalitions of multiple social service agencies, educational providers, and employers are needed to address their needs. In Angela's situation, the surface issues are homelessness, an inability to provide for her children, and a spotty work history. Additionally, Angela has few employment skills and a history of not being able to get along with others. She was also one of countless children unable to attend school regularly because of an unstable family and temporary periods in the foster care system.

Low-literate, low-income, and low-skilled citizens like Angela can take advantage of programs such as coping-skills workshops, family literacy programs, and basic skills development, particularly in reading, writing, and processing information that can increase their employability and sustainability opportunities. How the homeless or chronically poor access education and employment largely depends on where, when, and which agency refers them. For example, when an individual exits the foster care system at 18 years old, it is not rare for them to be homeless or rotating sleeping on different friends' sofas. If they completed high school or obtained their GED, they have a greater chance of gaining employment by participating in transitional education programs sponsored by many community colleges.

Great Expectations is a holistic program initiative housed at five of Virginia's community colleges. At The John H. Daniel Campus of Southside Virginia Community College, Great Expectations allows women and men who have aged-out of the foster care system to pursue and complete a college program. Great Expectations does this by providing intense advising, personal counseling, financial aid, and job placement referrals in conjunction with academic support services. Moreover, the Education and Training Vouchers Program (ETVP), a nationwide initiative, is designed to help youth who are aged-out or leaving the foster care system. The program is designed to provide tuition for up to $5,000 to attend vocational and technical schools, colleges, or universities.

Displaced Workers Programs

Displaced workers are adults who lost their jobs with little chance to go back to the same job. They will need to learn new skills to reenter the workplace. Choitz and Prince (2008) note a number of programs in community and technical colleges for dislocated workers, including bridge programs and career pathway programs. Bridge programs are designed for adults who lack basic academic skills to enter post-secondary education and training (Council for Advancement of Adult Literacy, 2005). Students are placed into courses and programs such as developmental education, literacy, and Adult Basic Education (ABE) so that they can learn reading, writing, and mathematics skills needed to pursue courses in a career track. Bridge programs and pathway programs are both relatively new and, therefore, there is insufficient information to be able to evaluate their effectiveness (Choitz & Prince, 2008).

Career pathway programs are long-term and are designed to allow individuals to enter and advance in a specific career (Council for Advancement of Adult Literacy, 2005). The programs combine initial training, work experience, and advanced training (Alssid, Gruber, Jenkins, Mazzeo, Roberts, & Stanback-Stroud, 2002). For example, the No Worker Left Behind (NWLB) program, initiated by Michigan's Governor Jennifer Granholm, is designed to facilitate "the transition of thousands of workers into good-paying jobs by providing up to two years worth of free tuition at any community college, university or other approved training provider" (State of Michigan, n.d., p. 1). Acceptance into the program requires that participants be at least 18 years old, a U.S. citizen, and have not graduated from high school within the last two years. Additionally, participants may not be full-time college students. Once an individual qualifies, they can receive benefits, including "tuition or instructional costs, books, materials, fees (such as application costs, registration, and laboratory fees) and academic supportive services (counseling and career advising). Tuition assistance is capped at $5,000 per year for two years, for a total of $10,000 per person" (State of Michigan, n.d., p. 6).

Already many community colleges are responding to the high numbers of displaced workers. For example, Thomas Nelson Community College (TNCM) is meeting employers' needs by offering technical training programs in manufacturing industries that are predicted to grow (Pulley, 2009). Other institutions are responding to the needs of their communities by adding more retraining courses in high-demand fields: "The demand is driven in part by people who need retraining because they have lost their jobs—or fear losing them—and in part by recent high-school graduates who turn to community colleges because they can't afford state or private colleges" (Biemiller, 2009, p. B11).

Funding remains of critical concern at community colleges across the nation (American Association of Community Colleges, 2009) because traditionally, they have not received the level of funding necessary to serve some of the neediest in society. Therefore, federal and state dollars are often sought to offset the costs of programming. For instance, through the Adult Education and Family Literacy Act (AEFLA), funding is made available to community and technical colleges as well as community-based organizations to assist adults in becoming literate and skilled for the workforce. In many technical and community colleges across the nation, thousands of students each year complete a General Education Development (GED)/High School Equivalency Diploma (HSED); participate in basic skills/career-oriented programs; or enhance their basic reading, writing, and mathematical skills to remain employed, or to secure employment.

Programs for Rural and Urban Citizens

In eleven states across the country, ABE, GED, and HSED are offered through community and technical colleges rather than as an extension of high school. In Wisconsin, for example, all 16 colleges offer ABE, GED and HSED, but only Milwaukee Area Technical College (MATC) offers the adult high school. In addition, students in both of these urban and rural Wisconsin districts have opportunities to take advantage of basic skills training through partnerships with community-based organizations and job centers. Through contracted services with community colleges, employers often provide targeted training to their employees to enhance basic skills and train their staff to meet new workforce needs.

According to Center on Wisconsin Strategy (2008), there is a wealth of untapped potential for employment opportunities for those who could obtain training. The Center on Wisconsin Strategy (2008) cites a skilled worker shortage for many industries with a high percentage of individuals on the "economic sidelines, neither engaged in education nor adequately skilled to fill these high-wage jobs" (Wisconsin Indianhead Technical College, n.d., para. 8). Occupational degree holders in Wisconsin who stay within the state earn about 23% more than those who hold only a high school diploma. With the closing of many plants and industries in rural areas in Wisconsin, there is a greater need to provide educational outreach to these communities.

Rural communities present challenging issues around access. In many cases, individuals are not aware of the services available in the general vicinity of their homes and often have misinformation about particular services. Although there may be colleges nearby, it is not uncommon for the residents to feel alienated from those schools. With both urban and rural populations, individuals often lack the basic foundational skills to pursue high wage/high skilled careers thereby prolonging the time needed to enter or reenter the workforce. With the current economic situation, this concern will become more evident and more challenging to address.

Prisoners, Pre- and Post-Incarceration

It is not surprising that the prison population is comprised of a disproportionate number of adults who are low-income, low-literate, and low-skilled. With the large increase in incarcerations over the last decade, it seems that the literacy skills could be explored as an answer to addressing the problems of recidivism (Vacca, 2004).

In the United States, there are currently more than two million incarcerated men and women. Of these prisoners, only 51% have a high school diploma or equivalent, compared to 76% of the general population. Prisoners are more likely to be male, minority, and young, and more than 90% of these inmates will one day re-enter society, and seek employment. Education plays a major factor in an individual's ability to adjust back into society and community colleges are well-equipped to provide programs, courses, and services that will serve this population because of their emphasis on occupational and vocational education.

Since 1953, both two-year and four-year colleges and universities have provided access to education, offering GED, HSED, ABE, and liberal arts courses to jail and prison inmates across this nation. According to Williams (1989), "The main objectives of these college-run programs are to provide a quality education for those inmates showing potential and enthusiasm; improve inmates' academic and vocational skills; change the inmates' attitudes regarding work and responsibility; and prepare inmates for the competitive job market they will face upon release" (p. 2).

Due to the current economic downturn, finding jobs upon release is becoming more difficult, placing an additional burden on the resources available for inmate re-integration. At the same time, it has become necessary to extend offerings beyond vocational and skills training to include associate degrees and other programs on a larger scale. Research has shown that inmates in education programs have lower recidivism rates than non-participants, and that the more extensive the educational program, the more likely they will be able to stay out of prison (Vacca, 2004).

Springfield Technical Community College in Massachusetts and its Continuing Education arm have offered five to seven college-level credit courses and GED preparation at the Hampden County House of Corrections (HCHC) for several years. In 2008, 123 inmates took courses and 117 inmates received their GEDs. Recognizing that this is often the students' first encounter with higher education, the college offers services in addition to classes. These services include GED testing at the prison site and assistance with required paperwork for the Free Application for Federal Student Aid (FAFSA), and assisting with higher education admission and registration forms. In an effort to build upon the relationship started while in prison, the college works with the HCHC Pre-Release Center to place ex-offenders in college upon their release. In 2007, 149 ex-offenders enrolled in college courses at Springfield Technical Community College (Massachusetts Board of Higher Education, 2008).

Through a partnership with the Correctional Education Association, the Youth Offender Program, and Milwaukee Area Technical College in Wisconsin, college-credit courses are offered to subscribing prison facilities via the satellite services of the Transforming Lives Network. Liberal Arts and Science courses are packaged and delivered to prisons across the nation, offering inmates the opportunity to learn from a college instructor and earn an associate of arts degree while incarcerated. The goal is to prepare inmates to leave prison and reenter society equipped with an academic degree.

Similarly, Wayne County Community College (WCCCD) in the greater Detroit metropolitan area, with the support of their office of Continuing Education, offers a reentry training and employment program in partnership with the Michigan Department of Corrections. The program is specifically intended to prepare low-literate, low-income, and low-skilled parolees for employment in such fields as culinary arts, building maintenance, hazardous material management, and construction. A unique feature of the program is that through a series of intake and assessment procedures, WCCCD staff members are able to identify compatibility skills and aptitude for their chosen field, and to identify individuals with learning disabilities. As a result, the reentry program is better able to align the individual's progress and program plan. Once they complete skills development and training courses, parolees are matched with local businesses that are willing to hire them. At the time of employment, a 90-day work plan is designed to assist the parolee to succeed at his or her work site. During their 90-day probationary period, the parolees are also required to participate in training on communication skills, conflict resolution, budgeting, and time management. After participants complete 90 days of successful employment, the company is expected to hire them.

There are more examples of community college partnerships with jails and prisons across the nation. Without these important programs and the need to view incarceration as an opportunity to transform lives, inmates would be released in a way that is no better off than when they arrived to jail or prison. Society cannot afford to ignore this population nor disregard their educational and skill development needs nor their potential. Without these programs and services, we further disenfranchise a group of individuals who could be productive citizens with the proper motivation, training, and academic preparation.

CLOSING THE GAPS

One of the biggest challenges low-literate, low-income, and low-skilled citizens face is committing to an academic and skill development program that leads to self-sufficiency. Some programs can take 18 weeks or more to complete, while in many instances participants are also trying to meet their basic needs, including childcare and transportation. Therefore, it is very important that social service agencies, the local community college, and local One-Stop Job Centers maintain a co-case management approach to serve these citizens. One way to implement a co-case management approach is for service agencies for displaced homemakers and re-entry services for ex-offenders to provide office space in their same facility where employers can hold pre-employment interviews. Mobile outreach services, specifically designed for meeting the needs of rural and urban low-income, low-literacy, and low-skilled adults are also recommended.

For aged-out individuals—those who are too old for foster care—the first step is to get them into a transition or support program at their local community college. Many aged-out citizens often have histories of truancy, shoplifting, and other delinquencies. Therefore, they need intense guidance and support to pursue post-secondary education that can lead to sustainability and greater economic development. Community colleges, in partnership with businesses and social service agencies, can develop specific programs to work with these citizens. Those who are periodically homeless, low-literate, and low-skilled are the group most likely to fall off the radar tracking screen from programs designed to boost participants' economic conditions. Once personal housing issues are addressed, participants immediately need to be linked to resources that can help them optimize their opportunities for self-sufficiency.

IMPLICATIONS FOR PRACTICE

Certain occupational fields require prospective employees to own their own tools related to the job. By community colleges, businesses, and occupational trade associations partnering together, there are possibilities for creating an equipment "loan" program. Moreover, companies can match experienced workers with low-literate, low-income, and low-skilled citizens to act as mentors, including them in all aspects of the training process until they achieve the necessary competencies or perhaps a certification. This new economy requires much more collaborative efforts than in years past, and it is expected that this trend will continue. Although many employers are often hesitant to hire individuals with criminal records—an unfortunate result of conditions of poverty and low literacy—community colleges, post-release programs, and prospective employers can design collaborative actions and initiatives that support successful reentry into the workforce and community.

Throughout this chapter, we have discussed the challenges of low-literate, low-income, and low-skilled citizens across the nation. We have referred to specific labels often attached to this group, including displaced homemakers, displaced workers, the homeless, ex-offenders, and individuals who live in urban and rural communities. These labels further identify the many obstacles these individuals must overcome in their quest for sustainable and meaningful employment as well as a good quality of life. We recommend purposeful and structured interventions that include goal setting, academic and skill enhancement, and comprehensive development and training focused on entry and re-entry into the workforce. These processes should include interim measures of success so that low-literate, low-income, and low-skilled citizens see their own progress.

Community colleges are at the cutting edge of innovations for redirecting past strategies for training and development into a new strategy of collaboration and partnership development. Community colleges realize that education is not a separate activity, that learners bring their lives to the classroom. It is imperative that adult educators recognize that in order to truly make a difference in the lives of these citizens, all the pieces of the puzzle or all parts of life must be addressed for true success to occur. While a more productive livelihood of low-literate, low-income, and low-skilled citizens can be realized through education, true success and self-sufficiency will only be realized when business, industry, and education work together to provide the needed services and skills development of these citizens. Although many support programs provide access to a community college education, it is recommended that a systematic approach reaching out to low-literate, low-income citizens who are residing in shelters, receiving services from churches, religious-based organizations, and living in rural and urban communities is needed. No one entity should be expected to solve these challenges.

REFERENCES

Adela, T., & Stintson, J. (2008 October). Russia among hardest-hit. *USA Today*. Retrieved September 8, 2009, from http://www.usatoday.com/news/world/2008-10-09-russia_N.htm

Alssid, J., Gruber, D., Jenkins, D., Mazzeo, C., Roberts, G., & Stanback-Stroud, R. (2002). *Building a career pathways system: Promising practices in community-college centered workforce development*. New York: Workforce Strategy Center.

American Association of Community Colleges. (2009, July 31). States expect tougher times for FY2010 budgets. *Community College Times, 21*(15), 14.

Biemiller, L. (2009, March 27). Bursting at the seams: As enrollments soar, some colleges offer round-the-clock classes—and still run out of space. *The Chronicle of Higher Education*, pp. B11–B13.

Center on Wisconsin Strategy. (2008). *The state of working Wisconsin 2008*. Retrieved September 1, 2009, from www.cows.org/soww

Choitz, V., & Prince, H. (2008). *Flexible learning options to adult students*. Washington, DC: U. S. Department of Labor.

Council for Advancement of Adult Literacy. (2005). *To ensure America's future: Building a national opportunity system for adults*. New York: Council for Advancement of Adult Literacy.

Dembicki, M. (2009, January 30). Pell grants, tax credits in the mix. *Community College Times, 21*(3), 1.

Displaced Homemakers Assistance Act, 20 Illinois Combined Statues 615/2 (2006). Retrieved August 29, 2008, from http://www.ilga.gov/legislation/ilcs/ilcs3.asp?ActID=252&ChapAct=20 ILCS 615/&ChapterID=5&ChapterName=EXECUTIVE+BRANCH&ActName=Displaced+Homemakers+Assistance+Act%2E

Displaced Homemaker Program. (n.d.). Work Force Investment Act of 1998. 29 U.S.C. § 2801 (1998). Retrieved August 29, 2009, from http://www.michigan.gov/printerFriendly/0,1687,7-122-1679_1821_2779—,00.html

Greenhouse, S. (2009, August 14). More white-collar workers turn to community colleges. *New York Times*. Retrieved June 17, 2010 from http://www.nytimes.com/2009/08/20/education/20COMMUN.html?_r=1

Hyde, J., & Spangler, T. (2008, December 11). Hope for rescue shifts to White House. *Detroit Free Press*. Retrieved September 8, 2009, from http://www.freep.com/article/20081211/BUSINESS01/81211121

Ivcic, M. (2009, May 13). Delphi closing part of Vandalia plant. [Radio Broadcast]. Retrieved September 1, 2009, from http://newstalkradiowhio.com/local-news/2009/05/delphi-closing-part-of-vandali.html

Massachusetts Board of Higher Education. (2008). *Performance measurement report: Performance goals for state and community colleges in the Commonwealth of Massachusetts*. Retrieved September 3, 2009, from www.mass.edu/library/2008pmr/springfield.asp

Pepitone, J. (2009, March 25). Michigan jobless rate hits 12%. *CNNMoney.com*. Retrieved June 10, 2010 from http://money.cnn.com/2009/03/25/news/economy/michigan_unemployment/index.htm

Pulley, J. (2009, March 27). Positioned to help reignite the economy. *Community College Times, 21*(7), 12.

Seminole Community College. (n.d.). *New Directions: Displaced Homemaker Program*. Retrieved August 29, 2009, from http://www.scc-fl.edu/newdirections/

State of Michigan. (n.d.). *No Worker Left Behind: Frequently Asked Questions*. Retrieved September 1, 2009, from http://www.michigan.gov/nwlb/0,1607,7-242-48049-,00.html

United States Department of Housing and Urban Development. (n.d.). *Housing choice vouchers fact sheet*. Retrieved May 3, 2009, from http://www.hud.gov/offices/pih/programs/hcv/about/fact_sheet.cfm

Vacca, J. (2004). Educated prisoners are less likely to return to prison. *Journal of Correctional Education, 55*(4), 297–305.

Williams, D. N. (1989). *Correctional education and the community college. ERIC Digest.* (ED321835). Los Angeles, CA: ERIC Clearinghouse for Junior Colleges.

Wisconsin Indianhead Technical College (n.d.). *WITC News and Events: Tech colleges 'bright spot' in workforce report*. Retrieved September 1, 2009, from http://www.witc.edu/news/2008/bright.htm

CHAPTER 3

RICHES FROM THE POOR

Teaching Humanities in the Margins

Janet Groen
University of Calgary

Tara Hyland-Russell
St. Mary's University College

INTRODUCTION

Leeann is a forty-something-year-old woman, living in a large Canadian urban center. Modest about her own abilities, she admits the difficult path her life has taken. She now lives in a supportive housing environment for women facing physical or mental challenges. We first met her as we researched several Canadian iterations of humanities programs that offer free university courses for poor people. Leeann was willing to sit down with us and tell us about her involvement with the program and what learning in the humanities means to her. Despite her shy demeanor, Leeann's passion for learning was evident from the beginning of the interview. She refers to philosophers Plato, Descartes, and Kant as "brilliant guys" who help guide her on her journey into intellectual engagement and a more engaged sense of

Learning for Economic Self-Sufficiency, pages 29–47

self in relation to the world. Feeling welcomed into courses on philosophy, critical thinking, and literature was crucial for Leeann, as life circumstances had taught her that learning was something she didn't merit and that her poverty would always exclude her from education. Leeann was amazed when she heard about a university program that was intended specifically for people like her, people living in poverty who did not have the means to attend school. As Leeann shares,

> When she mentioned that it was university courses for non-credit and that the marginalized, like myself, the poor like myself would be able to go, I just jumped on it not knowing a thing about it or how to help out with it or anything. I just put my body down on the chair and said, let me hear all about it. (Leeann)

Like Leeann, for a long time Kevin had no hope of being able to access further learning. In fact, it was far from his mind as he struggled daily to keep his head above water. A spiraling alcohol addiction led to Kevin living on the streets and in shelters for five years. He survived, but many of his relationships did not: he lost most of his former life. Yet Kevin didn't give up. He connected with people at an urban agency for people living in poverty. They supported him as he gave up drinking and encouraged him to look beyond his current bleak situation. When some people advised him to get back to work, Kevin realized he wasn't ready for that step and, instead, opted to take a few high school courses. That led to a renewed interest in learning and, when offered the opportunity to take a university-level history course for free, Kevin jumped at the chance. Several of these courses later, Kevin had proved to the instructors and to himself that he was more than capable of continuing in post-secondary education, so he enrolled in a local institution to pursue a degree. Wiry and engaging, Kevin tells his story with wry humor, passionate about sharing what he has learned in order to encourage others to move beyond what may seem to be the darkest moments of their lives.

> It's really important that students share the same background—poverty and addictions—and we understand each other. The program isn't in a hurry to change everything overnight. (Kevin)

Fraser is also no stranger to darkness and struggle. Proudly Aboriginal, Fraser lives on a small and isolated reserve; yet, he has spent more time off the reserve than on, both from necessity and by choice. While narrating how he has been bounced around from foster homes to living on the street, to migrating among several urban centers looking for work, Fraser acknowledges both the downsides and the benefits of his mobile life. He remains cheerfully optimistic and pins his hopes for a better future on learning and education. A single father, Fraser wants to break a generational cycle of poverty and violence to give his two-year-old son a better chance. Fraser wants to fulfill his dream of giving back to his community that he calls home.

> See that's why, that's why I'm in Humanities 101. I can help everyone else but I just can't seem to help myself. (Fraser)

We met each of these three students during our work and research into several Canadian humanities programs for the poor. Our involvement in the research project began with our local program, *Storefront 101*, in Calgary, Alberta. Janet's passion for adult literacy learning compelled her to volunteer as a member of the working committee at *Storefront 101* in 2003, while Tara's enthusiasm for teaching and social justice brought her to teach a course in English literature in the program in 2005. She subsequently joined Janet on the working committee in 2006.

It was our joint experience in the program, witnessing firsthand the powerful transformation in students' lives and in the lives of tutors, instructors, and program planners that led us to a three-year intensive case study of three Canadian programs.

Students' experiences and testimonies had convinced us that the programs changed lives, but we wanted to know what prompted the transformation, what makes an effective program, and how this change occurs. What we discovered through many interviews with students, instructors, program planners; analysis of written records and syllabi; and developing and administering surveys and questionnaires, were riches beyond our imagining: riches of understanding, riches of experience, and riches of hope. And, while we certainly had expertise to offer, it became very clear that we were not the source of most of the riches. Rather, as we spent time with people who had been marginalized by society and opened ourselves to learn, we discovered an abundance of riches coming *from* the poor[1].

HUMANITIES EDUCATION AS PATHWAY OUT OF POVERTY?

Canada has a growing number of humanities programs for the poor: free, university-level courses taught by top-notch faculty and attended by people who have been barred access to post-secondary education or who don't believe they're entitled to learning. The programs are designed to be deeply transformative, moving beyond the traditional vocational training that is the usual fare for low-income people *and* opening a learning space for critical, reflective thinking and a more engaged citizenship. Inspired by the Clemente Program founded in New York in 1995, the humanities programs in

Canada counter the external, material barriers to learning while attracting students into communities of learning that invite them to reflect on internal barriers to learning. Although each of the Canadian programs organizes its structure independently, the programs share an educational vision to resist the restrictive forces of poverty that often prove insurmountable for poor people wanting to learn.

Earl Shorris, founder of the Clemente program, provides a vivid metaphor for the restrictive forces of poverty. He describes the daily forces affecting the poor as a *surround,* a fence circling and pressing upon them, analogous to the circling manoeuvre used by hunters to gather and isolate prey and eliminate the possibility of escape. He cautions us not to imagine this surround as a force acting upon an abstract "poor," however, but upon individual people with names and lives:

> The forces of the surround do not affect the poor, they affect poor persons, not even families, but persons, one at a time. Everyone who lives within the surround lives alone. The weight of the forces separates them, splintering the body of the poor like glass underfoot, driving the shards of family, community, society into feckless privacy. (Shorris, 2000, p. 47)

Such force closes off any opportunity for change and growth, insists Shorris, because it cannot be reasoned with: "Unlike argument, which has a dialectical shape, involving thesis and antithesis, and lies at the heart of the political life at all levels of society, force closes off dialogue" (Shorris, 2000, p. 42).

Humanities programs that work in the margins of society, offering courses for people living in poverty, push back at the forces – the *surround* – pressing upon the poor, by constructing a space for dialogue, critical thinking and imagination. However, the very location of humanities programs in society's margins and their mandate for people living in poverty positions them as radical and concerned with social change. After all, these humanities programs are modeled on the liberal arts education that is typically the domain of the elite and privileged in society. Giroux (1992) outlined the ability of "radical education" to question relationships of power and knowledge and to create a more democratic society. As Jackson (1997) understands Giroux's (1992) view of the radical education project:

> Radical education... questions fundamental categories and is concerned with making society more democratic. It brings together theory and practice. Radical educators have a concern with the crucial role of pedagogy, in particular calling into question the relationship of knowledge to power, and a responsibility to engage with questions of difference, and questions of the experiential. (Jackson, 1997, p. 458)

There is no doubt that the humanities courses offered for people living in poverty are radical. They seek to uncover and disrupt relations of power that surround and immobilize the poor while they enact a pedagogy that transforms not only the students but all participants in the learning community. To mark and name this radical education that is rooted in social justice, we have coined the term *Radical Humanities* (Groen & Hyland-Russell, 2009).

Non-Traditional Adult Learners

As we learned, taught, and researched within a number of Radical Humanities programs, we sought to establish a profile of their students. The term "non-traditional adult learner" most closely captures the programs' students, though there is little consistency in the use of the term and no agreement on its definition. The use of the term seems to vary widely depending on context, country, institution, policy, demographic and enrolment patterns. Scheutze and Slowey (2002), however, provide a usable definition of non-traditional adult learners. As they note, the term

> usually refers to socially or educationally disadvantaged sections of the population ... those from working class backgrounds, particular ethnic minority groups, immigrants, and, in the past, frequently women ... it tends to relate to older or adult students with a vocational training and work experience background, or other students with unconventional educational biographies. (pp. 312–313)

The demographic survey we administered to students in three programs supports Scheutze and Slowey's (2002) definition as all of the students surveyed were socially, economically, or educationally disadvantaged and most had unconventional or interrupted educational backgrounds (Groen & Hyland-Russell, 2007). However, as we explain in more detail later, the scope and multiplicity of barriers facing the learners prompts us to further differentiate students in the Radical Humanities as "marginalized, non-traditional adult learners" (Groen & Hyland-Russell, 2009).

Based on Shorris' (2000) observations about the *surround* that circumscribes poor people's ability to move out of impoverishment and into learning, we knew it was important to understand the nature and dynamics of the barriers faced by the marginalized, non-traditional adult learners in our programs. According to Spellman (2007), in addition to a low income, non-traditional adult learners face the following barriers to learning: "lack of academic preparation, lack of finances, social issues, cultural issues, and overwhelming family responsibilities" (p. 63). Parnham (2001) found further barriers to learning such as the "lack of information and formal guidance about what is available; situation barriers ... family constraints; lack of support... and childcare" (p. 58). Perhaps as important as the *kinds* of barriers that non-traditional learners face is their *cumulative effect*. Cross (1981) stressed that students' difficulty starting or finishing educational projects increased with the numbers of barriers they experienced. According to Bowl (2001), "University entry is experienced as a dislocation and disjunction which is intensified if the learner is non-traditional in more than one sense" (p. 157).

The cumulative effect and intensification of dislocation due to multiple barriers was evident in the lives of the students we surveyed and interviewed but was prominent to a far greater degree than in the literature we reviewed. Each of the three learners we profile in this chapter experienced a number of barriers to ongoing learning; many of these barriers are interconnected. For example, as Leeann looked back on her childhood, she realized that her education was not important to her family. As she noted,

> They were so excited to get a little boy that I think they forgot about me along the wayside and thought, well, maybe she won't amount to anything because she is a girl. There was quite a stigma attached to that back then in some families—how the husband usually wanted a first born to be a boy to take after him. I wasn't given a lot of opportunities... I had to quit high school in grade 9 with only four credits. (Leeann)

In addition to having limited high school education, Leeann also finds a lack of social skills to be a barrier. As a result of her experiences with abuse, addiction, and schizophrenia, she has, according to her, "certainly acted out in the past to you know where I haven't had the coping skills to work things out." These combined barriers have, in turn, resulted in challenges related to her daily living conditions: she lives in subsidized housing, isolated and far from her family.

The challenges Fraser faces through his Aboriginal background also reflect the interconnectedness of barriers experienced by many marginalized, non-traditional learners. He reflects on generations of oppression perpetuated through government assimilation policies and residential schools:

> The damage that was done; now you go back a little bit–the racism, the government policy and everything else that was set out to destroy us destroyed a lot of people. I carried that anger. (Fraser)

His personal situation did not mitigate these systemic barriers; instead, early and ongoing traumatic events only served to build upon them.

> My mother was murdered when I was eight... she was married to, not my father, she was married to another guy. My father married somebody else. And he ended up killing her and so I ended up going to a foster home

> in . . . here. When I hit 16, 17 I had some family members say "Get on the bus and go" . . . All this time wasn't great, but the thing about Toronto was I was on my own still and ended up on the street in Toronto. So rather than pay my rent, I slept on a park bench. (Fraser)

Over time, barriers that were both systemic and relational led to deep psychological barriers as Fraser was led to question his heritage and place in society:

> I didn't enjoy, I didn't like being an Indian, I don't want to be an Indian. Why am I an Indian? I questioned that. . . . I'm at the back of the class because that's where I belonged. (Fraser)

When Kevin started the humanities program, it had been 25 years since he had been in school: he had spent the previous five on the streets and in shelters as a result of alcoholism. He asked himself the question that almost every other learner in a Radical Humanities program has asked: "Am I going to be able to do this?" Even after Kevin had successfully completed several *Storefront 101* courses, he continued to negotiate stable living conditions. For several years, he couch-surfed while trying to pursue further education. The one personal item he owned was a computer. He continually faced internal barriers of self-doubt and anxiety, even as he was determined to earn a degree in social work and to give back to society.

At first glance, the poverty that students in Radical Humanities programs share seems to be their single most defining feature; however, our ongoing research has complicated that view. We quickly became aware of the multiple and interrelated barriers the students faced and sought to understand how the multiple barriers affected their ability to participate in learning. Cross's (1981) analysis of adult learner participation provided a conceptual model through which to classify the kinds of barriers students faced. Cross suggested that barriers fall into three categories: situational, institutional, and dispositional. "*Situational barriers* are those arising from one's situation in life at a given time" (Cross, 1981, p. 98, emphasis in original). Situational barriers addressed by the students in our research included low income, lack of childcare or transportation, inadequate or unstable housing, inadequate food and medical care, lack of private study space, unsafe or violent living conditions. "*Institutional barriers*," according to Cross, are the "practices and procedures that exclude or discourage working adults from participating in educational activities" (1981, p. 98, emphasis in original). While a limited number of students in Radical Humanities programs are working, they nonetheless experience profound institutional barriers that are not limited to learning institutions. In addition to the scheduling, procedures, and red tape issues identified by Cross, students in our study noted barriers created by limited access to information about learning opportunities, lack of required documentation such as high school transcripts, shelter curfews, and vocational or training program demands linked to social funding.

While situational and institutional barriers provide significant impediments to learning, perhaps even more powerful are what Cross identified as "*Dispositional barriers*... those related to attitudes and self-perceptions about oneself as a learner" (p. 98). Magro (2006/2007) asserts that "psychological barriers such as fear, low self-esteem, and negative attitudes toward education are the most resistant to change" (p. 71). Willians and Seary (2007) supported this finding: "Many [adult learners] have been hindered by both their past and present educational, social or cultural circumstances and most doubt their ability to succeed in higher education" (p. 438). Certainly, as the personal experiences of Leeann, Kevin, and Fraser illustrate, the students we interviewed spent much of their time talking about the internal barriers to learning, barriers based on their perceptions that they were powerfully hindered from education by attitudes and beliefs—that school was just not for them due to some lack in their lives or selves.

These students' stories profoundly demonstrate that dispositional, situational, and systemic barriers often combine to restrict ongoing learning and lead to a denial of self as learner. This constellation of barriers, both internal and external, more accurately identifies the participants in Radical Humanities programs than the sole criteria of poverty. Describing the specific barriers for a particular student also helps name the oppressive practices that have led to students being pushed to the margins of society, where they feel invisible and ignored. For this reason, both to capture and name the profound effects of these multiple and interrelated barriers to learning, often arising from systems of social and institutional oppression, we have described the participants of Radical Humanities programs as "*marginalized*, non-traditional adult learners" (Groen & Hyland-Russell, 2009). With our deepening awareness of the complexity of the barriers facing marginalized, non-traditional adult learners, we were even more amazed at the students' courage, tenacity, and willingness to risk as they entered the Radical Humanities learning space. We turned to transformational learning theory, which will be further discussed below, to try and understand the dynamics involved when people who believe they do not merit education become animated and joyfully engaged with learning.

The Possibility of Transformational Learning

We began to question *how* people facing such significant and intertwined barriers begin to conceive of themselves as learners. Time and again, despite significant and multiple barriers, many of the marginalized, non-traditional learners in the Radical Humanities programs *did* experience a shift in their perception of self. At the beginning of a course, many learners were unable to identify learner goals or even themselves as learners, but a few weeks into the program they found themselves shaping learning goals and beginning to dream about the future in ways they never thought possible. Indeed, each of our three learners displayed what Mezirow (1978) called perspective transformation, where they experienced significant shifts in the way they conceptualized themselves and their relations to learning. For example, Kevin realized that even if he has some rough classes, he knows he can make it. As he explained, "[my marks] may not be all A's but I won't drop out." Kevin exhibits confidence and poise; where once he focused on the material poverty that dominated his life, now he said he "feels more higher up in company by taking university courses... inside is the feeling of being rich, though not materially."

As Leeann considered her success in the Radical Humanities course, she explained,

> It's making friends....That's a success for me. It's a success, I think, in life. And just to be able to come up with some answers to the questions that they give. It's not easy. When you're just learning it and you've been out of school for 30 years like me, and you haven't been following these kind of brilliant minds all your life, so yeah it's a challenge but I consider it a success to have gotten as far as I have, thank goodness. I am trying to improve myself. (Leeann)

Whereas Leeann once discounted herself from learning, now she feels a vital member of the learning community and feels she owns her education.

Similarly, Fraser believes that the *Radical Humanities* program has opened up possibilities for him.

> I come to this course and am having fun, and like you know, we're capable... I need the schooling, and this opened the door for it and made it enjoyable and because of my experiences it's made it seem like it's... it's challenging, I know it's going to be challenging. It's challenging. (Fraser)

The experiences of Fraser, Leeann, and Kevin, as well as other learners in the Radical Humanities programs, suggest that transformational learning is possible for adults who face significant barriers to learning. Cranton and King (2003) outlined the basic dynamic underlying transformative learning:

> At its core, the idea is elegant in its simplicity. We make meaning of the world through our experiences. What happens once, we expect to happen again. Through this process, we develop habits of mind or a frame of reference for understanding the world, much of which is uncritically assimilated. In the process of daily living, we absorb values, assumptions, and beliefs about how

> things are without much thought. When something different happens, we can be led to question our way of seeing the world. (p. 32)

Central to transformative learning, then, is a deep shift in the way people see themselves in relation to the world around them. A prerequisite to such a shift must be a new set of experiences that challenges people's assumptions and experiences. The fundamental nature of transformative learning has been agreed upon by educators and writers about pedagogy: Transformative learning entails a fundamental change in how people see themselves and the world (Clark, 1993). What remains as contested ground is *how* we can achieve transformative learning and *for whom* it is possible.

Over the last decade, transformative learning theory has broadened the base of Mezirow's (1991) rational cognitive learning approach to address affective, spiritual, ethical, and collaborative dimensions of the learning process (Dirkx, 1997; King & Wright, 2003; Taylor, 2000). Yet transformative learning theory has continued to restrict its focus to critically reflective learners. Mezirow (2003a, 2004) and Merriam (2004) suggested that a minimal level of education is a necessary pre-requisite for the rational discourse and critical self-reflection that prefigures perspective transformation. According to Mezirow (2003a), "Preconditions for realizing these values and finding one's voice for free full participation in discourse include elements of maturity, education, safety, health, economic security and emotional intelligence" (p. 15). "Hungry, desperate, homeless, sick, destitute, and intimidated people obviously cannot participate fully and freely in discourse" (Mezirow 2003b, p. 60).

Following these parameters, Fraser, Leeann, and Kevin did not meet the preconditions in order to undergo the perspective transformation they experienced. Despite their abilities to be active, contributing members to a dialogic and critically evaluative learning community, each of these students remained in situations with scarce resources. Indeed, other Radical Humanities students have completed courses *while living in homeless shelters or on the streets.* Their experience seems to fly in the face of Mezirow's claim that people who are "hungry, desperate, homeless, sick, destitute and intimidated obviously cannot participate fully and freely in discourse" (2003b, p. 60). Clearly, the learners in Radical Humanities programs challenge us to expand our understanding and our theoretical framing of where and how transformative learning can occur. Is there any validity in the claims for particular preconditions to transformative learning as outlined by Mezirow (2003a, 2004) and Merriam (2004)? What can we learn from the students of Radical Humanities that can enrich our knowledge of the processes of transformative learning?

Creating Spaces for Transformative Learning

To respond to the questions posed above, we turn to the programs themselves, particularly to the concrete and specific program planning elements. In their mandate and design, each of the programs addresses the intertwined situational, institutional, and dispositional barriers typically experienced by marginalized non-traditional adult learners. Each of the programs identifies its mandate as education for people living in low-income situations, poverty, or homelessness. A basic reading level is required, determined by a reading comprehension test, or by students self-identifying as having the ability to read a newspaper or tabloid.

To address external or situational barriers such as poverty and lack of material resources, each program makes a concerted effort to anticipate and remove all material barriers to learning. Students receive, at no cost, course materials such as binders, textbooks, course readings, paper, and pens. Tuition and registration fees are waived through unique arrangements with the host post-secondary institutions. Students are provided with transit tickets and child-care remuneration. Two of the programs provide hot meals prior to each class and tutorials twice each week, while the third program offers a snack during the class break and a hot meal prior to the weekly tutorial session.

Institutional barriers are also deliberately assessed and countered. Many students report the density and incomprehensibility of bureaucratic processes that have repelled them in previous attempts to pursue post-secondary learning. Though students may have had a deep desire to continue further learning, when faced with a maze of forms or an impersonal admission process, coupled with an already jeopardized sense of self as learner and insufficient material resources for even the application fee, they give up. Thus, the programs make deliberate efforts to mitigate the very real institutional barriers to accessing education. For instance, the application forms and processes are streamlined to diminish anxiety and fear of official forms; to address fears about losing their already tenuous, if meagre, income, students are repeatedly reassured that information will not be shared with government or other agencies; personal interviews are held as part of the intake process; and, in one program, the registrar of the host academic institution brings the equipment to take photos and create student ID cards right to the classroom. Connections between students and mentors are facilitated to help guide students through admission and application processes.

Each Radical Humanities program upholds a common political agenda of access and the belief in the power of humanities education to create a reflective space in which students can develop critical thinking capacities. In addition to the underlying common philosophy of access to knowledge, each of these programs situates itself in a physical setting rich with the symbolic power associated with the elite in our society—universities. Though many students have lived their whole lives in university communities, they have never felt entitled to inhabit the university space. As a result, when they first step foot on university grounds as Radical Humanities students, they see their act as highly symbolic and powerfully transgressive. For this reason, most Radical Humanities programs make a deliberate decision to physically situate the classes in a university. As students often felt excluded from the life of the university prior to participating in a Radical Humanities program, they also did not share in the cultural life of their community. Thus, throughout a typical term, students access a variety of cultural institutions within their communities such as museums, theatres, and public and university libraries. For many students, it is the first time they have seen a live performance or entered a public cultural space. Bringing students into cultural spaces powerfully conveys the message that they are legitimate members of society and that they are able and entitled to engage with cultural ideas and forms.

Inseparable from students' perceptions of institutional practices and barriers are the people within those institutions. Most students are fearful of professors, who are suspect, "alien," elite. Professors represent in a powerful way the chasm between students' negative experiences of learning and the learning for the elite that they feel is barred to them. Because the symbolic nature of professors is so heavily over-written for the students, it is crucial that the instructors for Radical Humanities programs be very carefully selected. The instructors who have been most able to connect with the marginalized, non-traditional adult learners and to bypass the real and symbolic barriers are those who possess a mature and grounded sense of self, what Cranton and Carusetta (2004) and Carusetta and Cranton (2005) called "authenticity." Qualities of authenticity include helping others, relating to others, and caring for others around us. Authenticity also involves knowing who we are within our social world, how we are shaped by the world, and how we position ourselves in that world (Cranton & Carusetta, 2004). Experience within the Radical Humanities programs has demonstrated that instructors must be experienced, confident in their own abilities, yet flexible in their approach. They need to be firm in their own sense of being in the world, and able to withstand the challenging relationships within the Radical Humanities classroom. They also need to be able to understand and question their part in the social construction of the relationships and power fields that operate in particular ways within the classroom.

Cranton and Carusetta (2004) posited a continuum of authenticity that ranges from a beginning authenticity to a mature authenticity. Instructors who are in the beginning stages of authenticity are concerned with maintaining their own status and base their teaching styles and student/teacher relationships on notions of rule-based authority, rather than with building relationships with students based on a recognition of student needs and differences. In fact, instructors in the beginning stages of authenticity locate themselves in "fragmented, authority-based perceptions" (Cranton & Carusetta 2004, p. 281) based on concrete rules but are unaware of power relations or how they inhabit positions of power in the classroom. In contrast, instructors with a more mature sense of authenticity have a "more integrated sense of self" (Cranton & Carusetta 2004, p. 281) and engage in complex critical reflection: The focus is on questioning the "premises underlying educators' conceptualization of themselves, their students, and the context within which they work" (Cranton & Carusetta 2004, p. 288). Most of the students entering the Radical Humanities learning space are at best tentative learners; it is therefore essential that instructors are maturely authentic both in their beings and pedagogy. Indeed, the success of nontraditional adult learners in a Radical Humanities program requires the presence of mature authenticity in their instructors.

While we acknowledge the central role the instructor plays in addressing and countering both dispositional and institutional barriers to learning, an additional critical role is fulfilled by a person who can connect students to academic and community resources. This role is typically formalized through the Program Coordinator or Program Assistant who helps establish the learning community from student recruitment through interviews and admissions to graduation. This coordinator keeps in close contact with students and follows up if they are absent from class. In addition to managing the practical aspects of the program such as class scheduling and the provision of meals and supplies, the coordinator also offers emotional and practical support throughout students' learning journeys. An instructor from one of the programs spoke about the significance of this role:

> [Our program assistant] who was helping there has been wonderful and just getting a spirit of friendship going.... [She was] just marvellous really and took care of us all of this through grungy details that you have to deal with. (Michael)

Although at one level, the instructors and coordinator offer the simple comfort of a supportive environment and a friendly contact, at another level they offer students a profoundly new way of viewing themselves in relation to learning. Much of the students' shift from a place of denial of self as learner to being fully engaged learners depends on the establishment of a deeply respectful, accepting, and safe learning space.

Safe Space and Building Community

Because the programs' learners have been marginalized and oppressed in many ways, often over a long period, they tend to be extra vigilant to issues of power and safety. Many students actively scope out the classroom before they settle in, planning for escape routes should that be necessary. Others only feel able to open up through discussion and participation when they feel physically, emotionally, and psychologically safe. As outlined above, the ways in which the instructors and program planners frame the course are critical in establishing safety. They model respect and acceptance and enforce healthy boundaries. After all, many of the students have been living isolated or marginal lives and thus have adopted defensive, even belligerent, modes of behaving that have protected them. However, those very behaviors interfere with the creation and maintenance of the community, an essential condition for transformative learning.

The building of community begins from the first encounter potential students have with program planners to the first class session. Most of the program participants point to the crucial role that the regular meals fill in building community. Although the provision of a warm meal prior to a class or a tutorial session might simply seem like a practical support, it physically and symbolically gathers learners, the instructor and tutors around a common goal and space. One instructor described the importance of the communal meal:

> We need to have a common table and eat together, you know and that's a big feature of this program . . . you get to be friends with the people. There are no barriers; they don't think of you as some exalted . . . person. They think of you as another learner in a way. (Ernie)

Attentiveness to the students' stress, anxiety and fears is another critical element in building safety and community. Surveys performed in three programs revealed that the vast majority of students had experienced multiple negative life experiences such as poverty, violence, addictions, homelessness, and chronic illness (Groen & Hyland-Russell, 2007). These experiences manifested in various ways as traumatic reactions. The students are highly attuned to anything that even suggests they may be in harm's way. According to Horsman (1999), there is a strong correlation between people who have experienced violence and those who have had negative experiences with education. Every aspect of the program must be considered in light of students' profound need for safety, trust, and respect. Our experience with Radical Humanities programs has shown that everyone involved in the program—from director to instructor to tutor—must be exquisitely aware of the most finely nuanced aspects of power and how they can be intimidating to a student, even if we are not experiencing the situation in the same way: "A reminder that the experience of trauma intersects with other hierarchies of power is crucial, since worker–learner is a hierarchical relationship. It is particularly important the instructor support learners to honour their own boundaries and avoid pushing them to override boundaries" (Horsman 1999, p. 111).

During her interview, Leeann underscored several times the high value she places on safety and its essential place in the program:

> It feels like a very safe place, yes it does, it really does. Believe me I have a violence detector going on inside of my head... I find as women we have a hard time speaking up. I'm one of those too unless I'm feeling really really comfortable in my setting, as I am right now. I'm very nervous of course but very comfortable in my setting. (Leeann)

Time and again, students spoke of their experiences of being silenced, shunned, ignored, threatened, or bullied by people who wield their power as weapons, whether it be an aid worker who demands a particular form of behavior before resources are allocated or a bus driver who demeans through name-calling or belittling. If poor students have previously experienced such demeaning behavior, then even when we *think* we are mitigating situational barriers through resources like hot meals or bus fares, we may unintentionally brush up against and activate reactions against former acts of oppression that hinder current learning. As we stated earlier, all barriers need to be addressed and their interconnectedness acknowledged. Students need to be helped to understand the intertwined nature of the barriers they face and be given access to resources, such as trained counselors and the insights from research findings such as Horsman (1999). These resources could be used to help them work through some of their habits of response that may not be useful in their current learning community. Yet we need to continually remind ourselves that this transformative process is a long and complex one. According to Magro (2006/2007), "while educational planners may be more successful in reducing situational or institutional barriers to learning, psychological barriers such as fear, low self-esteem, and negative attitudes toward education are the most resistant to change" (p. 71). This is so partly because the habits of mind and body to protect against oppression and trauma are deep-seated and often unconscious. Our experience and research confirm Horsman's (1999) findings that prevalent patterns of disassociation, memory lapses, triggering, and learned helplessness prevail among students who have previously experienced violence or trauma. Thus, even when students show up for class and are fully prepared to learn, their unbidden responses often interfere with their full class participation and grasp of material.

Our findings and experience are that issues of power and dominance, whether in current relationships or as embodied memories of former oppressive relationships, do significantly interfere with students' ability to learn. Thus, while we reject most of Mezirow's (2003) statement that learners who are "hungry, desperate, homeless, sick, destitute and intimidated people obviously cannot participate fully and freely in discourse" (p. 60), we concur wholeheartedly that when people are *intimidated,* they are not free to participate, converse, and learn. A central facet of any Radical Humanities program, then, must be to uncover relationships of power and domination, to counter oppressive practices so that we can create a safe space and build a community free from any form of intimidation. Educator and activist, bell hooks, suggests that "dominator culture promotes a calculated objectivism that is dehumanizing. Alternatively, a mutual partnership model invites an engagement of the self that humanizes, that makes love possible" (2003, p. 131). hooks made clear that radical pedagogy involves not only defining and naming oppressive educational and social practices but also naming and practicing counter-oppressive measures—such as the usually muffled concept of love. She defines love as "a combination of care, commitment, knowledge, responsibility, respect, and trust" (p. 131).

One of our interviewee–learners, Kevin, realized the necessity for this partnership model of learning when he experienced its absence. After completing a course in the *Storefront 101* program, he moved to another town, enrolling in its local college in order to test himself. He felt lonely, isolated, and afraid. "I really messed up [by leaving support behind and trying to do it himself]. I'm lonely, eh." In contrast, while in the *Storefront 101* program, he realized that when there was a program, he could overcome it because "there's help." He appreciated "being able to connect regularly with warm, caring people: planners, tutors, instructors, and people at post-secondary—people who care."

As we seek to remove ourselves from the center, the dominant social sphere, to meet people in a community of learning that straddles both the margins and the elite institutions, we do so in a relationship of mutuality of respect and love. We recognize the courage and resiliency of the learners and their willingness to name that which matters most—the importance of relationships, community, and care. In doing so, it is not only our students who experience the riches of learning in a Radical Humanities course. Indeed, as evidenced in the following statement by an instructor, it is the tutors, instructors, and program directors who believe that they have been enriched by their engagement with the students:

> I just felt incredibly privileged to be part of it. It was a real gift to me to have people so grateful for learning and so gracious....I felt learning was so hon-

> oured and so welcome and so not taken for granted. It was as if though every morsel [pause] was treasured. (Tara)

CONCLUSION

As we continue to work to build communities of learning at the margins of dominant learning institutions and discourses, we are constantly reminded of the need to reassess our assumptions—as researchers, theorists, and teachers—because we are frequently surprised. We are surprised and delighted by the zest and joy for learning manifested by learners in the Radical Humanities programs. We are also humbled by the students' persistent teaching as we become aware of the imbricated policies, practices, and structures that force them to the margins of society. Our students have taught us not only about the gritty, material impoverishment of many people in our current society, but more importantly, the resulting devastating beliefs that cause despair and a firm conviction that they do not merit education. Their perseverance, resilience, courage, and willingness to advocate for themselves and others has given us—all of us who work and research and teach in the field of adult learning—a deeper understanding of the possibilities of transformational learning at the margins of society.

When we diligently and sensitively heed the many aspects of material and non-material barriers to learning and the particular ways these act as forces to splinter the poor; when we deliberately counter these barriers and create a profoundly accepting, non-judgemental and safe learning community; and when we abandon our roles as authoritative teachers for more mature ways of being, then we open ourselves and others to the possibilities of transformation. Then and only then do we begin to change our current relations within systems of power and oppression that have kept the poor at the margins of society. Instead of believing we hold all the answers, we become able to enter into dialogue and become open to receive riches beyond imagining *from* the poor.

AUTHOR NOTES

We are grateful to our colleague Tim Heath who suggested the phrase "riches *from* the poor" during the plenary session of the Radical Humanities Symposium hosted at the University of Calgary, AB (October, 2008). Tim amended Earl Shorris' (2000) phrase "riches for the poor" from his book of the same name that launched the Clemente model to emphasize the wealth of experience, knowledge, and wisdom that the students bring to each other and to the program planners and instructors.

This research was supported by a grant from the Canadian Council on Learning and by the University of Calgary and St. Mary's University College. Our deep thanks go to the instructors, tutors, and program planners of *Radical Humanities* programs across Canada who were gracious in sharing their experience. Most especially, we are grateful to the students of the program who so willingly shared their stories of engagement with learning and who urged us to become learners about poverty.

REFERENCES

Bowl, M. (2001). Experiencing the barriers: Non-traditional students entering higher education. *Research Papers in Education, 16*(2), 141–160.

Clark, M. (1993). Transformational learning. *New Directions for Adult and Continuing Education, 57,* 47–58.

Carusetta, E., & Cranton, P. (2005). Nurturing authenticity: A conversation with teachers. *Teaching in Higher Education, 10*(3), 285–297.

Cranton, P. & Carusetta, E. (2004). Developing authenticity as a transformative process. *Journal of Transformative Education, 2*(4), 276–293.

Cranton, P. & King, K. P. (2003). Transformative learning as a professional development goal. *New Directions for Adult and Continuing Education, 98,* 31–37.

Cross, K. P. (1981). *Adults as learners: Increasing participation and facilitating learning.* San Francisco: Jossey-Bass.

Dirkx, J. (1997). Nurturing soul in adult learning. *New Directions for Adult and Continuing Education, 74,* 79–88.

Giroux, H. (1992). *Border crossings: Cultural workers and the politics of education.* New York: Routledge.

Groen, J., & Hyland-Russell, T. (2007). Radical humanities: Riches of learning for disenfranchised adult learners. In S. Walters & L. Cooper (Eds.), *Proceedings of the 5th International Conference on Researching Work and Learning* (pp. 291–296). Cape Town, South Africa.

Groen, J., & Hyland-Russell, T. (2009). *Radical humanities: A pathway toward transformational learning for marginalized non-traditional adult learners.* The Canadian Council on Learning Research Report. (Unpublished manuscript; manuscript submitted for publication)

hooks, b. (2003). *Teaching community: A pedagogy of hope.* New York: Routledge.

Horsman, J. (1999). *Too scared to learn: Women, violence and education.* Toronto: McGilligan.

Jackson, S. (1997). Crossing borders and changing pedagogies: From Giroux and Freire to feminist theories of education. *Gender and Education, 9*(4), 457–467.

King, K. P., & Wright, L. (2003). New perspectives on gains in the ABE classroom: Transformational learning results considered. *Adult Basic Education, 13*(2), 100–123.

Magro, K. (2006/2007). Overcoming the trauma of war: Literacy challenges of adult learners. *Education Canada, 47*(1), 70–74.

Merriam, S. (2004). The role of cognitive development in Mezirow's transformational learning theory. *Adult Education Quarterly, 55*(1), 60–68.

Mezirow, J. (1978). Perspective transformation. *Adult Education, 28,* 100–110.

Mezirow, J. (1991). *Transformative dimensions of adult learning.* San Francisco: Jossey-Bass.

Mezirow, J. (2003a). *Learning as transformation: Critical perspectives on a theory in progress.* San Francisco: Jossey-Bass.

Mezirow, J. (2003b). Transformative learning as discourse. *Journal of Transformative Education, 1*(1), 58–63.

Mezirow, J. (2004). Forum comment on Sharan Merriam's "The role of cognitive development in Mezirow's transformational learning theory." *Adult Education Quarterly, 55*(1), 69–70.

Parnham, J. (2001). Lifelong learning: A model for increasing the participation of non-traditional adult learners. *Journal of Further and Higher Education, 25*(1), 57–65.

Schuetze, H., & Slowey, M. (2002). Participation and exclusion: A comparative analysis of non-traditional students and lifelong learners in higher education. *Higher Education, 4,* 309–327.

Shorris, E. (2000). *Riches for the poor: The Clemente course in the humanities.* New York: W.W. Norton & Co.

Spellman, N. (2007). Enrollment and retention barriers adult students encounter. *The Community College Enterprise, 13*(1), 63–79.

Taylor, E. (2000). Fostering Mezirow's transformative learning theory in the adult education classroom: A critical review. *The Canadian Journal for the Study of Adult Education, 14*(20), 1–28.

Willans, J., & Seary, K. (2007). 'I'm not stupid after all'—changing perceptions of self as a tool for transformation. *Australian Journal of Adult Learning, 47*(3), 433–452.

CHAPTER 4

USING TECHNOLOGY TO IMPROVE PEDAGOGY AND EMPOWERMENT WITH LOW-LITERACY ADULTS

Kathleen P. King
University of South Florida

At a time when technology-driven functions permeate our lives, adult literacy students who have not mastered media literacies, technology literacies, and information literacies remain excluded from many experiences as well as economically viable opportunities. The world of work in the 21st century also is immersed in global economics, ubiquitous networks, multiple forms of technology communications, and the incessant, often frustrating changes in technology hardware, functions, and related skills. When college-educated professionals have to work hard to keep up with this breakneck pace of change, how well are we preparing adult literacy students to successfully survive? The solution to this dilemma is that our adult literacy educational orientation, instruction, and programs must incorporate the vital technology and related literacies listed above in their baseline definition of proficiency and services. Through relevant and accessible examples,

Learning for Economic Self-Sufficiency, pages 49–65

this chapter will demonstrate many opportunities for technology learning that are meaningfully and effectively integrated into literacy education. The purpose of these efforts is critical pedagogy: to use technology in instruction as a stepping stone for greater learning, economic opportunities, validation, and empowerment.

OPPORTUNITY IN A PINK SLIP

Martin and Barbeen live in rural South Carolina. Having been laid off from a closing retail store, Barbeen decided to try to retrain for a different career. The problem was she had to address the literacy issues she had hidden for so long. While she could follow conversation and speak quite well, the written word was a mystery.

Barbeen had delayed her return to school and training because her early education had been a terrible experience. Economic needs were such that the family of five needed two incomes; jobs were scarce for unskilled labor. The equation added up to Barbeen choosing to take the risk of learning, overcoming past failures and maybe, just maybe, opening new chapters of her life and somehow connecting with her family needs. Such an experience could be life changing for others as well: her children needed to understand how to succeed for themselves.

INTRODUCTION

Barbeen's family in the scenario above is like many others who are getting increasingly squeezed by the demand for greater academic and technology skills in the workplace. No longer optional skill sets, technology learning and use have become so fundamentally ingrained in employers' expectations that hiring technologically-inexperienced prospects is too great a risk and investment.

Moreover, workplace skill expectations include not only technology literacy, but also a constellation of related skills categorized under the umbrella term, 21st century learning. The composite elements include vital skills which are essential in the business context that has evolved alongside our global, technology-based, and 24–7 marketplace.

Demand for Literacy

Adults who have not conquered literacy challenges are necessarily excluded from 21st century skills. Many of these skills are text based, and most tasks required of employees revolve around data entry, information research, retrieval, analysis, synthesis, and reports. In addition, being able to record, read, and transfer or publish schedules, reports, and task progress or meeting notes are essential as much work continues to be done in team settings within businesses (King & Sanquist, 2009; The Partnership for 21st Century Skills, 2004).

When individuals are not text literate, they are outside the *entire* scope of such employment opportunities. Instead, they are relegated to lower paying, more transient employment. In hard-pressed financial times and increasing unemployment, many of these lower income jobs tend to become part-time positions. This situation demands that many heads of household juggle three to five underpaid part-time jobs in order for a family to survive.

In these ways, economic needs, employability, security, and advancement now become contingent on not only basic literacy, but also this aggregate of 21st century learning skills (The Partnership for 21st Century Skills, 2008). This chapter discusses how educators and trainers can incorporate empowering skills into literacy learning to better equip adult learners for 21st century workplace and living demands, thus addressing the cycle of lack of skills and low wage earning.

21ST CENTURY LEARNING: THE GLOBAL AND INFORMATION AGES

Today, we can recognize the signs of 21st century learning in many places in our society and in the literature. Organizations are demanding that employees of all skill levels have a greater capacity for language oral and written literacy, technology literacy, problem solving, self-directed learning, global communications, critical thinking, and basic information, research, and analysis skills (Enriquez, 2001; Gardner, 2006). A critical framing perspective among these individual skills is that effective 21st century workers need to be self-directed: able to recognize, plan and initiate learning through a variety of media and resources. It is no longer a work climate of "I'll wait until the employer provides a training class for me to attend." Instead, employers expect workers and job candidates to recognize what they lack in skills or information and find ways to address those needs, through formal or informal learning avenues (Gardner, 2006). The demand for self-directed learners is inescapable in a technology-driven and rapidly changing society (Kahle, 2002). In this section, critical characteristics of the 21st century learning in the global and information ages are described and discussed. The first focus is considering the nature of learning organizations.

Learning Organizations

Obviously, many employers do not explicitly articulate this statement today. However, if one examines the practice of training services, or lack thereof, the expectations of entry qualifications and workplace responsibilities, one sees just such a situation. Some organizations express employee learning expectations more fully than others. Still others have adopted a learning organization perspective that focuses not just on community and organization, mission, vision and structure, but also self-development, individual, and group initiatives.

Consider the following two quotes about learning organizations from very different sources. The first is an article by Marsick and Watkins (1994) published in the *Journal of Human Resource Development* about learning organizations. This article provides academic insight about the meaning of learning organizations during a time of heightened demand for change and performance on workers, and organizations. Although written in 1994, the contemporary relevance is clear:

> Learning is continuous, linked to daily work, developmental, strategic, and just in time. Learning is built into work planning, career paths, and performance rewards. Employees at all levels develop a habit of learning, asking questions, and giving feedback. They share their learning with others through networked structures, teams, and electronic bulletin boards so that it becomes part of the organization's memory. They are empowered to make decisions that affect their jobs. Learning is rewarded, planned for, and supported through a culture open to risk taking, experimentation, and collaboration. (Marsick & Watkins, 1994, pp. 354–355)

The next example is from one of many popular business speakers and futurists. In this excerpt, Kahle (2002) describes the essential skills he perceives are needed among business employees in the Information Age. Notice the skills, characteristics, and activities in which such typical workers will be involved:

> I believe there is one core skill which will define the most successful individuals. It's the ability and propensity to engage in self-directed learning. The only sustainable effective response to a rapidly changing world is cultivating the ability to positively transform ourselves and our organizations. And that's the definition of self-directed learning.
>
> In the face of a world that is different one week to the next, our most powerful positive response is to cultivate the ability to learn. By "learning," I don't mean just the acquisition of new information, although that is a necessary prerequisite. Rather, I mean the kind of "learning" that requires one to change be-

> havior on the basis of an ever changing understanding of the world. Learning without behavior change is impotent.
>
> The individuals who become disciplined, systematic self-directed learners will be the success stories of the information age. Likewise, those organizations that become learning organizations will have the best chance of surviving and prospering. (Kahle, 2002, para. 3–5)

This contemporary description of learning needs and expectations in organizations demonstrates that the nature of work in higher-earning job placement is drastically different from lower-pay-scale employment. In a technology-driven and rapidly changing society, people in modestly higher-earning positions; entry-level professional positions such as clerks, receptionists, sales; and technicians need to problem solve and engage in teamwork more frequently than other positions. Therefore, we know that the skills needed to prepare for and succeed in these responsibilities will necessarily be different. Through difficult experiences, many workforce training programs have learned that technical skills alone do not meet training needs: instead, the integration of soft skills is much needed for success in the 21st century workforce.

Soft Skills Integration

Furthermore, businesses across varied industries today expect workers to be able to fulfill tasks and responsibilities more independently and to suggest improvements and other initiatives (Enriquez, 2001). Consequentially, employees often are required to work in collaborative groups, requiring a range of interpersonal, language, and social skills that people from other classes with prior life experience and little formal training may not yet possess (King & Sanquist, 2009).

Such workplace expectations reinforce the need to emphasize integrated soft skills and technology skills in workplace training programs, and to use simulations, role playing, and internships to approximate and draw as close as possible to the transfer of learning experience (Galbraith, 2003). Since soft skills include communication, interpersonal, and social skills, preparation and training programs need to both explicitly and interactively include them in learning experiences in order for understanding and practice to occur. For instance, based on individuals' cultural history, personal preferences, and/or past personal experiences, working individually may be a preferred format. Therefore, the need to develop collaborative skills may include emotional adjustment, overcoming fear, and overcoming racism, separatism or religious mores, taboos, or traditions (Frankel, Swanson, & Sagan, 2005).

The need to help our low English literacy students prepare for these situations is paramount for their basic ability to interview well, enter a new work environment, and succeed. These are the very aspects of workplace training and placement our programs struggle with the most, and it is in part because those responsible for funding these programs devalue their importance (Longman, Atkinson, Miholic, & Simpson, 1999). Moreover, once placed, students are no longer directly within range of program services. However, as we continue, we will discover the learning need may also provide some solutions.

As people move up from low wage earning employment, they also are more involved in global communications—both with people from around the globe who are locally situated and with those who are in foreign nations. In addition to the interpersonal skills for business employment mentioned previously, other skills must be added to workplace preparation. Not only cross-cultural, multilingual, and international understandings of communication, etiquette, and protocol, but also how to effectively conduct each of these criteria through technology channels is needed for success in business today.

For instance, now a blue-collar worker adjusting to a new workplace must effectively navigate several additional layers of social norms, performance and communication expectations, and protocol. Specifically, not only do people have to learn how to effectively and appropriately communicate, build professional relationships, and conduct business across class, culture, and race, but they must also do so deftly via telephone, email, webcam, web conference, and online work communities (such as, wikis, blogs, LANS, WANS, and proprietary workspaces). Lack of life experience and degree of familiarity with different people, groups, and technologies are decided disadvantages for the poorly literate adults seeking to climb the professional ladder (Wlodkowski & Ginsberg, 1995).

In the midst of these multiple dimensions of responsibilities, differing communication streams and layers, workers will also find that these jobs often require rapid decision making. The expectations are for faster decisions, less routine operations, and more fluid critical thinking. As one climbs the pay scale, often the pressure, expectations, and demands also escalate.

With these simple examples, it is clear that people with less advanced educational and professional training have limited opportunities to advance their employment standing. Our workplace conditions today are such that not only English language literacy, but a complement of professional, cultural, and technology literacy skills, attitudes, perceptions, and behaviors are needed in order to retain a position and have a chance for advancement. In the next section, a specific case example provides a rich context to illustrate and discuss these and other dynamics of 21st century skills preparation.

CASE: Bronx NY: Reaching Upwards with Information Technology Certifications

An example of an educational effort to assist community and individual economic self-sufficiency comes from my experience with a Department of Justice grant that we were awarded at Fordham University RETC Center for Professional Development (http://www.retc.fordham.edu). Having accepted the leadership of this university center in the Bronx, I analyzed the lack of adult education and professional advancement opportunities available for this depressed and marginalized borough of New York City. The number of under-served people in this community is staggering on a city, state, and national scale.

The United States Census (2000) estimated population of the Bronx was 1.3 million people, 36% being Black and 48% being Latino or Hispanic; furthermore, based on 2005 census data, 28.9% of Bronx residents are below the poverty line. According to the 2003 report from the National Center for Educational Statistics, the Bronx had 41% of its population without basic literacy skills, while the state of New York was 22%, compared to the national rate at 14.5%.

Over the years, many of the most marginalized immigrants in New York City have settled, created their communities, and maintained their original languages and cultures in the Bronx. Since the 1970s, when the Bronx experienced severe economic crisis and race riots, there has been a slow rebuilding of economic opportunity. In that context, we examined the opportunities for Bronx residents to move up the pay scale and attain information technology jobs through entry level, intermediate, and advanced certifications. In 2006, while other boroughs had 10–30 centers for such training and testing available, the Bronx had none. Thus, the Department of Justice grant afforded the opportunity to develop such a center and provided exposure and service to parents and high school students through a local training and certification site off campus, in the midst of Bronx life. It was easy to demonstrate that these students were at-risk, because not only were the schools as a whole underperforming; the entire borough was at risk based on economic and social progress and crime rates.

The services and programs were well received. The center gained traffic, but it was difficult to publicize the opportunities other than through the schools. We found that not being a grassroots organization made it more difficult to connect with the community. Even though we made the costs of the service very modest due to the external funding, there was an expectation that the training services would be free. We had tried to make this a project that could be self-sustaining in the future, and it was difficult to get sufficient footholds, traffic, and awareness.

In addition, this project was only able to meet part of the larger community's and residents' educational and employment needs: the formal information technology training. Indeed, we took the parents, schools, teachers, and students a great distance in providing access and introduction to information technology and certifications by offering the following services:

- We provided free classes for parents.
- We introduced parents to computer and Internet use; these were parents who had never touched computers before.
- We helped teachers and parents become technology literate through offsite and in-school professional development programs.
- We provided free certification testing for high school students in special academic programs.
- We dialogued with parent groups about their technology and employment needs.
- We began building relationships to serve the community directly.
- Other services were provided as well.

However, the gaps in skills, experiences, opportunities, and resources remain so wide, and the population in need is so large, that a small project by one institution could not break through in significant numbers. We provided a model of community consensus building, teacher and parent training, community service, and technology and career education; we now need more organizations and companies to contextualize, replicate, and scale this model based on community membership, employment opportunities, and skills needed.

As this chapter continues our discussion of literacy in this volume, there are many terms used in this area of technology-related literacy, but they are neither all equivalent nor interchangeable. Indeed, carefully parsing the varied terms sheds greater light on the breadth of issues and scope of knowledge needed to be a 21st century learner. Just as our world of work is embedded within technology communications, facilitation, production assessment, and delivery, so is our educational process. Therefore, as we help students learn, we should be utilizing technology in order to cultivate the necessary technology-related literacies in the process.

MULTIPLE TECHNOLOGY RELATED LITERACIES

There are several categories of skills and practices related to technology literacies needed for success in the 21st century workplace. This section introduces, discusses, and differentiates among three major areas: multiple media literacies, technology literacy, and information literacy.

Media Literacy

Media literacy is one of the more basic communication literacies. It includes the finding, researching, retrieving, and understanding of content communicated through the media. Such content may include TV, radio, newspaper, magazine, journals, movies, blogs, wikis, and websites because today the media uses all of the above to deliver their messages to the public and targeted constituencies.

How does media literacy impact the literacy practices of adult learners? In fact, not only is it an added layer of context, language, vocabulary, communication, and culture, but it is also a vehicle that often is dominated by hegemonic purposes and values (Dines & Humez, 2003). Even in democratic societies, the media work fervently to try to sway or control public opinion of government, policy, politics, and crises, to name a few. Certainly, in societies where the government dictates the decisions, values, or opinions of the people, such control is more overt.

In recent years, the literature has increasingly addressed the bias of media and false depiction of groups to serve political agendas or as a form of control and moral purposes (Dines & Humez, 2003). Lull (1995) articulates the state of this situation:

> In the United States, advocacy of alternative political ideologies, parties, and candidates, or suggestions of viable consumer alternatives to the commercial frenzy stimulated and reinforced by advertising and other marketing techniques are rarely seen on the popular media. Radical ideas typically appear only on underfinanced, noncommercial radio, TV stations and in the low budget print media. (p. 64)

With such one-sided representation in the media, even everyday consumers need to hone their critical thinking skills to read between the lines and question motives, methods, and message. Those unschooled in these perspectives or strategies are at a decided disadvantage in society and are being controlled by those constituencies who control the popular media outlets and are eager to reinforce the disenfranchisement of the illiterate and the poor (hooks, 1994).

Effective activities that expose the need for media literacy and the issues of media bias often focus on learner-created content. We find it valuable for learners to investigate a media story, pose questions individually or in the group, and then, based on the questions that are proposed, initiate additional research. This process helps adult learners experience how to proceed from an original artifact (media piece), develop critical questions, plan a course of investigation, and pursue development of a brief essay, poster, or demonstration of their opinion of the original media selection. By incorporating critical literacy, critical thinking, and media literacy into the experience, the activities are not disjointed, but taught as a process that may be genuinely followed in the life or work of a self-directed learner.

Technology Literacy

Since the 1980s and the introduction of the personal computer, microcomputers, and ATMS, technology use has proliferated in many sectors of our lives. While in 1980, one might have had a seemingly easy option to avoid personal computer use, in 2009 that is no longer possible. The ability to use varying forms of technology to meet daily living and work needs is an essential prerequisite for banking, shopping, learning, filing for benefits, and working today. Rather than solely focusing on using a laptop or desktop computer, educators need to broaden their concept to include the multitude of technologies we employ every day. Consider what technology interaction may be required in order to function successfully in society for just one day:

- Use a self-checkout terminal at a grocery store
- Make bank transfers at an ATM
- Complete medical, health, and federal compensation forms electronically (phone, computer, online, kiosk)
- Find books via a database in the library
- Complete initial and renewal forms for department of motor vehicles (online or kiosk)
- Configure contact list, calendars, and ringtones on cell phones
- Send and respond to texts, instant messages, and e-mail with cell phones, smart phones, or computers
- Search for essential health information, school notices, community laws/regulations, community and legal service availability online.

It is has come to my attention that in the past year, more community assistance programs, federal programs, and state agencies are not only making their information available online (that was circa 2000–2003), but *solely* available via online portals (Kakissis, 2002). While this reduces the cost of publication designing, printing, and distribution, it decidedly excludes people who are not technology literate.

Building experiences of exposure, learning, understanding, and meaningful dialogue around these technology uses in the literacy classroom is indispensable for helping adult learners develop greater economic viability. Moreover, embedding technology literacy learning in situated learning, real-life contexts and settings is much more powerful for apprehending concepts and for ultimate transfer of learning than teaching isolated tasks and skills (Argyris & Schon, 1974; Lave & Wenger, 1991).

Information Literacy

The idea that community resources and assistance are available online certainly raises issues of equity, access, rights, and literacy information beyond the scope of solely *technology literacy*. Adults need to master identifying, understanding, and applying information literacy skills. The American Library Association (ALA) describes information literacy as a set of abilities allowing individuals to "recognize when information is needed and have the ability to locate, evaluate, and use effectively the needed information" (2000, p. 2)

How important are information literacy skills in helping literacy learners make gains in economic self-sufficiency? One demonstration of the need may be seen in the 2007 Online Nation report by Allen and Seaman. Community and two-year colleges are often valuable support systems for successful literacy students who seek to pursue their associate's or bachelor's degree. This report from the Sloan Foundation (Allen & Seamen, 2007) reveals that over the last five years, community colleges remain the clear leaders in online learning growth: "Two-year associate's institutions have the highest rate of growth rates and account for over one-half of all online enrollments for the last five years" (p. 1). Therefore, for adult learners to succeed in their preparation for sustainable economic gains at community colleges, they will need full competencies in information literacy.

There is a vast difference between being able to use the Internet and being able to use it to effectively research needed information. Such a task requires the ability to determine, plan, and conduct effective, accurate searches, as well the ability to discern among valid and invalid sources of content. To my growing disbelief, I increasingly hear the remark, "If it is on the Internet, it must be true," from inexperienced technology users. In addressing this learning need, one sees an illustration of the critical connections among media literacy understanding, technology literacy, and information literacy in bringing all those skills together.

Understanding issues of purpose, sources, authorship, as well as the technology-based publishing processes via an organizational or company website versus a private blog or wiki need to be explored, discussed, and mastered. The following questions should be considered:

- What is the difference?
- Are there checks and balances in any of these forums?
- How public is the information and who is the real source author of the content?

Some of these answers can be difficult to resolve in the case of websites, blogs, discussion boards, and online environments.

Because all of these technologies are used in business and educational settings, it is vital that literacy education students have valuable leadership and instruction regarding these issues. Learners can gain valuable real-life experiences through situated learning environments in practicing multiple literacy skills in different formats if guided via dialogue, explorations, and discussions through custom designed activities such as WebQuests, curricula, or student-selected topics. An example of such a curriculum is *Web Wisdom by* Tate and Alexander (1999). Information literacy investigations may be conducted individually or in small groups, and projects may include multimedia presentations, oral reports, leading class discussions, or posting countering comments at the source site. When students realize they can not only accurately find and analyze technology-delivered information, but they can also participate in the global discussion, voice and empowerment are unleashed (Tapscott, 2009).

Using Technology-Based Tools

Another approach to increase the professional preparation as well as technology and information literacy skills of low literate adult learners is to improve the pedagogy/andragogy that could empower them. By introducing and continuing technology activities and skills in meaningful, in-depth, and truly integrated ways across their content areas of study, instructors will introduce adult learners to a greater breadth of technology skills as well as other benefits:

- Productivity applications of technology (rather than only social or entertainment use such as that with which many young adults are familiar)
- Research skills for academic study that incorporate online resources, better translating to work environments
- Critical thinking skills to assess how situations of using technology are similar and different and, thereby, develop strategies to address those
- Problem solving skills in negotiating new learning and the usual technical snafus
- Self-directed learning strategies to find computer-based, online, or other technical support for technical needs
- Greater self-efficacy in business, technology, and professional skills
- Increased variety and expertise with skills suitable for a broader range of better wage-earning employment (for example, computer use, online technologies, email, word processing, or perhaps spreadsheets or databases).

Furthermore, based on the specific applications used in the classrooms, the learning may also result in:

- Technical skills and behaviors to facilitate collaborative learning and interactions
- Multiple strategies as teachers introduce technology skills through their own learning approaches
- Additional development of soft skills and multicultural communication skills through technology based communications: phone, email, text message, Voice Over Internet Protocols (VOIP), discussion boards, to name a few
- Increase viable and low-cost options for international communication with prospective employers, current employers, family, friends, medical services, and educational institutions
- Integrating technology in the learning experiences of low literacy adults prepares them to actively engage in the workplace and community while advancing formal content skills. This involvement provides a vital foundation for participation, voice, and advocacy.

ACTION: FIRST STEPS OF ADULT LITERACY EDUCATORS

Guidelines for creating meaningful technology-integrated literacy instruction include several imperatives for organizations, adult educators, and trainers to consider (Clarke, 2008). As in most approaches to adult learning, this situation needs to emphasize context and learner needs. The preparation aspect of this instruction is essential for success with literacy learners in pre-employment and workplace training. Instructors who study their learners carefully discuss their needs; they also dialogue about their aspirations, learning styles, barriers, and preferences and are better able to design instructional activities that will match the needs, abilities, and skills of their students.

In a simple three-step process we might consider Preparation, Delivery, and Assessment as our major stages of instructional technology delivery, as in most approaches to instructional design. However, we need to be even more attentive to students' needs, resources, and responsiveness. Similarly, we need to be mindful of the following observations: When are students asking more questions? Does their body language indicate confusion? Are they hesitant to ask for help? Which of their key interests can be used as research assignments to assist them in conquering their hesitations, barriers, or fears?

Adult literacy programs will find it most effective if they can design and schedule classes and resources for not only computer lab environments where students can access computers, internet, printers, and scanners throughout the day, weekends, and evenings, but also classrooms that have one or more computers in each. In this way, as learners work in various content areas and on assignments, they can use computers for researching, writing, editing, or developing media. By experiencing truly integrated technology in their literacy instruction, learners begin to realize a shift in their worldview of technology. In these situations, technology becomes part of their environment—one of the many tools they use throughout the day, rather than an isolated, mysterious, or untouched resource.

Concomitant with adult literacy instruction that is integrated with technology is professional development for teachers that helps them develop new skills and perspectives of integrating technology meaningfully to their classroom teaching, preparation, and assessment. Such change in teaching practice, and sometimes philosophy, is not superficial. In order to support educators in this learning and professional evolution, ongoing professional development is needed. Furthermore, the training for the educators should be practical, hands-on, and supportive of their own learning needs. Professional development, which addresses the needs of teachers as adult learners, provides individual support, group work, and peer discussion. Through carefully designed professional development using adult learning principles, teachers may experience the building of reflective practice and instructional technology integration while effecting perspective transformation (Cranton & King, 2003; King, 2002, 2003).

Based on the literature, such teacher professional development should incorporate the following essentials:

- Activities for each educator to self-assess, reflect upon, and consider each
  - Learning style (Advanogy, 2003, 2003–2007)
  - Teaching style (Grasha & Riechmann-Hruska, 1996)
  - Educational philosophy (Kellerman, 2001)
- Exploration of the potential of technology integration in literacy instruction through
  - Cases
  - Sample lessons
  - Evaluations of the merits and difficulties of each example
- Identification and incorporation of the needs of their students in the technology assisted learning
- Strategies for facilitating collaborative and small group instruction
- Exploration of different classroom management and layout designs to incorporate computers in the classroom space and instructional time frame

- Incorporation of reflective journaling to encourage educators to consider the learning they experience and its meaning for their practice and perspectives of teaching and learning.
- Design and evaluation of lessons that are meaningful and incorporate
  - Critical thinking
  - Dialogue
  - Real-life application (King, 2002, 2003; King, Melia, & Dunham, 2008).

CONCLUSION

Looking Forward: Building on Practice, Developing New Pathways

Realizing the potential to prepare low literacy adult learners for employment in better compensation jobs has many benefits. Not only will learners gain more comprehensive and integrated educational experiences, they will also build lifelong skills of self-directedness, research, technology skills, information literacy, media literacy, critical thinking, problem solving, cross-cultural communication, interpersonal skills, and other soft skills. Certainly exclusive focus on workbooks, worksheets, and test scores in literacy education will not prepare adult learners for the challenges ahead in better wage-earning employment.

Today, employers demand more initiative, preparation, and critical thinking from workers at every level (Enriquez, 2001; Gardner, 2006; Marsick & Watkins, 1994). If educators and organizations are to assist in solving the issues of cyclical welfare generations and low skills/low income, we must incorporate the skills needed in the workplace into our literacy and workplace training classes today. This chapter has provided an overview of the scope of the problem and recommended approaches and strategies to plan and deliver 21st century learning that will leverage literacy practices for greater earning power.

REFERENCES

Advanogy. (2003). *Memletics Learning Styles Inventory ver 1.2.* Des Plaines, IL: Author. Retrieved December 1, 2009, from http://www.learning-styles-online.com/inventory

Advanogy. (2003–2007). *Learning styles overview.* Des Plaines, IL: Author. Retrieved December 1, 2009, from http://www.learning-styles-online.com/overview/

Allen, L., & Seaman, J. (2007). *Online nation.* Needham, MA: Sloan-C Foundation. Retrieved January 20, 2009, from http://www.sloan-c.org/publications/survey/pdf/online_nation.pdf

American Library Association (ALA). (2000). *Information literacy competency standards for higher education.* Retrieved November 12, 2009, from http://www.ala.org/ala/mgrps/divs/acrl/standards/standards.pdf

Argyris, C., & Schon, D. A. (1974). *Theory in practice.* San Francisco: Jossey-Bass.

Clarke, M. (2008). Understanding and managing employability in changing career contexts. *Journal of European Industrial Training, 32*(4), 258–284.

Cranton, P., & King, K. P. (2003). Transformational learning as a professional development goal. In K. P. King & P. A. Lawler (Eds.), *New perspectives on designing and implementing professional development for teachers of adults: New Directions for Adult and Continuing Education* (pp. 31–38). San Francisco: Jossey-Bass.

Dines, G., & Humez, J. M. (2003). *Gender, race and class in media* (2nd ed). Thousand Oaks, CA: Sage.

Enriquez, J. (2001). *As the future catches you: How genomics and other forces are changing your life, work, health and work.* New York: Three Rivers Press.

Frankel, R., Swanson, S., & Sagan, M. (2005, September). The role of individualism/collectivism in critical classroom encounters: A four country study. *Journal of Teaching in International Business 17*(1/2), 33–59.

Galbraith, M. (Ed.). (2003). *Adult learning methods: A guide for effective instruction* (3rd ed). Malabar, FL: Krieger.

Gardner, H. (2006). *Five minds for the future.* Cambridge, MA: Harvard Business School Press.

Grasha, A., & Riechmann-Hruska, S. (1996). *Teaching styles survey: Grasha-Riechmann.* Retrieved January 25, 2009, from http://www.longleaf.net/teachingstyle.html

hooks, b. (1994). *Teaching to transgress: education as the practice of freedom.* New York: Routledge.

Kahle, D. (2002). *The ultimate survival skill for the information age.* Retrieved January 30, 2009, from http://www.davekahle.com/article/ultimate.html

Kakissis, J. (2002, Feb. 28). Paper tax forms hard to find in North Carolina; IRS encourages online filing. *The News & Observer.* Retrieved January 10, 2010 from http://findarticles.com/p/articles/mi_hb5553/is_200202/ai_n21595979/

Kellerman, J. (2001). *PAEI (Lorraine Zinn instrument) online.* Baltimore, MD: University of Maryland. Retrieved January 25, 2009, from http://www25.brinkster.com/educ605/paei_howtouse.htm

King, K. P. (2002). *Keeping pace with technology: Educational technology that transforms. Vol. I.* Cresskill, NJ: Hampton Press.

King, K. P. (2003). *Keeping pace with technology: Educational technology that transforms. Vol. II.* Cresskill, NJ: Hampton Press.

King, K. P., Melia, F., & Dunham, M. (2008). Guiding our way: Teachers as learners in online learning. In C. Van Slyke (Ed.). *Information communication technologies: Concepts, methodologies, tools and applications* (pp. 2193–2208). New York: Information Science Reference.

King, K. P., & Sanquist, S. (2009). 21st century learning and human performance. In V. Wang, & K. P. King, (Eds.). *Fundamentals of human performance and train-*

ing. Series: Adult education special topics: Theory, research and practice in lifelong learning (pp. 61–88). Charlotte, NC: Information Age.

Lave, J., & Wenger, E. (1991). *Situated learning: Legitimate peripheral participation.* Cambridge, UK: Cambridge University Press.

Longman, D., Atkinson, R., Miholic, V., & Simpson, P. (1999). Building long-range workplace literacy projects. In J. L. Higbee & P. L. Dwinell (Eds.), *The expanding role of developmental education* (pp. 31–42). Morrow, GA: National Association for Developmental Education. Retrieved February 2, 2009, from http://www.nade.net/documents/Mono99/monp99.all.pdf

Lull, J. (1995). *Media, communication, culture: A global approach.* Cambridge, UK: Polity Press.

Marsick, V. J., & Watkins, K. E. (1994). The learning organization: An integrative vision for HRD. *Human Resource Development Quarterly, 5*(4), 353–360.

National Center for Educational Statistics. (2003). *National assessment of adult literacy (NAAL)* Retrieved February 3, 2009, from http://nces.ed.gov/naal/estimates/overview.aspx

Tapscott, D. (2009). *Grown up digital.* New York: McGraw-Hill Professional.

Tate, M., & Alexander, J. (1999). *Web wisdom: How to evaluate and create information quality.* New York: Lawrence Erlbaum.

The Partnership for 21st Century Skills. (2004). *Framework for 21st century learning.* Tucson, AZ: The Partnership for 21st Century Skills. Retrieved January 28, 2009, from http://www.21stcenturyskills.org/documents/frameworkflyer_072307.pdf

United States Census. (2000). New York by county: GCT-PL. Race and Hispanic or Latino. Retrieved February 2, 2009, from http://factfinder.census.gov/

Wlodkowski, R., & Ginsberg, M. (1995). *Diversity and motivation: Culturally responsive teaching.* San Francisco: Jossey Bass.

CHAPTER 5

THE CONNECTION BETWEEN HEALTH LITERACY AND ADULT LITERACY IN DEVELOPING ECONOMIC SELF-SUFFICIENCY

Lilian H. Hill
The University of Southern Mississippi

Imagine being a single parent struggling with low literacy and poverty and your child is about to enter kindergarten. Several vaccinations are required before she can be enrolled, and the school provides you with a pamphlet containing information regarding reasons why vaccinations are required, where the shots can be obtained, their cost, contact phone numbers, and documentation needed by the school to verify that your child received them. Once you understand the information, you must schedule an office visit, which involves calling for an appointment, locating the clinic on a map, organizing and paying for transportation, answering questions about your child's health and previous vaccinations, and paying for the expense. Many childhood vaccinations involve a schedule of shots, meaning you must track them on a calendar. Accessing the services of an agency that provides

Learning for Economic Self-Sufficiency, pages 67–83

reduced cost or free vaccinations for low-income parents involve comprehending more written information. For parents with the lowest literacy, the skills embedded in this seemingly simple requirement are complex (Foulk, Carroll, & Wood, 2001).

Estimates of the prevalence of low health literacy range between one third to almost half of the U.S. population (Golbeck, Ahlers-Schmidt, & Paschal, 2005; Kutner, Greenberg, Yin, & Paulsen, 2006). Research indicates a clear discrepancy between the skills "needed to understand and comply with health-related materials and instructions (e.g., patient education brochures, medication labels, consent forms, verbal instructions, and discharge instructions) and the health literacy abilities of many Americans" (Schwartzberg, Cowett, VanGeest, & Wolf, 2007, p. S97). Low literacy has been linked with not only poverty but also poor health outcomes, delayed/incorrect diagnosis, compromised disease management skills, and higher healthcare costs. Literacy has a direct influence on patient "access to crucial information about their rights and their healthcare, whether it involves following instruction for care, taking medicine, comprehending disease-related information, or learning about disease prevention and health promotion" (Rudd, Moeykens, & Colton, 1999, para. 9). Indeed, lower health literacy levels are associated with poor self-assessment of health, lack of access to health insurance, and difficulties with accessing and interpreting health information (Kutner, Greenberg, Jin, & Paulsen, 2006).

DEFINING HEALTH LITERACY

Given this information, it is not surprising that both health professionals and adult educators are concerned about health literacy. The term has acquired various meanings since the early 1990s and now ranks as one of four key public health priorities in the United States, alongside disease prevention, eliminating health disparities, and public health preparedness (Office of the Surgeon General, n.d., p. 1). A frequently cited definition from the Institute of Medicine (2004) describes health literacy as "the extent to which individuals have the capacity to obtain, process, and understand basic health information services needed to make appropriate health decisions" (p. 2). Other definitions involve the cognitive and social skills that affect people's motivation and abilities for gaining access to, understanding, and using information in ways that promote health and describe it as a "critical empowerment strategy to increase people's control over their health, their ability to seek out information and their ability to take responsibility" (Wait, Kickbusch, & Maag, 2005, p. 8). Useful foundational knowledge includes health-related vocabulary and conceptual knowledge regarding health (Baker, 2006). These are related to basic literacy skills, but health literacy is context-specific. Understanding the demands of the healthcare setting is impeded for people who are unfamiliar with its concepts and vocabulary.

The definitions above present health literacy as individual capacities with which people acquire and process health-related information. An alternate perspective is to view health literacy in relationship to a person's interactions with the healthcare system, and in this more dynamic perspective it can be recognized that a person's health literacy may fluctuate depending on the complexity of medical conditions and the interactions between patients, healthcare providers, and healthcare systems (Baker, 2006). One perspective that is gaining currency is to view health communications as a mutual responsibility between patients, health providers, and health systems. In other words, the meaning of health literacy refers to patients' ability to find and use health information, providers' ability to communicate, as well as health systems policies that either facilitate or impede communication with patients (Jupka, 2008). One of the original authors of the Institute of Medicine's definition proposed the following revision: health literacy refers to the "capacity of individuals, organizations and communities to obtain, process, understand and share basic health information and services needed to make appropriate health decisions" (Smith, 2008). This view emphasizes the need to create more accessible patient information and to confirm that patients can understand, retain, and use health information.

Health literacy involves a wide range of skills, including some knowledge of biology and preventive self-care; the ability to navigate the health systems environment, understand diagnoses, comprehend health explanations and instructions; and the skills to follow medical directions. Reading comprehension is one of the most important literacy skills required to negotiate healthcare demands, but prose, document, and numeracy skills are also needed (Gazmararian, Parker & Baker, 1999). Patients are routinely expected to read and understand medication labels, participate in diagnostic screenings, measure liquid medications, follow dosing schedules, comprehend informed consent documents and insurance forms, make follow-up visits on schedule, and read and comprehend health materials. Greater literacy burdens fall on those with chronic illnesses such as asthma and diabetes, which involve sophisticated knowledge about managing the condition, changing health habits, and handling acute situations. Health literacy assists people to learn about the medical conditions they have and accept lifestyle changes that a diagnosis may necessitate (Foulk, Carroll, & Wood, 2001).

Language is not a neutral medium of communication but, instead, is situated in a person's larger social world. Greenberg (2001) noted that many definitions of health literacy ignore the reasons why patients have difficulty knowing what to tell doctors and complying with medical treatments. These include the "receptive and expressive oral communication skills that are necessary to navigate the health environment" (p. 70). According to Greenberg (2001), the Institute of Medicine's definition of health literacy, the definition used in the introduction of this chapter, may be particularly problematic. The Institute of Medicine's definition

> ignores English as a second language, medical jargon, and vernacular issues. Secondly, it assumes that the onus of responsibility is on the patient, when in many cases it is a shared responsibility, with the medical professional knowing what, how, and when to ask or state comments and questions. Third, it does not address the assumed shared knowledge of the medical profession. For example, many individuals have misconceptions that are not addressed by health professionals.... Not surprisingly, many patients commonly complain that physicians do not explain their illness or treatment options in terms they can understand. (Greenberg, 2001, p. 70)

Freire and Macedo (1987) noted that for literacy to be meaningful, it must be "situated within a theory of cultural production and perceived as an integral part of the way in which people produce, transform, and reproduce meaning" (p. 142). Literacy must be seen as a "political phenomenon, and it must be analyzed within the context of a theory of power relations and an understanding of social and cultural reproduction and production" (Freire & Macedo, 1987, p. 142). Communications between health providers and low literate patients are compromised by unequal power relationships and the ways in which language, vocabulary, and communication styles are used.

PREVALENCE OF LOW HEALTH LITERACY

The 2003 National Assessment of Adult Literacy (NAAL; Kutner, Greenberg, Jin, Boyle, Hsu, & Dunleavy, 2007) used the same definition of literacy as the 1993 National Adult Literacy Survey, but the 2003 NAAL testing instrument differed in two important ways: (1) the scale used to rate adults' literacy was changed, and (2) health literacy items were incorporated (Kutner, Greenberg, Yin, & Paulsen, 2006). The 2003 NAAL categorized each of the health literacy tasks as clinical, prevention, or health systems navigation, and mapped to the performance scales used throughout the NAAL of Proficient, Intermediate, Basic, and Below Basic. Examples of health literacy tasks included: "filling out patient information forms for an office visit" (clinical); "identifying signs and symptoms of health problems" (prevention); or "understanding what a health insurance company will and will not pay for" (health systems navigation) (Kutner, Greenberg, Ying, & Paulsen, 2006, p. 3). Health literacy tasks were classified along with other tasks as prose, document, or quantitative literacy problems (Kutner, Greenberg, Ying & Paulsen, 2006).

Of the 19,000 adult participants surveyed for the 2003 NAAL, the majority were rated at intermediate health literacy (53%), 12% were rated as proficient, 22% had basic health literacy, and 14% were below basic literacy (Kutner, Greenberg, Jin, & Paulsen, 2006). The real-world implications for the 36% of participants who scored at either basic or below basic indicate that these individuals would have difficulty with many of the tasks involved with navigating the healthcare system and caring for their health. Women, Whites and Asian–Pacific Islanders tended to have higher average health literacy than men, Blacks, Hispanics, American Indians/Alaska Natives, and multiracial adults. Higher average health literacy rates existed in participants who spoke only English before beginning school compared to participants who spoke other languages and those who spoke both English and another language. Average health literacy increased with each level of educational attainment, beginning with high school and GED completion, while 49% of those participants who had not completed high school were ranked at below basic literacy. Those living in poverty also tended to have low health literacy. Participants who received health insurance through their (or their family member's) employer, the military, or private insurance companies tended to have higher average health literacy.

LITERACY AND ECONOMIC SELF-SUFFICIENCY

A powerful determinant of health is socioeconomic status, resulting from a mix of income, education, and employment, and it has been documented that people of higher socioeconomic status tend to adopt healthy lifestyles and participate in health screenings, partially because they can afford them and they can more easily comprehend the information (Foulk, Carroll, & Wood, 2001). Literacy has been described as a form of currency in modern society, linked with "social and economic variables such as voting, economic status, weeks worked, and earnings reported" (Foulk et al., 2001, p. 8), and those with limited literacy will find it more difficult to attain their personal goals for earning a living, making consumer decisions, participating as a citizen, and achieving self-sufficiency (Foulk et al., 2001). Low health literacy has been found to be prevalent among those with lower socioeconomic status (Porr, Drummond, & Richter, 2006) as well as among racial and ethnic minorities, the elderly, and people living in rural areas (Schwartzberg et al., 2007).

Health is an integral part of maintaining self-sufficiency and is also an important factor in securing and maintaining employment. The results of the NAAL indicate that adults with lower literacy skills tended to be unemployed more often, employed part-time rather than full-time, and to earn less than their counterparts with higher literacy. Half of adults with the lowest literacy were not participating in the labor force. Adults with lower literacy were more often employed in service, construction, production, and transportation while adults with higher literacy were found in professional and management positions. Not surprisingly, adults with lower literacy earned lower salaries. Overall, the higher the literacy level a person had the higher his/her household income (Kutner et al., 2007).

The NAAL (2003) found that individuals with low literacy also experience reduced access to health insurance because the treatments they are prescribed may be unaffordable, especially prescription medicines. For example, some medications for rare conditions can cost more than $10,000 annually, and cancer treatments may cost many times more than that. Even with health insurance coverage, increasing co-payments require that patients with limited resources make choices between which treatments and medications they can and cannot afford. Individuals living in poverty, especially the elderly, make difficult choices between medical treatment, heating their homes, and buying food. Furthermore, despite pervasive public health messages encouraging healthy eating, the necessary foods are often inaccessible in low-income communities due to an absence of grocery stores that stock a variety of healthy foods. In some areas, the only store may be a convenience store that carries high-calorie snack foods, making it impossible to follow healthy eating guidelines.

Subban (2007) noted that "low-level literacy negatively affects a person's level of income, ability to access to employment and institutions, and sense of self-worth" (p. 68). Subban (2007) further explained that economic status and low literacy interferes with community participation, meaning that people have less influence on community initiatives that affect them. Literacy skills contribute to better problem solving and critical assessment of information, and these may contribute to "better coping mechanisms, improved access to health services and the adoption of health practices, all crucial for sustaining psychological, mental and physical health" (Feinstein & Hammond, 2004, p. 201). Lacking these skills makes health decisions and navigating the healthcare system difficult indeed.

CONSEQUENCES OF LOW HEALTH LITERACY

When health providers communicate the benefits and risks of recommended treatments, low health literacy can impair their patients' understanding (Davis, Williams, Marin, Parker & Glass, 2002). Consequences may include an "incorrect use of medications; failure to comply with medical directions; unhealthy lifestyle practices; greater prevalence of disabilities and chronic illnesses; risk of injury in the workplace, the community, and at home; and inability to access and to make effective use of the healthcare system" (Porr et al., 2006, p. 329). Patients with low health literacy may have limited economic resources as well as health beliefs that interfere with their ability to follow healthcare provider's instructions. As a result, they will often be labeled "noncompliant." Low health literacy has been found to be strongly associated with medication nonadherence (DiMateo, 2004) and poor health outcomes (Mayeaux et al., 1996).

Individuals with low health literacy are less likely to seek out preventive care such as dental or vision checkups, osteoporosis screening for women, prostate screening for men, and colon cancer screening (White, Chen, & Atchison, 2008). Low health literacy skills make it more difficult to navigate the complexities of paying for health services and applying for assistance, while poverty makes it less likely that people will have access to health insurance. Although the U.S. is known as one of the world's wealthiest countries, healthcare costs are among the leading cause of individuals filing for bankruptcy—and many who file do have medical insurance (Health Insurance Costs, p. 21).

A common misconception is that the poor receive free medical care. However, even when a person qualifies for this type of free medical care, there are significant costs involved. The patient may not receive treatment in a timely manner, allowing the condition to progress, sometimes to the point that treatment is more drastic than might have been needed or is ineffective. A patient may be treated in a hospital system that trains health providers, engendering a loss of privacy and dignity for the patient.

Potential Strategies

Due to the complexity of the issues regarding health literacy and economic self-sufficiency, there is no single solution and instead, a multiple-pronged approach is recommended, which is, in fact, already occurring: (1) health providers are working to communicate more clearly, (2) community empowerment projects are reaching out with health information, and (3) adult educators and members of the healthcare sector who believe that health literacy is a mutual responsibility are forming partnerships to improve health literacy.

Health Communications

Considerable interest in health literacy within the healthcare sector is leading to growing efforts to communicate in more intelligible ways. In a study of how health providers adjusted communication for low literate patients, the most common strategies used were using simple language, providing simplified printed materials, speaking more slowly, reading instructions out loud, writing down instructions, and presenting a limited number of concepts (Schwartzberg et al., 2007). The healthcare system relies heavily on patient education materials such as brochures and other printed materials; however, the value of these health communications is dependent on whether patients find them accessible and useful. Patients' perceptions of health communications relate extensively to their readability and cultural sensitivity (Wilson, Baker, & Brown-Syed, 2000). A consistent problem is that the reading level demanded by many health-related materials exceeds that of many adults (Bottrel, Alpert, Fischbach, & Emanuel, 2000; Bryant et al., 2001; Clerehan, Buchbinder, & Moodie, 2005; Paasche-Orlow, Parker, Gazmararian, Nielsen-Bohlman, & Rudd, 2005). For example, a review of informed consent documents at a southeastern medical cancer center found none that were written at or below an eighth-grade literacy level, and that they were complex and lengthy enough that patients would be unlikely to read them or comprehend the information the forms are intended to communicate (Sharp, 2004).

Suggestions for improvement of written materials include simplifying the vocabulary used, highlighting the most salient information with graphic elements such as bullets and headings, and adding illustrations (Campbell, Goldman, Boccia, & Skinner, 2004). Simple materials that are attractive and illustrated appeal to many users, including those who read well (Hill, 2008). Illustrations, including pictograms, can aid comprehension, recall, and even adherence with medical information. Visual images do not communicate the same meaning to everyone and may be culturally inappropriate or misunderstood, leading to potentially dangerous consequences. Therefore, it is recommended that visuals be developed in consultation with the cultural group for whom they are intended. Other techniques employed use video and computer-based presentations because video may be more effective than print communication alone (Campbell et al., 2004). An advantage of computer-based presentations is that the user can control the pace of the presentations.

Changes needed to make medical information more accessible extend beyond changing the medium of communication and reducing the reading demand. Medical concepts and vocabulary must also be clearly explained to ensure comprehension. No technique should be considered fully effective without patient counseling in which the health provider spends enough time to be sure that the patient fully understands the information and is able to follow the instructions. "Comprehension is a critical factor in patient decisions to seek care and the patients' ability, once care is sought, to act on the health information or instructions received" (Schwartzberg et al., p. S97). To ensure comprehension has taken place, health providers often employ the teach-back method in which the patient is asked to repeat in his/her own words what has been taught. Another strategy is to ask the patient to demonstrate a technique that he or she has been using. For example, a patient may be asked to demonstrate drawing up liquid medication into a syringe. Using this technique, my former colleague learned that a diabetic patient who was struggling to achieve glycemic control did not understand the meaning of the measurement markings on the syringe, so that the doses she injected would always vary.

Significant challenges to patient education are the intersection of diverse cultures and increasing complexity within the healthcare system, meaning that another aspect of effective health communications is cultural appropriateness and sensitivity (Lasch et al., 2000). Increased diversity within the U.S. population is demonstrated in the various languages, dress and diet practices, and in the multiple ways patients perceive illness, health beliefs and health practices (Núñez, 2004). Poor, culturally diverse patients shoulder a disproportionate share of poor health conditions (National Medical Association, n.d.). Health providers lacking cultural understanding may contribute to the health disparities and stereotypes that can impede clinical decision-making (Geiger, 2001).

To address potential misunderstandings created by language, communication styles (including differing standards for directness, body language, and eye contact), health beliefs, and practices, the Office of Minority Health, U. S. Department of Health and Human Services (2001) created *National Standards for Culturally and Linguistically Appropriate Services in Healthcare* (CLAS) with the aim of improving the cultural competence of healthcare organizations and health providers. CLAS standards have been incorporated into accreditation requirements for healthcare organizations, and the three components address translation of medical materials, revision of health systems policies and procedures, and education of health providers The aim is to institutionalize attitudes, knowledge, and skill changes that foster greater inclusivity within healthcare systems. Patient educators have found that representation of specific cultural groups in patient education materials may have a positive impact on use and retention of health information (Baty, Kinney, Ellis, 2003; Guidry & Walker, 1999; Weintraub, Maliski, Fink, Choe, & Litwin, 2004). For example, culturally and linguistically appropriate interventions were found to enhance the rate of cervical screenings in Chinese women residing in North America (Taylor et al., 2002).

Community Empowerment for Health and Wellness

Community-wide empowerment projects can engage both health professionals and adult educators in communicating health information where people live and work. Studies have indicated that when health interventions focus on empowerment at the community level, residents have the opportunity to learn about healthier lifestyles and wellness and are enabled to make systemic, health-promoting community changes (Syme, 2000). One project in Massachusetts trained adult basic education and English as a Second

Language students to become community health advisors (Garner, 2008). Once trained, they presented health information, sometimes in their native language, to fellow students and participated in community health events. The presentations were accompanied by health screenings and explanations of the state's new health insurance laws. Students gained leadership skills and the project gained access to diverse communities where the health advisors lived that might not otherwise have been reached.

University faculty in nursing, nutrition, and adult education in Nova Scotia partnered with community-based literacy programs and rural, tri-county health authorities to explore community health literacy needs and strategies to build on community members' existing skills in order to improve health (Gillis, 2004). A participatory approach was employed to achieve the project goals of changing policies and practices and to build capacity for community health. For the study, 46 adults whose experiences were affected by low literacy were interviewed. Findings revealed the complex interactions between literacy and health. The resulting publication emphasized priorities for improvement and was distributed to research participants, community leaders, and government decision makers. Several community health initiatives have been undertaken in response to the publication. The authors concluded that health literacy involved not only accessing suitable health information but also learning to make personal choices, speaking up about health needs, and gaining control of the factors that promote health.

Community residents often initiate projects regarding issues that most affect them. Residents of the Excelsior District of San Francisco, including many families of color and immigrants, experience noise and air pollution from the large highway and busy city thoroughfares that surround it (Sciammas, Rivard, Wier, Seto, & Bhatia, 2008). The intense traffic caused levels of emissions that exceed public health recommendations and are associated with the community's high levels of asthma hospitalizations, as well high levels of ischemic heart disease, stroke, and lung diseases, including cancer. Community residents, researchers at the city department of public health, and People Organizing to Demand Environmental and Economic Rights (PODER) worked together to conduct a health impact assessment and made recommendations that diesel buses be replaced with hybrid vehicles; truck traffic be minimized near homes, schools, and playgrounds; and truck routes be established that minimize health impacts on neighborhoods. The Municipal Transportation agency has committed to plans to use more hybrid vehicles, and PODER is working to address the problems caused by excessive pollution caused by truck traffic.

Community-based health promotion is perceived as an effective approach that employs community development strategies, respects local concerns, and involves community leaders. A wide variety of settings and community partners can be involved, and, when it is used as a preventive strategy, the "role given to community residents... in setting priorities for health promotion, in determining how these programs will be established, in monitoring progress and evaluating results" (Easterling, Gallagher, & Lodwick, 2003, p. 3) is central. Adult educators may be concerned they lack sufficient health knowledge to participate in community partnerships, but they need not be health experts; rather the expertise they bring is their knowledge of students' needs and the ability to analyze the literacy tasks adults in their community must undertake to improve their health (Rudd, 2007).

Partnerships Between Adult Education and Healthcare

Interest is growing in forming partnerships between the healthcare and adult education sectors to address low health literacy with the understanding that cooperation between adult educators and health providers may enrich adult basic education or literacy classes. Health literacy is of concern to adult educators as a social justice issue related to diversity and social inequities (Hill, 2007); it is similarly related to the healthcare sectors' goals to alleviate health disparities. In both cases, health education contributes to social justice because of the focus on social, economic and political forces that influence people's health (Glanz, Rimer, & Lewis, 2002). Incorporating health education as a component of adult education courses can assist adults to acquire the skills, knowledge, and attitudes needed to affect positive change in their health behaviors and make responsible choices regarding social and environmental issues affecting their lives (Obilade, 2005).

"Adult educators can help health practitioners understand the underlying assumptions in public health and in healthcare, the nature of the demands made on adults, and the need for a better match between these demands and adults' skills" (Rudd, 2007, p. 35). In partnering with adult educators, health providers can provide relevant health information and gain opportunities to better understand their patients' literacy abilities and health needs. At the same time, adult learners gain health knowledge and confidence in navigating the healthcare environment, which may otherwise feel foreign and uncaring. For example, the New York City mayor's office formed a fellowship that places first-year medical students in adult literacy classrooms. The students learned from trained literacy teachers and were able to assist through sustained interaction with adult learners. The program avoided the deficit approach to low literacy that often prevails and familiarized fellowship students with the "struggles and triumphs" of low-income adults rather than "having their experiences collapsed into a description of the 'presenting problem' that clinicians would read on a medical chart" (Tassi & Ashraf, 2008, p. 4). The presence of the fellowship students in the adult literacy classroom helped to demystify the medical profession and healthcare system, and adult learners indicated that they felt more comfortable approaching doctors for information.

Partnerships can involve literacy educators inviting health providers to address specific issues of concern to class members; outreach programs; and task forces and research initiatives that influence health policy (Bennett, Pinder, Szesniak, & Culhane, 2008; Gillis, 2004; McKinney, 2008). The *Take Charge of Your Health* program in Pennsylvania partnered health and literacy educators in order to create a curriculum for mothers of premature infants. The program was distributed by making home visits to women who scored below 6th-grade level on the Test of Adult Basic Education (TABE). The authors noted that this low level of literacy has been linked to a less frequent use of pediatric care services (Bennett et al., 2008). After an unsuccessful classroom initiative, the home visit phase of the program focused more on health systems navigation skills and less on the development of formal literacy skills. Although the process was labor intensive, participants completing the program were complimentary about what they learned and contacted instructors with follow-up questions.

In North Carolina, the division of public health created a task force with the goal of improving health literacy in the state. Forty-nine groups from the areas of healthcare policy, medical education as well as clinical groups and literacy providers collaborated to publish a needs assessment analysis and recommendations to the state's legislature. According to McKinney (2008), collaborators were able to

> build better relations between members of the health and literacy fields, including a better understanding of how each field can benefit from the expertise of the other... the medical professionals in particular were surprised to learn how much adult educators could do for them in terms of guidance in how to reach their patients and making recommendations for clear language. (p. 27)

A project in New York State employed the Health Literacy Study Circles curriculum developed by the National Center for the Study of Adult Literacy to provide professional development for literacy educators. Students pilot-tested written education materials, took tours of hospital departments, and provided feedback to hospital administrators regarding how to improve navigation signage for patients with low literacy skills. Another part of the project was the development of a guide for health professionals about how to form partnerships between health providers and adult educators. The guide is used as part of a program in which "the expertise of adult educators [is employed] to train healthcare providers in effective communication with lower literate patients and the development of appropriate educational materials" (McKinney, 2008, p. 29). In addition, adult educators acquired health knowledge, while students gained tools to access the healthcare environment, communicate with healthcare providers, and advocate for their own needs.

Adult literacy educators may be concerned that studying health topics would interfere with students' ability to learn literacy skills; however, a study using a health literacy curriculum at 42 adult basic education sites in Illinois found that participants increased their literacy scores as well as their health knowledge and skills for navigating the health system (Levy et al., 2008).

Reybold and Johnston-Polacek (2006) caution, however, that an "ideology of health empowerment is insufficient to challenge inequities" (p. 153). Rather, people involved in the partnership must take the time to familiarize themselves with the culture and community, and learn how "race, ethnicity, and class frame relationships among university faculty, community educators and community members" (Reybold & Johnston-Polacek, 2006, p. 156). Adult educators and health providers involved in health literacy projects must accept that the needs are communal and not out there in the community; in other words, they must act as community members. What is also clear is that a program developed for one community cannot necessarily be transferred to another without considerable research, and programs are most effective when individually tailored to the community.

CONCLUSION

Health literacy is a serious concern, both for adult educators and healthcare providers. Definitions differ and include individual patient capabilities to acquire, process, and act on healthcare information; empowerment strategies for using healthcare information to promote health; and a sociocultural activity involving mutual respect and responsibility between patients and health providers. What is agreed upon is that low health literacy affects at least one third of the adult population and that consequences can include nonadherence to medical recommendations, failure to seek preventive care, and poor health outcomes.

Health literacy is integral to achieving and maintaining self-sufficiency, and low health literacy is linked to low socioeconomic status. Strategies for addressing health literacy include community empowerment and outreach, efforts by healthcare providers to communicate more clearly, and partnerships between adult educators and healthcare providers that educate students engaged in literacy classes and adult basic education. These efforts offer opportunities for fostering social justice in which adult educators can be of service.

REFERENCES

Baker, D. W. (2006). The meaning and the measure of health literacy. *Journal of General Internal Medicine, 21,* 878–883.

Baty, B. J., Kinney, A. Y., & Ellis, S. M. (2003). Developing culturally sensitive cancer genetics communications aids for African Americans. *American Journal of Medical Genetics, 118A,* 146–155.

Bennett. I., Pinder, P., Szesniak, R., & Culhane, J. (2008). Taking charge of your health: A collaborative health literacy intervention linking adult education and maternal-infant healthcare. *Focus on Basics, 9B,* 14–20.

Bottrel, M. M., Alpert, H., Fischbach, R. L., & Emanuel, L. L. (2000). Hospital informed consent for procedure forms. *Archives of Surgery, 135,* 26–33.

Bryant, L. D., Murray, J., Green, J. M., Hewison, J., Sehmi, I., & Ellis A. (2001). Descriptive information about Down's syndrome: A content analysis of serum screening leaflets. *Prenatal Diagnosis, 21,* 1057–1063.

Campbell, F. A., Goldman, B. D., Boccia, M. L., & Skinner, M. (2004). The effect of format modifications and reading comprehension on recall of informed consent information by low-income parents: A comparison of print, video, and computer-based presentations. *Patient Education and Counseling, 53,* 205–216.

Clerehan, R., Buchbinder, R. & Moodie, J. (2005). A linguistic framework for assessing the quality of written patient information: Its use in assessing methotrexate information for rheumatoid arthritis. *Health Education Research, 20,* 334–344.

Davis, T. C., Williams, M. V., Marin, E., Parker, R. M. & Glass, J. (2002). Health literacy and cancer communication. CA: *A Cancer Journal for Clinicians, 52*(3), 134–149.

DiMateo, M. R. (2004). Variations in patients' adherence to medical recommendations: A quantitative review of 50 years of research. *Medical* Care, *42,* 200–209.

Easterling, D. V., Gallagher, K. M., & Lodwick, D. G. (2003). *Promoting health at the community level.* Thousand Oaks: Sage Publications.

Feinstein, L., & Hammond, C. (2004). The contribution of adult learning to health and social capital. *Oxford Review of Education, 30*(2), 199–221.

Foulk, D., Carroll, P., & Wood, S. N. (2001). Addressing health literacy: A description of the intersection of functional literacy and healthcare. *American Journal of Health Studies, 17*(1), 7–14.

Freire, P., & Macedo, D. (1987). *Literacy: Reading the word and the world.* South Hadley: Bergin & Garvey.

Garner, B. (2008). Literacy students as health advisors. *Focus on Basics, 9B,* 10–13.

Gazmararian, J. A., Parker, R. M., & Baker, B. D. (1999). Reading skills and family planning knowledge and practices in a low-income managed-care population. *Obstetrics and Gynecology, 93*(2), 239–244.

Geiger, H. J. (2001). Racial stereotyping and medicine: The need for cultural competence. *Canadian Medical Association Journal, 164,* 1699–1670.

Gillis, D. (2004). A community-based approach to health literacy using participatory research. *Adult Learning, 15*(1/2), 14–17.

Glanz, K., Rimer, B. K., & Lewis, F. M. (Eds.). (2002). *Health behavior and health education: Theory, research, and practice.* San Francisco: Jossey-Bass.

Golbeck, A. L., Ahlers-Schmidt, C. R., & Paschal, A. M. (2005). Health literacy and adult basic education assessments. *Adult Basic Education, 15*(3), 151–168.

Greenberg, D. (2001). A critical look at health literacy. *Adult Basic Education, 11*(2), 67–79.

Guidry, J. J., & Walker, V. D. (1999). Assessing cultural sensitivity in printed cancer materials. *Cancer Practice, 7*, 291–296.

Health Literacy Study Circles. Retrieved May 6, 2009, from http://www.ncsall.net/index.php?id=25

Hill, L. H. (2007). Health literacy is a social justice issue that affects us all. *Adult Learning, 15*(1/2), 4–6.

Hill, L. H. (2008). The role of visuals in communicating health information to low literate adults. *Focus on Basics: Connecting Research and Practice, 9B*, 40–46.

Institute of Medicine. (2004). *Health literacy: A prescription to end confusion.* Washington: National Academies Press. Retrieved July 15, 2008, from http://www.iom.edu/?id=19750

Jupka, J. (2008, November 7). *Response to Health Literacy Discussion List.* Retrieved November 15, 2008, from http://www.nifl.gov/mailman/listinfo/Healthliteracy

Kutner, M., Greenberg, E., Jin, Y., Boyle, B., Hsu, Y., & Dunleavy, E. (2007). *Literacy in everyday life: Results from the 2003 National Assessment of Adult Literacy* (NCES 2007–480). Washington, DC: U.S. Department of Education, National Center for Education Statistics.

Kutner, M., Greenberg, E., Jin, Y., & Paulsen, C. (2006). *The health literacy of America's adults: Results from the 2003 National Assessment of Adult Literacy* (NCES 2006–483). U.S. Department of Education. Washington, DC: National Center for Education Statistics.

Lasch, K. E., Wilkes, G., Montuori, L. M., Chew, P., Leonard, C., & Hilton, S. (2000). Using focus group methods to develop multicultural cancer pain education materials. *Pain Management Nursing, 1*, 129–138.

Levy, S. R., Rasher, S. P., Carter, S. D., Harris, L. M., Berbaum, M. L., Mandernach, J. B., et al. (2008). Health literacy curriculum works for adult basic education students. *Focus on Basics, 9B*, 33–39.

Mayeaux, E. J., Murphy, P. W., Arnold, C., Davis, T. C., Jackson, R. H., & Sentell, T. (1996). Improving patient education for patients with low literacy skills. *American Family Physician, 53*(1), 205–211.

McKinney, J. (2008). Partnerships in North Carolina, Wisconsin, and New York. *Focus on Basics, 9B*, 26–30.

National Medical Association Cultural Competence Primer. (n.d.). Retrieved June 20, 2005, from http://www.askme3.org/pdfs/NMAPrimer.pdf

Núñez, A. E. (2004). Transforming cultural competence into cross-cultural efficacy in women's health education. *Academic Medicine 75*, 1071–1079.

Obilade, O. O. (2005). Health education. In L. M. English (Ed.), *International encyclopedia of adult education* (pp. 274–277). London: Palgrave Macmillan.

Office of Minority Health (2001). *National standards for culturally and linguistically appropriate services in healthcare: Executive Summary.* Washington, DC: U.S. Department of Health and Human Services.

Office of the Surgeon General. (n.d.). *Public health priorities.* Retrieved October 30, 2008, from http://www.surgeongeneral.gov/priorities

Paasche-Orlow, M. D., Parker, R, M., Gazmararian, J. A., Nielsen-Bohlman, L. T., & Rudd, R. R. (2005). The prevalence of limited health literacy. *Journal of General Internal Medicine, 20,* 175–184.

Porr, C., Drummond, J., & Richter, S. (2006). Health literacy as an empowerment tool for low-income mothers. *Family and Community Health, 29*(4), 328–335.

Reybold, L. E., & Johnston Polacek, G.N.L. (2006). A critical perspective of health empowerment: The breakdown of theory-to-practice in one Hispanic subculture. *Family and Community Health, 29*(2), 153–157.

Rudd, R. (2007). Let's become partners: Practitioners in the health and education fields need to cooperate. *Adult Basic Education and Literacy Journal, 1*(1), 32–36.

Rudd, R. E., Moeykens, B. A., & Colton, T. C. (1999). Health and literacy: A review of medical and public health literature. *Review of Adult Learning and Literacy* (Vol. 1). San Francisco: Jossey-Bass. Retrieved December 13, 2008, from http://www.ncsall.net/index.php?id=494

Schwartzberg, J. G., Cowett, A., VanGeest, J., & Wolf, M. S. (2007). Communication techniques for patients with low health literacy: A survey of physicians, nurses and pharmacists. *American Journal of Health Behavior, 31*(Supp 1), S96–S104.

Sciammas, C., Rivard, T., Wier, M. Seto, E., & Bhatia, R. (2008). Traffic causes death and disease in San Francisco neighborhood. *Race, Poverty and the Environment, 15*(2), 77–78.

Sharp, S. M. (2004). Consent documents for oncology trials: Does anybody read these things? *American Journal of Clinical Oncology, 27,* 570–575.

Smith, W. (2008, December 4). *Response to Health Literacy Discussion List.* Message posted to Health Literacy listserv. Retrieved March 3, 2009, from http://www.nifl.gov/mailman/listinfo/Healthliteracy

Subban, J. (2007). Adult literacy education and community development. *Interdisciplinary Community Development, 15*(1/2), 67–90.

Syme, S. L. (2000). Community participation, empowerment, and health development of a wellness guide for California. In M. A. Jamner & S. Arokola (Eds.), *Promoting human wellness: New frontiers for research, practice, and policy* (pp. 78–98). Berkeley: University of California Press.

Tassi, A., & Ashraf, F. (2008). Health literate doctors and patients: The New York City Health Literacy Fellowship for first-year medical students. *Focus on Basics, 9B*(1), 3–8.

Taylor, V. M., Hislop, T.G., Jackson, J.C., Tu, S., Yasui, Y., Schwartz, S.M., Teh, C., Kuniyuki, A., Acorda, E., Marchand, A., & Thompson, B. (2002). A randomized controlled trial to promote cervical cancer screening among Chinese women in North America. *Journal of the National Cancer Institute, 94,* 670–677.

Wait, S., Kickbusch, I., & Maag, D. (2005). *Navigating health: The role of health literacy.* Alliance for Health and the Future. Retrieved January 8, 2008, from http://ns1.siteground169.com/~healthan/healthandfuture/images/stories/Documents/navigating%20health%20-%20the%20role%20of%20health%20literacy.pdf

Weintraub, D., Maliski, S. L., Fink, A., Choe, S., & Litwin, M. S. (2004). Suitability of prostrate cancer education materials: Applying a standardized assessment tool to currently available materials. *Patient Education & Counseling, 55*, 275–280.

White, S., Chen, J., & Atchison, R. (2008). Relationship of preventive health practices and health literacy: A national study. *American Journal of Health Behavior, 32*(3), 227–242.

Wilson, F. L., Baker, L. M., & Brown-Syed, C. (2000). An analysis of the reading level and cultural sensitivity of information on the National Cancer Institute's Web site: CancerNet. *Oncology Nursing Forum, 27*, 1403–1409.

CHAPTER 6

ADULT LEARNERS IN URBAN COMMUNITIES

Challenges and Opportunities for Economic Independence

Larry G. Martin
University of Wisconsin-Milwaukee

Low-income adult learners in urban areas face a number of challenges in their efforts to obtain economic independence. This chapter discusses the meaning of financial self-sufficiency in American society; highlights the challenges to low-income urban residents' economic independence; explores the resources, knowledge, and skills required for financial independence; and presents several approaches adult educators and continuing educators can employ to assist low-income urban residents to develop and grow their economic assets via the provision of financial literacy education and training programs.

Learning for Economic Self-Sufficiency, pages 85–102

THE CASE OF DONNELL BROWN

I grew up during the 1950s and '60s in a small city (13,000 people) in a racially segregated Jim Crow-dominated Mississippi. My home was located in a community of self-sufficient African American families who lived on the outskirts of the city. Although most of the families in the community were extremely poor, to my knowledge, none of them received state or federal financial assistance. My father was the son of a successful farmer. His dad had owned over 500 acres of land and consistently produced successful crops; however, my father was unsuccessful at farming and entered construction work as a laborer. Around the community, he was known as a tight-fisted and stingy man, but as he transitioned from a common laborer to a skilled cement finisher, and then to a cement sub-contractor, he managed his income to the point where he was able to accumulate wealth.

During that period, most of our neighbors remained among the working poor. They stayed in dead-end, unskilled jobs that paid minimum wages; hunted and fished for food; retrieved stale and unwanted food discarded from grocery stores; raised and slaughtered livestock (e.g., pigs and chickens); and raised gardens and produced canned vegetables. With our father's financial support, most of my seven siblings and I were able to afford to go to college. Most of my neighbors' children, however, took the same types of low-wage jobs as their parents. During the 1960s and 70s, some of them also experienced out-of-wedlock births and became welfare recipients.

One of my neighbors' sons escaped this economic pattern. Donnell Brown was the son of an ice man. His father, Mr. Joseph Brown, had a large family of ten children. He worked his entire life at an ice plant, delivering ice to families and businesses before refrigerators became widespread. Donnell's sisters and brothers all lived the same low-income lifestyle as his parents. Donnell, however, apparently noticed the alternative financial success experienced by my farther and many of his children. He started to visit my father and talk to him on a regular basis. My father was very free with his financial advice about never living outside of one's income and the value of savings. He shared his advice about the value of hard work and about living a good life. Even his Christian faith and beliefs and his habit of going to church two to four days/nights a week entered these conversations. Donnell listened intently to that advice and shared with my father the decisions he faced at different junctures in his life. While in high school, Donnell worked during the summers for my father's cement finishing business. After he graduated from high school, he moved away from his parents' home, took a job in a larger southern city about one hour's drive from his home town and went to college part-time. He later completed his B.S. degree and worked his way up to being a supervisor in the company that had hired him.

He is now married, has several children and, for all practical purposes, he and his family are financially independent.

INTRODUCTION

Former welfare recipients and some low-income workers receive state and federal support such as child care assistance and state-supported health insurance in their efforts to obtain jobs and to permanently leave the welfare system. These programs, however, were not necessarily designed to be anti-poverty programs to assist individuals and their families toward becoming self-sufficient and financially independent. To achieve that next level of success often requires not only employment that pays family-supporting wages but also a different mindset. As in the case of Donnell Brown, these individuals and their families must often change how they think about money, employment and careers, financial transactions, savings, and asset development. The formula followed by Donnell Brown is still available (with adjustments) to low-income urban families. Like Donnell, they must identify and draw upon the informational assets via financial literacy programs and others in their communities, contact and consult these resources, and possess the personal will and discipline to follow good advice. This chapter discusses the meaning of financial self-sufficiency in American society; the challenges to low-income urban residents' economic independence; the resources, knowledge, and skills required for financial independence; and financial literacy education and training programs.

THE MEANING OF FINANCIAL SELF-SUFFICIENCY IN AMERICAN SOCIETY

According to the American Heritage Dictionary, self-sufficiency is the ability to provide for oneself without the help of others; that is, to be independent (Self-sufficient, 2009). The "independent" American character can trace its historical roots from life on the frontier. Like the racially segregated community in which I grew up, individuals and their families had to maintain a largely independent lifestyle when they were cut off from the vital sources of support often found in towns and cities. Huffstetler (2008) similarly argued that financial independence has three definitions: (1) not relying on others to pay your bills, (2) freedom from all debt, and (3) freedom from having to work for income. Whereas the terms self-sufficiency and financial independence suggest that individuals and families have appropriate and adequate resources and the knowledge to use them, the concept of poverty suggests the opposite. Poverty connotes a lack of resources and related knowledge. Payne (1998) defined poverty as the extent to which an individual does without resources. Payne additionally explained the difference between situational poverty and generational poverty. Generational poverty was defined as an individual or group being in poverty for two generations or longer, whereas situational poverty was considered shorter and often resulted from a situational circumstance like death, illness, divorce, and other unforeseen circumstances that could impact individuals and their families (Payne, 1998).

According to Lind (2006), both self-sufficiency and financial independence are typically achieved via the accumulation of assets (namely, investments that appreciate over time) in the form of investments that can be converted into cash (e.g., savings, equities, 401(k) retirement accounts, and individual retirement accounts), material possessions that hold monetary value (e.g., a house, an automobile, a business), and investments in non-tangible property (e.g., education and training). Financial independence is known to be one of the main pillars of the American dream. This dream, however, is only realized for the top 20% of American households that possess 83% of the nation's wealth (Lind, 2006). For the 40% of American households who possess less than one percent of the nation's wealth (Friedman, 2005; Lind, 2006), and who are trapped in generational poverty, this is a distant dream that is often perceived to be beyond reach during their lifetime.

Over 25% of U.S. households have insufficient resources to subsist for three months without other support if their income ends abruptly (Lind, 2006). For minority populations, the lack of assets is acute: 60% of African American families and 26% of Latino families have either zero or negative net wealth (Lind, 2006). The previous federal welfare program, Aid to Families with Dependent Children (AFDC), provided support for women in poverty. The Personal Responsibility and Work Opportunity Reconciliation Act (PRWORA) passed in 1996 redirected the effort to lifting oneself and one's family from poverty. In this legislation, the goal of economic independence or self-sufficiency was not defined as sustained economic independence from debt. It was defined as a lack of dependence on government support. Characterized by its insistence on universal participation in approved work activity (Alfred, 2005), this legislation assumes that low-income workers can become economically independent by eliminating their reliance on government agencies for assistance.

Constrained by current economic difficulties, the goal of attaining complete and sustained economic independence has been a difficult challenge for even the most financially astute families and business organizations. During the economic recession of 2009, previously wealthy, world-wide corporations like General Motors, Chrysler, American International Group (AIG), and many others now seek economic relief from the federal government in the form of multi-billion dollar bailouts. If these corporations struggle to maintain long-term and sustained economic independence, the path to economic self-sufficiency is particularly vexing for low-income residents of urban communities. There are no guarantees that anyone can live a self-sufficient lifestyle without ever seeking intervention from social institutions. The goal, however, should be to assist individuals and their families to develop a comprehensive plan to build their economic assets and develop a safety net that will allow them to successfully cope with unanticipated expenses and emergencies including unemployment, accidents, and illnesses. Successfully building and growing financial assets should assist these families to significantly and consistently minimize their need for financial assistance from government, community, friends, family, and other sources, thus becoming more self-sufficient.

CHALLENGES TO LOW-INCOME URBAN RESIDENTS' ECONOMIC INDEPENDENCE

The goal of financial independence for a low-income individual is similar to the goal of an individual from a family that has experienced generational obesity to lose a considerable amount of weight while remaining in the family. It is more difficult to achieve financial independence for long-term residents of low-income urban communities. The urban context presents a number of challenges to low-income residents that inhibit and constrain their efforts to acquire, maintain, and grow financial assets. The term "urban" refers to all territory, population, and housing units located within an urbanized area (UA) or an urban cluster (UC) (U.S. Census Bureau, 2002b). The United States Census in 2000 delineated UA and UC boundaries to encompass densely settled territory that consists of core census block groups, or blocks that have a population density of at least a thousand people per square mile, and surrounding census blocks, which have an overall density of at least five hundred people per square mile. Particularly relevant for adult educators in the urban context, Daley, Fisher, and Martin (2000) argue that the principle features of the urban context are density and diversity, and their consequences, namely, anonymity and complexity.

The Challenge from Extreme Poverty

One of the overriding characteristics of low-income urban communities is severe poverty. Payne (1998) noted that poverty is interrelated with other factors like parental employment status and earnings, family structure, and parental education. According to DeNavas-Walt, Bernadette, and Mills

(2004), the 2003 U.S. Census reported the poverty rate in 2003 at 12.5%. According to the U.S. Census (2002a), a disproportionate number of poor people live inside central cities: 40.7% compared with 28.9% of people who do not. While poverty is a marker of financial status, it is also symptomatic of a number of other socio-structural and personal factors that affect the ability of individuals and their families to acquire and develop assets.

Social–Structural Challenges

In addition to poverty, modern urban centers share several other interrelated socio-structural characteristics that affect the ability of individuals to attain and grow economic assets. One characteristic of modern urban centers is the interlocking patterns of racial and income discrimination that have become synonymous with inner-city urban living (Galster & Keeney, 1988; Greer, 1989; Martin, 2004). This discriminatory practice is most noticeable in residential segregation that is driven by a mutually reinforcing events: (1) White racial prejudice, (2) overly aggressive police patrols in predominantly White communities that inhibit movement (Luzinski, 2004), (3) continuing housing market discrimination (Hacker, 1992) that constrains geographical mobility, (4) labor market discrimination that inhibits employment opportunities and upward mobility, and (5) resulting large-scale unemployment and interracial economic disparities (Kantor, 1999). Obtaining consistent long-term employment that could develop into career opportunities becomes a major obstacle to overcome for individuals who are seeking economic independence.

Additional threats to financial stability and the growth of assets in low-income urban communities include: (1) street gangs (Barton, 2002; Patton, 1998) that promote neighborhood violence such as drive-by shootings, maintenance of drug houses, control of neighborhoods via intimidation and threats, marking territory via unsightly graffiti and overall making life insecure; (2) struggling and failing majority–minority K–12 schools that do not impart the necessary knowledge and skills to compete in the broader society for employment and advanced educational opportunities (Wilson, 1987); (3) the widespread presence and visibility of homeless individuals; and (4) decreased property values, which may make such neighborhoods less desirable places to live.

Personal Challenges

The context of low-income urban communities presents the economically minded resident with a number of other problems and issues that could quickly derail economic advancement efforts. For example, personal issues to be avoided or managed include: (1) the prospect of illegal drug addiction and use by a family member who may consequently require financial support from other non-addicted family members; (2) street gang membership by a family member that puts the household at risk of violence from rival gang members; (3) interpersonal violence at the hands of a family member that threatens one's personal health and safety; Payne (1998) indicated that poor inner-city youths are seven times more likely to be the victims of child abuse or neglect than are children of high social economic status (citing Renchler, 1993); (4) single-parenthood that places the burden of childrearing of one or more children on a single individual; (5) teenage pregnancy; (6) low literacy skills acquired in the local, low-achieving schools; (7) the frequent use of alternative language structures like Black English, slang, and foreign languages (Flowers, 2000) that conflict with the expected use of standard English in mainstream communities and institutions; and (8) learning and other types of disabilities that could affect an individual's ability to acquire and process new information. Interventions by adult education programs that assist low-income inner-city urban residents to develop their economic assets and become economically independent should involve appropriate cooperating agencies and organizations to arrange both educational and non-educational strategies and approaches to address residents' challenges. A first step in this process is to identify and isolate the effects of the urban low-income inner-city community context on the ability of residents to achieve upward economic mobility. This problem was the focus of a national housing mobility experiment.

Housing Mobility Experiments

To test whether or not residence within high-poverty urban neighborhoods affects individual economic outcomes, Ludwig, Duncan, and Pinkston (2000) conducted a randomized housing mobility experiment, with measures of economic self-sufficiency taken from state administrative records. The Moving to Opportunity (MTO) project was based in five U.S. cities: Baltimore, Boston, Chicago, Los Angeles, and New York. The program was designed to test the impact of helping families move from low-income housing in high-poverty urban areas to low-poverty neighborhoods with better housing, education, and employment opportunities.

Ludwig, Duncan, and Pinkston (2000) found that providing low-income families living in public housing units with private-market rental subsidies that can only be redeemed in very low-poverty neighborhoods reduces rates of welfare use by approximately 15%. The majority of the 15% reduction appeared to be explained by differences in welfare-to-work transitions. Ludwig, Duncan, and Pinkston (2000) also found that providing families with unrestricted housing vouchers has little effect on economic outcomes beyond the first year. Researchers concluded that these results emphasized the effects of the social capital provided by employed neighbors in the form of information about job openings and job references and that the social composition of neighborhoods may also affect local social norms supporting work versus welfare. Ludwig, Duncan, and Pinkston (2000) observed that despite the very low average earnings and employment rates reported in the study, most families did not enroll in MTO to gain access to better job opportunities. Around 80% of MTO applicants reported that escaping gangs and drugs was the first or second most important reason for joining the program. Ludwig, Duncan, and Pinkston (2000) argued that this motivation is not surprising given that over half of the MTO applicants also reported that at least one household member had been victimized by a crime during the past six months. The MTO experiment demonstrated modest effects on the challenges from extreme poverty and socio-structural challenges to economic independence. Consequently, there is an important role for improving residents' resources, knowledge, and skills for attaining financial independence.

RESOURCES, KNOWLEDGE, AND SKILLS REQUIRED FOR FINANCIAL INDEPENDENCE

Payne (1998) argued that low-income individuals and families seeking to escape the poverty of the lower class should possess the knowledge and skills to enter the middle class. They, therefore, need to obtain several key internal and external resources. The internal resources include the following: (1) financial—having the money to purchase goods and services, and (2) emotional—being able to choose and control emotional responses, particularly to negative situations, without engaging in self-destructive behavior. Payne (1998) indicated that this resource shows itself through stamina, perseverance, and choices. Other personal resources are (1) mental—having the mental abilities and acquired skills (i.e., reading, writing, computing) to deal with daily life; (2) spiritual—believing in divine purpose and guidance; (3) physical—having physical health and mobility; (4) support systems—having friends, family, and backup resources available to access in times of need. She argued that these are external resources: (1) relationships/role models—having frequent access to adult(s) who are appropriate, who are nurturing to the individual, and who do not engage in self-destructive behavior; and (2) knowledge of hidden rules—knowing the unspoken cues and habits of a group. A review of Donnell's case suggests that through his mentoring relationship (a community resource) he managed to obtain the knowledge and skills required to acquire several of the key resources mentioned in previous research (Payne, 1998).

The resources, knowledge, and skills required for financial independence can be examined within the context of generational poverty via an embedded class structure (Payne, 1998). The Kiplinger online newsletter (Kiplinger.Com, n.d.), however, addressed more general issues regarding the types of knowledge and skills that should be mastered in order for anyone to achieve financial independence. These include:

- investing—how to start investing and build strong stock and fund portfolios, develop an understanding of bonds, and pick a financial planner
- money management—how to create a budget, effectively cut spending, increase savings, learn about bank and savings accounts and loans
- credit and debt—how to manage personal and family debt, acquire and manage credit cards, shop for manageable interest rates, and obtain and monitor credit scores
- buying and selling a home—how to pick the right house to purchase, the economics of renting vs. buying a home, how to calculate and select mortgage rates, how to sell a home
- family finances—questions that should be addressed prior to marriage, planning for money management during the marriage, financial considerations during divorce, how to budget for children, and how to support aging parents
- saving and paying for college—consideration of 529 plan, FAQ, availability of financial aid programs
- retirement—retirement benefits, the Roth, IRA, 401(k), buying an annuity, and Social Security benefits
- insurance—life insurance, health insurance, auto insurance, and long-term care insurance
- estate planning—the steps to producing a good will
- taxes—tax planning and how to calculate and pay federal and state income taxes
- value living—how to spend money wisely (e.g., car buying skills, grocery shopping on a budget, buying on sale, using coupons, going green inexpensively, etc.)
- careers—the basics of careers, resume writing, how to choose the right job, negotiating a raise, and job interviewing skills.

While these are clearly knowledge and skills that would assist low-income urban residents to develop their economic assets, Freidman (2005) argued that offering this information via mainstream agencies and institutions would likely intimidate the intended audience. She suggested a more appropriate approach that would involve the design and development of financial literacy programs tailored specifically for low-income families.

FINANCIAL LITERACY PROGRAMS

Adult and continuing educators can assist low-income urban residents to develop and grow their economic assets via the provision of financial literacy education and training programs. These programs represent only one of several elements of a multi-strategy approach to asset building (Lind, 2006); however, they can be effective in assisting these individuals and their families to develop their knowledge, skills, and behaviors in important financial and economic matters. Lind (2006) cited two studies by Rand (2004) and Moore et al (2001) that found that financial literacy education and training programs positively influenced the savings efforts of low-income families and workers. One of the studies found that participants believed financial literacy classes were useful and influenced their motivation to save. Another study evaluated Financial Links for Low-Income People, a program that tracked participants in both financial management training and individual development account (IDA) programs. It found that most participants changed the way they budgeted, tracked household expenses, or paid bills.

Many workers who live in low-income urban communities have not acquired the knowledge and skills regarding the resources mentioned by Payne (1998) and Kunjufu (2006), nor have they mastered all of the financial knowledge and skills presented by Kiplinger.com (2009). Many employees live from paycheck to paycheck. They are often challenged to manage expenses incurred with employment, including child care, transportation, and car maintenance that can increase the burden on limited finances (Friedman, 2005). Given additional challenges, employees often lack the knowledge and tools necessary to make sound decisions with regard to budgeting, savings, and investments. Many traditional savings mechanisms exclude low-income families because they are based upon tax benefits for which low-income families do not qualify. Also, accumulating assets may disqualify these families from participating in income benefit programs like food stamps if their assets exceed specific levels (Welfare Information Network, 2002).

Principles for Financial Literacy Programs

The goal of financial literacy programs is to provide participants with the skills needed to effectively manage personal financial matters and make positive financial choices (Friedman, 2005). Friedman proposed three sequential principles and funding sources for designing and operating financial literacy programs for low-income adults and youth. First, choose a program that incorporates relevant information and practical examples that enable participants to personalize the concepts being taught and apply them to individual or family needs.

Second, choose an appropriate program provider and setting (Friedman, 2005). Organizations that have designed and delivered financial literacy trainings include community-based organizations that tend to focus on the learning needs of local residents. Banks and the Cooperative Extension Service offer general financial literacy programs geared to the general public. Colleges and universities often provide financial literacy programs to increase the financial knowledge of their students. Godfrey (2006) noted that 45% of college students are in credit card debt, with an average debt of $3,000 annually. Godfrey (2006) noted that approximately 150,000 young adults between the ages of 18–24 declare bankruptcy in one year. Employers are interested in offering financial literacy classes to enhance employees' personal financial literacy skills. Davis and Carnes (2005) studied employers and found that executives rated credit card use and budgeting as the most important personal financial literacy skills that employees should possess. When workers struggle with their personal finances, there is an increased tendency toward absenteeism, more frequent personal phone calls, inability to concentrate, and the risk of fraud and/or theft (Davis & Carnes, 2005). They argued that highly developed personal finance skills would free employees to focus on work activity and productivity. Lastly, adult literacy programs can offer valuable financial literacy information via math classes and other literacy related coursework.

Third, choose a model that encourages participants to complete the program (Friedman, 2005). Planners should make sure that the programs address learners' needs by taking their cultural and logistics needs into account. For example, a program targeting first-time home buyers could include lessons addressing the differences between a broker and a banker, the threat of predatory lenders, how to budget, and what the process of home ownership entails. Incentives could be used to encourage participation. These may include calculators, monetary stipends, the opportunity to meet with a financial advisor, or a certificate that can be used to start a savings account. Financial literacy programs might instead address several more general topics.

General Topics for Financial Literacy Programs

The actual topics addressed by financial literacy programs should vary to address the specific needs of the targeted population of potential learners.

Programs can include a number of general topics that address the learning needs of low-income residents living in an urban context seeking to achieve greater financial security and success. Topics could include the following:

- financial management, primarily money management skills through the development of a comprehensive long-term financial plan
- setting financial goals
- developing and maintaining a family budget
- building savings
- acquiring sound investment practices
- managing credit to include understanding credit reports, managing debt and bankruptcy, and repairing poor credit
- managing insurance, which includes selecting and maintaining insurance
- selecting financial services providers
- planning for retirement

In addition to these topics, financial literacy programs can offer specialized information on other asset building strategies.

Specialized Topics for Financial Literacy Programs

Low-income residents of urban communities would likely benefit from financial literacy programs that address a range of specialized topics, which will be further discussed below: access to mainstream financial services, caution on predatory lending practices, accessing insurance, individual development accounts, family self-sufficiency escrow accounts, the federal earned income tax credit, individual learning accounts, cost free financial planning, and community sustaining employment opportunities.

Access to Mainstream Financial Services

Financial literacy programs can assist participants to learn how to gain access to mainstream financial services, and allow them to avoid the exploitative alternative outlets in their communities. Approximately 22 million U.S. households do not have a checking or savings account (Lind, 2006). Therefore, they tend to rely on a number of convenient, but highly expensive, alternative financial service providers including check-cashing stores, payday lenders, title lenders, rent-to-own stores, and tax preparers to meet their banking and financial needs (Lind, 2006). By charging significantly higher fees and interest rates than their more mainstream counterparts, these institutions have payment plans that can trap users in a recurring cycle of debt. Exploration of this topic in courses and programs can help participants to eliminate their reliance on such services.

Caution on Predatory Lending Practices

Predatory lenders are a fixture in low-income communities. They tend to aggressively market financial products and services that typically contain significant risks and hidden costs that can contribute to debt, financial hardship, and a loss of assets. These practices include excessive points and fees, balloon payments, higher interest rates than are warranted by the risk, high prepayment penalties, loan flipping, and excess foreclosures (Lind, 2006). Financial literacy programs can offer opportunities for participants to discuss these practices and to avoid being victimized.

Accessing Insurance

Too often, low-income residents of inner city communities do not have appropriate or even adequate insurance to cover the costs associated with unexpected liabilities. A lack of appropriate coverage can leave individuals and their families vulnerable to a depletion of their limited savings and assets, all which can negatively affect their credit scores (Lind, 2006). Financial literacy programs can assist participants to learn about federal, state, and employer-subsidized insurance initiatives and to evaluate and acquire a variety of insurance instruments, like health, life, automobile, and rental/homeowners, which can assist in protecting their savings and assets.

Individual Development Accounts

Individual Development Accounts (IDAs) are dedicated savings accounts containing deposits by low-income workers that are matched by either private or public sources (Welfare Information Network, 2002). The interest in including low-income workers in programs similar to Individual Retirement Accounts (IRA) increased with the focus on welfare reform (Welfare Information Network, 2002). The Assets for Independence Act of 1998 provides federal funds for the operation of IDA programs at the state and local levels. The money accumulated in these accounts is restricted to postsecondary education and training, business capitalization, and home ownership. Additionally, the account balances held in IDAs that are funded through Temporary Assistance for Needy Families (TANF) are excluded from eligibility determination for all means-tested federal benefits (Welfare Information Network, 2002).

Family Self-Sufficiency Escrow Accounts

For low-income public housing residents who are not eligible for IDAs, Family Self-Sufficiency (FSS) escrow accounts can offer an opportunity to significantly increase savings. The FSS program was enacted in 1990 and is administered by the U.S. Department of Housing and Urban Development (Sard, 2001). The FSS program is designed to provide employment and savings incentives for low-income families who have Section 8 vouchers or live in public housing. The program allows public housing authorities to create escrow accounts that assist participants to increase their savings. The FSS program offers case management services that help participants pursue employment and other goals and provides escrow accounts into which the public housing agency (PHA) deposits the increased rental charges that a family pays as its earnings rise (Lind, 2006). Families that complete the program may withdraw funds from these accounts for any purpose after five years.

Sard (2001) reported that at the time of her publication, approximately 560,000 families in the public housing and Section 8 voucher programs received income from TANF or state general assistance programs. Fewer than 1.5% of these families appeared to be participating in FSS programs (Sard, 2001). Sard (2001) also reported that in November of 2000, about 48% of FSS participants who had been enrolled in FSS for 12 months or more had positive escrow balances. These families had an average escrow balance of about $2,400 and were adding to their accounts at the average rate of about $300 per month. In addition, about 45% of the families who were considered to have successfully completed the FSS program between the fall of 1999 and November 2000 received escrow funds averaging nearly $5,000 per family. However, fewer than half of public housing agencies offer the FSS program to residents. In addition, most agencies that do offer FSS sharply limit program size. As a consequence, Sard observed that fewer than five percent of families with children in the public housing and Section 8 voucher programs participated in FSS. Although these programs have demonstrated success, they still appear to be underutilized by low-income individuals.

The Federal Earned Income Tax Credit

The Federal Earned Income Tax Credit (1975) is a refundable tax credit for low-income workers. It has been credited with enhancing financial stability among low-income families and, according to Lind (2006), lifts more than 4 million people out of poverty each year. Many credit recipients use the refunds to make investments, like paying off debt, investing in education, and obtaining alternative housing (Lind, 2006).

Individual Learning Accounts

An Individual Learning Account (ILA) is a specified amount of resources such as dollars, hours, or learning technology tools (such as access to the internet and the use of government computers away from the office), or a combination of the three, that are set aside for an individual worker to use for her or his learning and development (ILA, 2004). The ILA program is a voluntary initiative; all employers do not participate. For employers who do, these accounts can generate a partnership between managers and their employees to design and fulfill employees' long-term career objectives. They provide a vehicle for supporting training efforts that are customized to the specific skill requirements of the individual and the strategic human resources development goals of the employing agency. They can be used to obtain the continuous learning necessary for an individual to enhance her/his overall professional development and, therefore, the employer can use them as a recruitment and retention incentive.

The use of ILAs shifts an employer's focus on training from a one-time learning event to a continuous learning effort—from required training to strategic workforce development—and integrates resources for training with efforts to balance work and learning time. The accounts may be centrally designed and universally applied across the employing organization, or they could be decentralized to allow individual components of the organization the flexibility to create accounts that target their specific skill gap needs (ILA, 2004). Participation in these programs increases workers' awareness of the varied learning opportunities available to them and allows them to tailor their learning and development efforts to their individual needs, thereby assisting them to gain the necessary skills to allow them to advance in their careers (ILA, 2004).

Cost-Free Financial Planning

Financial literacy programs can also draw upon the expertise of local financial planning professionals. Cost-free financial planning can be found on the Internet (Project for Financial Independence, 2009). Financial services professionals are often encouraged to provide public service. A financial professional may provide financial education or financial planning services for no compensation to people of limited means through public service or charitable organizations.

Community-Sustaining Employment Opportunities

Financial literacy programs can share opportunities for obtaining or subsidizing employment with participants. Similar to the self-sustaining community in which I grew up during the 1950s, an exciting and innovative urban sustainable farming system is currently transforming the cultivation, production, and delivery of healthy foods to underserved, urban populations (Allen, 2009).

Will Allen, a 2008 MacArthur Fellow, recognized that the unhealthy diets of low-income, urban populations and related health problems such as obesity and diabetes are largely attributable to limited access to safe and affordable fresh fruits and vegetables. In 1995, he began developing the farming methods and educational programs that are now the foundation of a national non-profit organization and land trust, known as Growing Power, which he co-founded and directs (Allen, 2009). According to their website,

Growing Power supports people from diverse backgrounds and the environments in which they live by helping to provide equal access to healthy, high-quality, safe, and affordable food for people in all communities. Allen's holistic farming model incorporates both cultivating foodstuffs and designing food distribution networks in urban settings. Through a unique synthesis of a variety of low-cost farming technologies such as the use of raised beds, aquaculture, vermiculture, and heating greenhouses through composting, Growing Power produces vast amounts of food year-round at its main farming site consisting of two acres of land located within Milwaukee, Wisconsin's city limits. Recently, cultivation of produce and livestock was begun at other urban and rural sites in and around Milwaukee, Wisconsin and Chicago, Illinois. As this organization expands its network and distribution systems, it will increasingly offer opportunities to low-income residents of urban communities to become urban farmers—that is, to learn how to grow self-sustaining crops for the substance of their communities.

CONCLUSION

Living and being raised in an urban context presents a number of complex challenges that can, and often do, derail any efforts of low-income residents to become financially independent. Many of us have learned our financial knowledge and skills from our parents. For low-income individuals and their families, this knowledge was often not available. This chapter explored the types of issues and challenges low-income urban residents face and identified the types of financial management knowledge and skills that is often available to middle class families that could enhance opportunities for self-sufficiency among those of low-income. Financial literacy programs for low-income individuals and their families were presented as a means to provide more specialized and customized knowledge regarding their pressing financial planning decisions.

REFERENCES

Alfred, M. V. (2005, February). *The invisible realities of welfare reform in Wisconsin: Perspectives of African American women and their employers.* Paper presented at the Academy of Human Resource Development International Conference (AHRD). Estes Park, CO. Eric Document: ED492294 (pp. 1087–1094).

Allen, W. (2009). *Growing power—Growing farmers.* Retrieved March 18, 2009, from http://www.growingpower.org/

Barton, G. (2002, October 3). Profiles: Crime, gangs and broken homes play a large part in boys' lives. *Milwaukee Journal Sentinel,* p. 1A, 16A.

Daley, B., Fisher, J. & Martin, L. (2000). Urban contexts for adult education practice. In A. L. Wilson & E. R. Hayes (Eds.), *Handbook for adult and continuing education* (pp. 539– 555). San Francisco, CA: Jossey-Bass.

Davis, R., & Carnes, L. (2005). Employers' perspectives of employees' personal financial literacy. *Delta Pi Epsilon Journal, 47*(1), 11–19.

DeNavas-Walt, C., Bernadette D., & Mills R. J. (2004). *Income, Poverty, and Health Insurance Coverage in the United States: 2003.* U.S. Census Bureau, Current Population Reports, P60-226, U.S. Government Printing Office, Washington, DC.

Flowers, D. A. (2000). Codeswitching and ebonics in urban adult basic education classrooms. *Education and Urban Society, 32*(2), 221–236.

Friedman, P. (2005). *Strategy brief: Providing and funding financial literacy programs for low income adults and youth.* The Finance Project. Washington, DC: Economic Success Clearinghouse.

Galster, G. C., & Keeney, W. M. (1988). Race, residence, discrimination, and economic opportunity: Modeling the nexus of urban racial phenomena. *Urban Affairs Quarterly, 24*(1), 87–117.

Godfrey, N. S. (2006). Making our students smart about money. *Education Digest: Essential Readings Condensed for Quick Review, 71*(7), 21–26.

Greer, S. (1989). Urbanism and urbanity: Cities in an urban-dominated society. *Urban Affairs Quarterly, 24*(3), 341–352.

Hacker, A. (1992). *Two nations: Black and white, separate, hostile, unequal.* New York, NY: Ballantine Books.

Huffstetler, E. (2008). What does financial independence mean to you? Retrieved January 19, 2009, from http://frugalliving.about.com/b/2008/06/02/what-does-financial- independence-mean-to-you.htm

Individual Learning Accounts. (2004). Retrieved January 20, 2009, from http://www.feddesk.com/freehandbooks/051004-1.pdf

Kantor, H. (1999). Race, education, and joblessness in the inner city, 1970–1990. *The Urban Review, 31*(3), 225–242.

Kiplinger.Com. (n.d.). *The basics of money: How to invest, manage your money and spend wisely.* Retrieved January 20, 2009, from http://www.kiplinger.com/basics/

Kunjufu, J. (2006). *An African centered response to Ruby Payne's poverty theory.* Chicago: Images.

Lind, C. (2006). *Strategies to build assets among low-income families: Mapping the field.* Washington, DC: The Finance Project. ERIC Document: (ED499582).

Ludwig, J., Duncan, G.J., & Pinkston, J.C. (2000). *Neighborhood effects on economic self-sufficiency: Evidence from a randomized housing mobility experiment.* Washington, DC: Georgetown Public Policy Institute.

Luzinski, T. (2004). *How police training and police social learning intersect and influence police racial profiling.* Unpublished doctoral dissertation, University of Wisconsin–Milwaukee, Milwaukee, WI.

Martin, L. (2004) Adult education in the urban context. In L. G. Martin & E. Rogers (Eds.), *Adult education in an urban context: Problems, practices, and programming for inner-city communities* (pp. 3–16). San Francisco: Jossey-Bass.

Moore, A., Beverly, S., Schreiner, M., Sherraden, M., Lombe, M., Cho, E. Y. N., Johnson, L., & Vonderlack, R. (2001). *Saving, IDA programs, and effects of IDAs: A survey of participants* (St. Louis, MO: Washington University, Center for Social

Development). Retrieved June 12, 2009 from http://gwbweb.wustl.edu/csd/Publications/2001/shortsurveyreport.pdf.

Patton, P. L. (1998). The gangstas in our midst. *The Urban Review, 30*(1), 49–76.

Payne, R. K. (1998). *A framework for understanding poverty.* Highlands, TX: aha! Process, Inc.

Project for Financial Independence. (2009). Retrieved January 19, 2009, from http://www.consultaplanner.org/

Rand, D. (2004). *Financial education and asset building programs for welfare recipients and low-income workers: The Illinois experience.* Washington, D.C.: The Brookings Institution. Retrieved June 12 from http://www.brookings.edu/metro/publications/20040413_doryrand.htm

Renchler, R. (1993). *Poverty and learning.* ERIC Digest, No. 83. ERIC Clearinghouse on Educational Management, Eugene, OR ED357433.

Sard, B. (2001). *The family self-sufficiency program: HUD's best kept secret for promoting employment and asset growth.* Washington, DC: Center on Budget and Policy Priorities.

Self-sufficient, *adj.* (2009). *The American Heritage Dictionary of the English Language* (4th ed.). New York: Houghton Mifflin. Retrieved January 19, 2009, from http://www.thefreedictionary.com/self-sufficient

U.S. Census Bureau. (2002a). Poverty in the United States: 2001 Current population reports: Consumer income. Retrieved October 5, 2008, from http://www.census.gov/prod/2002pubs/p60-219.pdf

U.S. Census Bureau. (2002b). Census 2000 Basics. Retrieved January 20, 2009, from http://www.census.gov/mso/www/c2000basics/00Basics.pdf

Welfare Information Network. (2002). Encouraging asset development for low-income workers. *Resources for Welfare Decisions, 6*(7). Retrieved October 5, 2008, from http://www.financeproject.org/Publications/encouragingassetdevelopmentRN.htm

Wilson, W. (1987). *The truly disadvantaged: The inner city, the underclass, and public policy.* Chicago: The University of Chicago Press.

CHAPTER 7

NO WORKER LEFT BEHIND

Low-Wage Workers' Equitable Access to Workplace Learning

Laura L. Bierema
University of Georgia

Work is steeped in United States culture and embraced as the path to the "The American Dream." Approximately 154 million people participate in the paid workforce in the United States as either employed or looking for work. Of these, 30 million workers are stuck in dead-end, low-paying jobs where they make less than $9.00 per hour (Hansen, 2009). Whether in desirable or undesirable jobs, workers in the U.S. and Canada work longer hours now than they did during the 1950s, logging nearly nine full weeks or 350 hours longer per year than workers in other industrialized countries (Take Back Your Time, 2009). People are working more, yet hard work does not necessarily translate into job security or good wages.

Today "non-standard" employment is becoming more common. Many North American companies employ people on a part-time and short-term basis in what some refer to as "McJobs." Other workers may be employed full-time, but they work in low-wage jobs, usually in the service industry that

Learning for Economic Self-Sufficiency, pages 103–120

offer few (or no) benefits, inadequate training, and few opportunities for advancement. According to the U. S. Bureau of Labor Statistics (2003), 17 out of the 20 largest growth occupations from 2002–2012 require job seekers with limited education and provide minimal training. This represents approximately six million jobs (Hansen, 2009).

Organizations promote learning as their new strategy, expecting workers to outlearn the competition and spend billions on training, with 2006 expenditures estimated to be nearly $130 billion (Workforce Management, 2008). Workplace learning has been the topic of enduring and increasing interest, yet what learning and educational opportunities are available for workers in low-status, low-wage, and low-skill jobs? The purpose of this chapter is to examine the marginalized group of low-wage workers and critically assess approaches to and investment in their workplace learning.

Workplace learning is full of contradictions and challenges for adult education. It has been criticized as co-opting workers into advancing a capitalist agenda and preserving hegemonic power relations (Ashton & Green, 1996; Gee, Hull, & Lankshear, 1996; Kincheloe, 1999). Learning at work, however, is important in promoting workers to achieve financial independence and job advancement, allowing them to move out of marginalized social positions. Bratton, Mills, Pyrch, and Sawchuck (2004) note that industrialized capitalism and adult education have developed "hand-in-hand" (p. 6) with contemporary adult education often sought for instrumental ends. Bratton and colleagues (2004) explain that adult education and training from a trade union and workers' perspective has historically been viewed as a means of improving job security and job-related skills. Our conceptualization of work and workplace learning may be too narrow in a complex world (Bratton et al., 2004).

Not all work is paid, and our workplaces cannot be isolated from the broader social contexts and the learning that occurs within them. Bratton et al. (2004) assert that workplace learning must be considered in terms of how it connects to the informal economy, social movements, and adult education—connections that are largely ignored. Our task, according to Bratton et al. (2004), is to expand our notions of work beyond the job site to include life purpose and vocation that may or may not be tied to paid work.

Learning is happening all the time in the workplace, both formally and informally.

There is a great amount of rhetoric about the current age of the learning organization and a knowledge economy, but although "we might live in a 'knowledge society,' we are a long way from a 'knowledge economy' as immense amounts of skill and knowledge currently go unused" (Bratton et al., 2004, p. 5). "The popular management rhetoric around e-commerce and 'knowledge work' should be tempered by a recognition that in all economies there is still an army of low-skilled, low paid workers—the 'McWorld'"

(Bratton et al., 2004, p. 40). These authors further underscore the systematically non-educative nature of work, arguing that these workers receive little opportunity for formal or informal learning (Bratton et al., 2004).

LOW-WAGE WORKERS

Much of the workplace learning literature and rhetoric assumes that the worker is skilled, well-paid, and relatively secure in his or her work in an organization that is willing to invest in her development. Corresponding with the rise in the service industry however, low-wage jobs have grown in the U.S. (The Working Poor Families Project, 2008). These include jobs such as cashiers, custodians, childcare workers, healthcare aids, security guards, restaurant workers, hospitality workers (motel, hotel, resort), housekeepers, retail workers, and several others (Low-Wage Occupations, 2009; The Working Poor Families Project, 2008). These workers can expect few opportunities for training or advancement.

Bernstein and Gittleman (2003) used the National Compensation Survey to examine the skill content of low-wage jobs. They focused on the following job factors: knowledge required, complexity of the job, guidelines to follow, scope and effect of the work, supervision received, supervision duties, personal contacts, purpose of contacts, physical demands, and work environment. There is no consensus among economists about the definition of low-wage work, so Bernstein and Gittleman (2003) offered three definitions: total hours worked for low wages, wages falling into the bottom quintile of wage distribution, and the number of hours for which earnings were below $8 per hour. Bernstein and Gittleman (2003) found:

- The lowest paid sectors of the economy include retail trade and services.
- A discrepancy exists in low wages based on unionization and firm size. Specifically, unionized workers receive better pay and wages are higher in establishments with 2,500 or more employees.
- On average, low-wage workers earn $8.00 per hour as compared with a mean of $18.37 for the rest of the jobs in the labor market.
- The combination of low wages and low skills results in 23% less pay than other jobs.

Bernstein and Gittleman (2003) concluded that low-wage work is disproportionately concentrated among low-skill jobs.

The Working Poor Families Project (2008) reports that the American Dream is fleeting for many American families who, despite working hard, earn incomes too low to achieve economic security. Hansen (2009) notes that today, approximately 30 million workers between the ages of 18 and 64 earn less than $9.00 per hour, or a full-time annual income of $18,800. This is the income level that delineates the federal poverty line for a family of four. More than one out of four U.S. working families with children is considered low income. Low-wage families are defined as those earning less than double the poverty rate. This equates to an annual income of $41,228 or less in 2006 for a family of four. A total of 42 million adults and children struggle to achieve economic security. The Working Poor Families Project (2008) reports that from 2002–2006, the number of low-income working families increased by 350,000, almost 10%, to approximately 9.6 million. Low-wage workers in the U.S. keep arduous hours working on average 2,552 hours per year, or one and one-half times the average of full-time workers. Not only do low-wage workers work long hours, pay taxes, and seek economic security for their families, but they also pay a larger percentage of their income for housing and tend not to have health insurance. They often also lack the requisite education and skills that would make it easier to advance up career ladders.

The Low-Wage Labor Market

The low-wage labor market has been the target of welfare reform as states attempt to help welfare recipients' transition to employment. Carrington and Fallick (2001) used the Current Population Survey to examine the minimum wage career progression of workers, and they concluded that the less educated, blacks, women with young children, and workers outside urban areas appear to get stuck in low-wage jobs, spending substantial portions of their early careers in minimum wage jobs. Kaye and Nightingale (2000), in a report sponsored by the U.S. Department of Health and Human Services, concluded that the low-wage labor market is not monolithic. Instead, it has a primary sector where people move into gainful employment, but also a secondary sector that "has few ladders to job advancement, little job stability, and more gender and racial discrimination than the primary market" (Kaye & Nightingale, 2000, p. 9). The secondary market, and subject of interest to this chapter, includes workers with low hourly wages, workers with low skills, and workers whose annual earnings are low because they work only part-time or intermittently. Workers making low earnings are widespread. For instance, in 1997, over one third of female workers' hourly wages would be insufficient to raise a family of four above the poverty level even if they worked full-year, full-time (Kaye & Nightingale, 2000). Workers with low earnings increased from 36 to 41% over the past decade, with recession taking a toll on these numbers. Given the current economy, the situation is likely to worsen.

Kaye and Nightingale (2000) described barriers to exiting the low-wage labor market as skills mismatch (including basic job readiness, lack of transportation), discrimination, spatial mismatch, and lack of access to informal information networks. Low-wage workers become stranded in these jobs because high paying jobs are not available, they are discriminated against, or they do not pursue or qualify for higher pay, including achieving more education (Theodos & Bednarzik, 2006). Kaye and Nightingale (2000) confirmed that job turnover is higher in industries where disadvantaged workers tend to find employment and that it is accompanied by high costs leading to more periods of joblessness, reduced earnings, and reduced opportunities for formal training. Real wage growth is minimal for many low-wage workers who leave welfare for work. According to Kaye and Nightingale (2000), wage growth for these workers is approximately 4.5% over a year (which translates into only about $400 per year for a low-wage worker), and other studies have cited even lower estimates.

Discrimination and the Low-wage Worker

Discrimination plays a key role in the dynamics of the low-wage labor market. It has a negative impact on the employment rates of African Americans, even when differences in skills have been accounted for (Kaye & Nightingale, 2000). Kaye and Nightingale (2000) reported that informal hiring networks account for between 25 and 60% of hires into blue collar and small enterprise jobs requiring no college education. These networks tend to promote discrimination since they are usually tightly knit, ethnically homogenous networks. African American workers are especially excluded from such networks.

Low-wage workers are predominantly women with almost 2 out of 5 working in low-paid jobs (Kim, 2000). Women are likely to make low-wages if they are young, single, or less educated, or work in service occupations where 41% of low-wage workers are concentrated (Kim, 2000). "The consequence of low-paying employment is often living near the poverty level. One-third of women who are paid low-wages live below 150 % of the poverty level" (Kim, 2000, p. 29). Kim (2000) also reports that among all adult women who earn low wages, 17% lived in poverty and 31% lived below 150% of the poverty level. Kim (2000) found proportional representation based on race among low-wage women; however, ethnicity was a factor with a slight overrepresentation of Hispanic women. Kim (2000) also found women who are not U.S. citizens to be overrepresented in low-paid employment.

Opportunities for women's workplace learning are still highly gendered. According to Probert (1999), current emphases on workplace learning will likely only reproduce existing inequities since "the dominant discourses continue to rely on abstracted conceptions of work and workers that privilege men" (p. 113).Women tend to develop expertise but not authority to gain power or advancement within their organizations (Probert, 1999).

Career structures are also highly feminized. The influx of women into the labor market has made the supply plentiful and the incentive to develop them for further advancement negatively impacted. Women also tend to represent the majority of part-time and contingent workers, sidelining them from developmental opportunities. Training may be offered during their non-working hours or they may not have equal access to apprenticeship training programs based on part-time schedules.

Johnson and Corcoran (2003) examined how the quality of employment outcomes and job transition patterns of former/current TANF recipients are affected by the skill content of work experience and by changes in economic conditions. Johnson and Corcoran (2003) used survey data from employers and longitudinal data from former/current welfare recipients covering the period 1997–early 2002 in order to analyze the relationships of schooling, the skill content of work experience, and different types of employment patterns with less-skilled women's job quality outcomes. Johnson and Corcorran (2003) examined the extent to which a lack of employment stability, job skills, and occupation-specific experience impede welfare recipients' abilities to obtain "good jobs" or transition into them from bad ones. The job quality and job transition patterns of former/current recipients are negatively affected by the current economic downturn. Welfare-to-work programs in the United States were introduced during a time of economic prosperity and a labor shortage. Times are very different now, and these programs emphasize work over training and put workers at more risk during a time of recession.

WORKPLACE LEARNING

Workplace learning holds the potential to help low-wage workers improve their income and advancement prospects. This section offers definitions of workplace learning and a discussion of its contested nature with respect to low-wage workers.

Workplace Learning Defined

"A key assumption about learning at work here is that it has something to do with individuals . . . apprehending experience reasoning, or logically thinking through their work experience and giving that experience 'meaning'" (Garrick, 1999, p. 226). According to Avis (2004), workplace learning must be (1) distinguished from learning in the workplace, (2) influenced significantly by economic and market needs, and (3) shaped significantly by elements of performativity and instrumentalism. Avis (2004) questioned how well workers are being prepared for their work roles, while simultaneously learning to be informed citizens in society. Bratton, Mills, Pyrch, and Sawchuck (2004) suggested, "The term workplace learning has become a metaphor for capturing formal, nonformal, self-directed, collective and even tacit informal learning activities" (p. 2). Bratton and colleagues (2004) described workplace learning as influencing contemporary discourse and drawing on multiple disciplines including adult learning, management theory, industrial relations, and sociological theory and opening inquiry to an understanding of both work and learning. "Work," according to Bratton and colleagues' definition, extends beyond paid work in formal organizations to consider unpaid work in the home and community. They suggest it is imperative to be familiar with both perspectives and that workplace learning discourse has become one of the most controversial elements of adult education.

Garrick (1999) identifies four dominant discourses of workplace learning: (1) human capital theory, (2) experience-based learning, (3) cognition and expertise, and (4) generic skills, capabilities, and competence. Human capital theory views human capabilities as having productive capacity. These capabilities are purchased by the employer and command a price in the market depending on their ability to produce goods and services. Investing in learning is viewed as a means of improving organizational performance.

The notion that human beings would be invested in as capital has been the source of powerful debate in adult education. Proponents suggest that human, intellectual, and cultural capital is beneficial when workplace learning is promoted for employees. Opponents suggest that the human capital approach "makes employees economically active but politically passive" (Garrick, 1999, p. 218). Indeed, learning for the low-wage worker in this discourse would be discouraged, as employers are often not relying on them for skill or longevity.

Experience-based learning assumes that experience is the foundation of and stimulus for learning and that learners actively construct their own experience. Learning is viewed as holistic, socially and culturally constructed, and influenced by the socioemotional context of work. Experiential learning may hold more promise for low-wage workers in that they can use their work experience to upskill and move on to better jobs either within their organization or elsewhere.

The cognition and expertise discourse is concerned with how the mind works. Garrick (1999) noted that uncertainties between cognitive and social contributions to thinking have created an erroneous view that the mind can be isolated from the social world. Our understanding of problem solving has been developed within this discourse and is viewed as a means of knowledge construction. The development of expertise is discussed within this discourse. Because low-wage jobs are often low-skilled, this discourse may be of little benefit to improving work-based learning for this population whose expertise is not valued by employers.

Generic skills, capabilities, and competence are concerned with attributes desired in organizations such as teamwork, problem solving, communication, attitude, and other job-specific skills. Helping low-wage workers develop generic skills may help them move into better jobs. Although the discourses of human capital, experience, cognition, and generic skills are helpful for understanding the learning of low-wage workers, a more critical analysis provides a richer understanding of the dynamics characterizing the low-wage worker's plight.

Bratton et al. (2004) distinguish between managerial and critical perspectives of workplace learning, noting that a managerial perspective is focused on organizational efficiency and profitability. This perspective is aligned with the human capital discourse and invests in workplace learning as a means of signaling intent to develop "human assets" and foster worker loyalty, commitment, and market competitiveness. The managerial paradigm is steeped in the discourses of economics, globalization, deregulation, privatization, and sustainable innovation (Bratton et al., 2004). The contrasting critical perspective considers how "organizational economic imperatives and disparities of power affect working people and society in terms of equity, environmental degradation, and democracy" (Bratton et al., 2004, p. 3). It is concerned with how interlocking systems of gender, race, class, and other factors shape workplace learning. Typical concerns in this paradigm include how workplace learning enforces cultural control, how training of competencies can make work more visible and manageable, how power shapes and impedes learning, and creating new forms of oppression. The notion of the learning organization, which was widely heralded as creating a unitary perspective in which the goals of workers and management were shared, has been critiqued for its ignoring of power relations and tensions in the employment relationship (Coopey, 1996). A critical analysis of low-wage work and learning is essential to both understanding and changing the dynamics that perpetuate it.

The Contested Nature of Workplace Learning

The employment relationship is economic, legal, and social (Bratton et al., 2004). Billett (2001) acknowledged that the saliency of learning opportunities depends on the work context and how workers elect to engage with workplace activities that contribute to learning. Workplace learning is a process of co-participation between the worker and the environment created by the organization (Billett, 2001). That is, it is an interaction of how the workplace supports or inhibits workers' engagement in work activities and access to both the direct and indirect guidance that promotes learning. Billett (2001) terms these interactions "learning affordances"; however, they are not equally available to all workers. Rather, the basis for such affordances includes perceptions of individual competence, race, gender, status of work, employment status, workplace demarcations, personal relations, and workplace cliques and affiliations (Billett, 2001). Low-wage workers are often invisible to management and at a disadvantage for access to learning affordances. Further, workplace learning access can be contested between different groups of workers such as newcomers versus more seasoned workers, full or part-time workers, teams with varying roles and standing in the workplace, goal sets (personal and vocational goals), and groups representing workers such as unions versus management or supervision (Billett, 2001).

Workplace learning is situated in context and dependent upon social interaction. Billett (2001) stated that a central concern of workplace learning is how individuals or groups are invited to participate in workplace learning since they may be encouraged or inhibited based on positionality. Fully understanding workplace learning requires an analysis of asymmetrical power relationships that shape organizations. Key variables of workplaces are (1) the nature and focus of strategic decisions, (2) power relations, and (3) the employment relationship (Rainbird, Fuller, & Munro, 2004). Rainbird, Fuller, and Munro remind us that employers' first concern is with product markets and competitive strategy, followed by concern over work organization, job design, and people management, and observe that this prioritization affects the extent and distribution of learning opportunities across the organization.

EDUCATING THE LOW-WAGE WORKER

Persisting at a low-wage job is insufficient to prevent poverty. Half of families with children with incomes below 200% of the federal poverty line have at least one full-time, year-round worker (Richburg-Hayes, 2008). The labor market is highly inhospitable to low-skilled workers who have little power to lobby for access to education or career advancement (Hansen, 2009). Effectively educating low-wage workers will involve mitigating their marginalization in job assignments and workplace learning, and better preparing them for more advanced jobs.

Mitigating Marginalization

Several factors marginalize low-wage workers, making attaining education challenging. Real wages have risen more significantly for workers with education, increasing the disparity between workers with and without post-secondary education (Richburg-Hayes, 2008). Between 1979 and 2005, real hourly wages for workers with advanced degrees rose by 28%, wages for college graduates rose by 22%, wages for high school graduates remained stagnant, while wages for high school dropouts decreased by 16% (Mishel, Bernstein, & Allegretto, 2007).

A key variable in low-wage employment is education level. Women with a high school education or less make up 21% of low-wage women workers, but only 11% of all women workers. Among women lacking a high school education, 74% work in low-wage jobs whereas only 14% of college educated women do (Kim, 2000).

Theodos and Bednarzik (2006) analyzed data from the Panel Study of Income Dynamics from 1995–2001 and found that persons who start out in low-wage jobs, but who work full time, maintain good health, and attain more education have an upwards earnings mobility, but that the opposite is true for those who are not working or begin at the lowest end of the income scale. Neither race nor gender was found to be a significant mobility factor among low-wage workers.

Johnson and Corcoran (2003) outlined several issues related to the marginalization of the low-skill, low-paid worker including skill requirements of jobs, job quality, transitioning from "bad" to "good" jobs, and local labor market conditions. Regarding the skill requirements of jobs, they found over a three decade increase of earnings inequality within groups defined by education and age/experience. Employers place a growing importance on cognitive skills in wage determination among all workers, including those less educated. According to Johnson and Corcoran (2003), a lack of "basic" skills—reading, writing, simple arithmetic, basic familiarity with computers—may explain why some welfare recipients have difficulty obtaining good jobs, combined with employers' desire for workers to possess desired attributes such as reliability, a positive attitude, and a willingness to work hard, as well as soft skills such as the ability to work in diverse groups and communicate effectively. With current unemployment levels in the U.S. surging, at issue are the educational levels of the workforce and training availability. Goodman and Healy (2009) reported that a key to economic recovery will be more emphasis on retraining workers who have lost jobs. Recently $4.5 billion was designated for job training as part of the economic stimulus bill. This compares in current dollars to 1979 expenditures of $20 billion a year. These numbers indicate that the U.S. has some distance to go in providing serious job retraining, given the current conditions. Goodman and Healy (2009) also found that education is correlated with job loss, with 12.6% of those who became unemployed in February 2009 having attained less than high school or its equivalent, as compared with 8.3% being high school graduates, 7.0% having some college, and 4.1% possessing a bachelor's degree or higher.

Improving Preparation of Low-wage Workers for "Good" Jobs

The Working Poor Families Project (2008) cited the U.S. educational system for poorly preparing workers for jobs that require higher skills, compounded by an economy that has created 4.7 million jobs that pay poverty-level wages between 2002 and 2006. According to this report, almost half of all job openings require more than a high school diploma, yet 88 million adult workers are not prepared for these positions and 25 million lack a high school diploma or its equivalent. Existing federal and state adult education programs serve approximately only one tenth of the need.

Employment projections from 2006–2016 show a continued trend: nearly one third of new jobs during this time frame will fall into the "short-term on-the-job-training category" (qualifications can be acquired during short demonstrations of job duties or within one month of on-the-job experience) (Dohm & Shniper, 2007). Almost 52% of new jobs projected during this timeframe require minimal training and are classified by the U.S. Department of Labor as "short-term on-the-job training" or "moderate-term on-the job training" (skills can be acquired between 1 and 12 months of combined on-the-job experience and informal training). Further, the effectiveness of education and basic skills training programs for low-wage workers is mixed (Richburg-Hayes, 2008). Sixty-two percent of students who viewed themselves as workers first and students second did not complete their community college goals after six years as compared with 39% of those who viewed themselves as students first (Richburg-Hayes, 2008).

Workplace learning opportunities can be the basis for exclusion and competition between groups in the workplace. Unskilled workers are relatively easy to recruit and usually experience what Bratton et al. (2004), describe as a "low trust" "low learning" regime (p. 39). For example, workers who are employed part-time, contractually, or who telecommute may not have the same access to participate in work experiences and learning that full-time employees do. Peripheral and part-time workers tend to receive the least amount of training (Ashton & Feldstead, 2001; Conference Board of Canada, 2002). Lower-level workers do not have the same access to experiences as do higher status workers. Whom you know also has an impact here as the strength of one's relationships and networks can also shape learning.

Hoddinott (2004) argued the following:

> In the workplace, the unequal nature of the employment relationship and the requirement for programmes of education or training to have a measurable impact on profitability tend to conflict with the need for the dispassionate and unthreatening assessment required in programmes of fundamental education. This tendency has been magnified in the recent past as performance on literacy, numeracy and language proficiency assessments has been interpreted as a consummate indicator of 'fitness' for work. (p. 89)

Hoddinot critically examined the use of basic skills assessments by and for employers, arguing that their use has resulted in increased and often unwarranted scrutiny of workers in low-skill, low pay work and cautioned that this practice has the potential to further marginalize already disadvantaged workers. She instead suggests that often assessments have little relationship to the actual skills required by the work and instead may serve to unfairly screen out individuals who might be highly capable of doing the work, but whose educational attainment or linguistic skills limit their ability to successfully pass the assessments. In addition to preventing workers from access to needed jobs, the use of assessments in this way may cause the loss of promotion opportunities and pay increases and force workers to participate in basic skills education over and above their normal working hours, and ultimately face job loss.

Educating the low-wage worker is not just a matter or organizing a training class. It is more complicated, involving compensation for dynamics that serve to maintain their marginalization, including a vicious cycle that keeps these workers trapped in "bad" jobs by limiting their access to educational experiences and skill development that would help them move into "good" jobs. These workers are also victims of poor preparation to be successful in the job market.

LEAVING NO WORKERS BEHIND: MOVING FROM LOW-WAGE TO GAINFUL EMPLOYMENT

The potential of low-wage workers to find gainful employment is closely linked with the economy's strength. Given the current worldwide economic downturn, it is likely that low-wage workers will have even more difficulty finding and keeping work, especially since the jobs they often qualify for will be low wage, offering few fringe benefits and little opportunity for advancement, not to mention high job turnover. Local labor market demand conditions also affect the job experience of low-skill and low-wage workers since they are often the first to be let go or be furloughed during business downturns.

Although the prospects of moving into good jobs are challenging, some economists predict that a systemic labor shortage will transform the workplace over the next 25 to 30 years as the gap between baby boomers and entrants of college-educated workers widens due to the boomers' mass retirements (Atwater & Jones, 2004). The U.S. economy has kept a consistent growth rate of three percent per year since 1948. Assuming this rate, the workforce will have to increase by 58 million employees over the next three decades in order to maintain the same levels of productivity. Yet, based on current population trends, the number of workers will only increase by 23 million, creating overall U.S. labor shortage of 35 million workers (Atwater & Jones, 2004). The contracting supply of labor may propel some employers to make better investments in the long-term learning of all workers.

Addressing the problem of marginalized, low-wage workers requires a systemic response with strong policies and incentives for employers to acknowledge this invisible group of workers. It will take several levels of reform, including individual initiatives, organization leadership, innovative community partnerships, and strong policy development and implementation to holistically address the workplace learning of low-wage workers and their subsequent success in the labor market.

Individual Initiatives

The plight of low-wage workers is not their fault; they are caught in a system that functions by ensuring their marginalization. Yet, part of the systemic solution is for individuals who are low-wage to take initiative to change their status. These initiatives include

- seeking career counseling through their local communities
- identifying skills acquired in life and work and how they would transfer to a better job
- developing mentoring relationships within their organization or field of interest
- building networking skills
- finding the right employers
- pursuing educational opportunities, especially through tuition reimbursement programs (Hansen, 2009)

Individuals may also want to affiliate with or seek the help of associations that work to address low wages such as the Annie E. Casey Foundation Jobs Initiative, Association of Community Organizations for Reform Now

(ACORN), CareerGear, Corporate Voices for Working Families, Economic Policy Institute (EPI), and several others. Finally, becoming community advocates of employer and policy reform to pressure employers to increase training opportunities, health care, and other benefits can help improve the outlook for low-wage workers. Taking these initiatives are good starting points, but they are only part of the equation as low-wage work is a systemic problem that will require policy, community, and employer cooperation to effectively address the problem.

Organizational Leadership

Organizations have a responsibility to address the plight of the low-wage worker. This means making access to workplace education equitable in comparison to other classes of workers. One approach to improving workplace learning equity would be to ensure that what Billett (2000) refers to as "workplace affordances" exist for low-wage workers. Based on an examination of three worksites, Billet (2000) found an interdependence between workplace affordances (how much access workers had to activities and resources for learning) and individuals' participation in work (their level of engagement in knowledge generating activities). He concluded that workplace learning is best supported when both workplace affordances and individual participation are high. When there were inconsistencies, learning was compromised. He also found that encouragement by leaders could offset weak learning environments where the workplace affordances were compromised, which means supervisors need to understand their role in improving workplace affordances and making learning more accessible and supported.

Adult educators and human resource developers working in organizations are also in a position to advocate for better learning access for low-wage workers and to see that the curriculum and pedagogy are meeting the needs of low-wage workers. Adult educators and Human Resource Development (HRD) practitioners have a tall task to provide meaningful development to low-wage workers that will result in good jobs and a career trajectory. Education serves a dual role of preparing learners for careers while simultaneously promoting independent and critical thinking for their social roles (Bratton et al., 2004). Balancing a vocation and social function of training and education is a critical task. Learners need the vocational skills to move up the career ladder, while also the capacity to critique power relations and practices that keep them invisible and stuck in dead-end, low-wage jobs.

Workplace education will need to address this tension between vocational and social learning if change is sought both with workers and management. This means locating workplace education in what Rainbird, Munro, and Holly (2004) recognized as the context of the tensions between performance and profitability and worker learning. It is important to link educational access and opportunity to unequal power relations and consider how workplace learning affordances link to career progress and how job assignments and work groups affect access to informal learning and advancement. Workplace educators are positioned to give the low-wage worker voice in educational decision making. HRD can also help employers define skill requirements and career ladders for entry-level jobs, as well as on-the-job training to help low-wage workers move into good jobs.

Innovative Community Partnerships

Communities have long played a role in economic development and literacy. A more strategic use of such partnerships could help strengthen low-wage workers' prospects. Community colleges can play an important role and have the infrastructure in place to assist organizations. Richburg-Hayes (2008) profiled programs within community colleges that were successful at helping students complete job training programs. A combination of advisement, community building, and incentives was a common thread across these programs. Strategies included creating learning communities where students were assigned to take three linked credit courses together and received vouchers for text books. Another example is where students were assigned to a dedicated advisor with whom they were required to meet frequently. These students were also eligible for a $150 scholarship for each of two semesters after meeting with the advisor. In another example, students were eligible for a $1000 scholarship for each of two semesters if they maintained at least half time enrollment and had a "C" average. Another program involved assigning students to a two-semester guidance course that provide academic support and advisement.

In another example, a national association is partnering with community colleges and employers for certification. The National Association of Manufacturing, the largest industrial trade association in the U.S., is advocating for a national certification system known as the "National Career Readiness Certificate" that would be evidence of both academic and workplace competencies needed by manufacturing firms (No Worker Left Behind, 2009). The goal is to work with community colleges to integrate workplace competencies and industry-wide technical skills into academic programs based on the recognition by the association president, John Engler, that "The day when unskilled but willing workers could show up [for a job] has passed.... We have to align worker skills with the educational pathway" (No Worker Left Behind, 2009).

Strong Policy Development and Implementation

Policies to support the workplace learning of low-wage workers are needed to help them improve labor market access and job retention, such as continued funding and support for programs that provide labor market information, job networking, job retention counseling, and career planning (Kaye & Nightingale, 2000). Effective policies will incorporate services such as child care and transportation, as well as building in incentives to help low-wage workers improve their advancement and mobility prospects. Policies are also needed that will help raise the incomes of low-wage workers and enhance employment security, such as the Earned Income Tax Credit, living wage campaigns, targeted public and community service jobs strategies, and minimum wage policies. The Working Poor Families Project (2008) advocates policy changes to support low-wage workers including investing in programs to advance the skills of adult workers. This can be accomplished by investing in adult workers through improved education and skill-development policies that make workers more competitive.

CONCLUSION

This chapter has introduced the plight of the low-wage worker as being stuck in a dead-end job with little access to workplace learning, advancement opportunities, or benefits. The U.S. can no longer afford to ignore this growing segment of the labor force, particularly in light of the economic decline and future labor shortages. It is imperative to provide advancement opportunities and financial rewards for workers who commit long, often back-breaking hours to their low-wage jobs. Educators, employers, communities, and policy makers must be mindful of mitigating low-wage workers' marginalization in job assignments and workplace learning, and better preparing them for more advanced jobs. Individuals need to take initiative by taking advantage of services available to them such as career counseling and job training and by identifying how life skills translate into employable skills. Individuals should actively seek mentoring and pursue education, taking advantage of tuition reimbursement programs where available. Organizations must ensure equal access to workplace learning and provide meaningful development that leads to stable employment and advancement opportunities. Individuals and organizations need the support of their communities and policy makers to create and sustain changes for low-wage workers. It is in the interest of workers, organizations, communities, and our nation to invest in workplace learning for *all* workers to ensure that no worker is left behind.

REFERENCES

Ashton, D., & Feldstead, A. (2001). From training to lifelong learning: The birth of the knowledge society? In J. Storey (Ed.) *Human resource management: A critical text* (pp. 165–189). Minneapolis: University of Minnesota Press.

Ashton, D., & Green, F. (1996). *Education, training and the global economy.* Brookfield, VT: Edward Elgar Publishing.

Atwater, D. M., & Jones, A. (2004). Preparing for a future labor shortage. *Graziado Business Report, 7*(2). Retrieved March 9, 2009, from http://gbr.pepperdine.edu/042/laborshortage.html

Avis, J. (2004). Work-based learning and social justice: 'Learning to labour' and the new vocationalism in England. *Journal of Education and Work, 17*(2), 197–217.

Bernstein, J., & Gittleman, M. (2003, November/December). Exploring low-wage labor with the national compensation survey. *Monthly Labor Review,* 3–12.

Billett, S. (2000). Guided learning in the workplace. *Journal of Workplace Learning, 12*(7), 272–285.

Billett, S. (2001). Learning through work: Workplace affordances and individual engagement. *Journal of Workplace Learning, 13*(5), 209–214.

Bratton, J., Mills, J. H., Pyrch, T., & Sawchuck, P. (2004). *Workplace learning: A critical introduction.* Aurora, Ontario: Garamond Press.

Carrington, W. J., & Fallick, B. C. (2001, May). Do some workers have minimum wage careers? *Monthly Labor Review,* 17–27.

Conference Board of Canada. (2002). *Performance and potential 2002–03.* Ottawa, Ontario: Conference Board of Canada.

Coopey, J. (1996). Critical gaps in the "learning organization." In K. Starkey (Ed.), *How organizations learn* (pp. 525–542). London: International Thompson Business Press.

Dohm, A., & Shniper, L. (2007, November). Employment outlook 2006–2016: Occupational employment projections to 2016. *Monthly Labor Review,* 86–125.

Garrick, J. (1999). The dominant discourses of learning at work. In D. Boud & J. Garrick (Eds.), *Understanding learning at work* (pp. 216–231). London: Routledge.

Gee, J. P., Hull, G., & Lankshear, C. (1996). *The new work order: Behind the language of the new capitalism.* Boulder, CO: Westview Press.

Goodman, P. S., & Healy, J. (2009, March 7). Job losses hint at vast remaking of U. S. economy. *New York Times,* p. A1, A10.

Hansen, R. S. (2009). Surviving and moving beyond low-wage jobs: Solutions for an invisible workforce in America. *Quintessential Careers.* Retrieved March 5, 2009, from http://www.quintcareers.com/surviving_low-wage_jobs.html

Hoddinott, S. (2004). The assessment of workers' 'basic skills': A critique based on evidence from the United States, Canada, and England. In H. Rainbird, A. Fuller, & A. Munro (Eds.), *Workplace learning in context* (pp. 89–106). London: Routledge.

Johnson, R. C., & Corcoran, M. E. (2003). The road to economic self-sufficiency: Job quality & job transition patterns after welfare reform. *Journal of Policy Analysis and Management 22*(4), 615–639.

Kaye, K., & Nightingale, D. S. (Eds.). (2000). *The low-wage labor market: Challenges and opportunities for economic self-sufficiency* Washington, DC: U.S. Department of Health and Human Services Office of the Secretary Assistant Secretary for Planning and Evaluation.

Kim, M. (2000, September). Women paid low wages: Who they are and where they work. *Monthly Labor Review,* 26–30.

Kincheloe, J. L. (1999). *How do we tell the workers? The socioeconomic foundations of work and vocational education.* Boulder, CO: Westview Press.

Mishel, L., Bernstein, J., & Allegretto, S. (2007). *The state of working America, 2006/2007.* Ithaca, NY: Cornell University Press.

No Worker Left Behind. (2009, March 5). *Inside Higher Education.* Retrieved March 25, 2009, from http://www.insidehighered.com/layout/set/print/news/2009/03/05/certification

Probert, B. (1999). Gender workers and gendered work: Implications for women's learning. In D. Boud & J. Garrick (Eds.), *Understanding learning at work* (pp. 98–116). London: Routledge.

Rainbird, H., Fuller, A., & Munro, A. (Eds.). (2004). *Workplace learning in context.* London: Routledge.

Rainbird, H., Munro, A., & Holly, L. (2004). The employment relationship and workplace learning. In H. Rainbird, A. Fuller, & A. Munro (Eds.), *Workplace learning in context* (pp. 38–53). London: Routledge.

Richburg-Hayes, L. (2008). Helping low-wage workers persist in education programs. Lessons from research on welfare training programs and two promising community college strategies. *MDRC Working Paper.* Retrieved March 8, 2009, from http://www.mdrc.org/publications/472/abstract.html

Take Back Your Time. (n.d.). Retrieved March 5, 2009, from http://www.timeday.org/default.asp#why

Theodos, B., & Bednarzik, R. (2006, July). Earnings mobility and low-wage workers in the United States. *Monthly Labor Review,* 34–47.

U.S. Bureau of Labor Statistics (2003). Earnings by educational attainment and sex, 1979 and 2002. Retrieved March 5, 2009, from http://data.bls.gov/cgibin/print.pl/opub/ted/2003/oct/wk3/art04.htm

Workforce Management. (2008, June 9). 2008 training providers. *Workforce Management: Training & Development.* Retrieved February 18, 2009, from http://www.workforce.com/section/11/feature/25/72/12/index.html

The Working Poor Families Project. (2008). Still working hard, still falling short. Retrieved March 5, 2009, from http://www.workingpoorfamilies.org/pdfs/NatReport08.pdf

CHAPTER 8

THE ROLE OF THE BLACK CHURCH IN DEVELOPING CONGREGANTS FOR THE WORKPLACE

E. Paulette Isaac
University of Missouri-St. Louis

INTRODUCTION

Employee layoffs are a common problem shared in any industrialized society, and in the United States, where, recently, employees have been laid off in significant numbers, it is often a signal of a troubled economy. When the economy takes a nose dive, some corporations find themselves having to lay off hundreds of employees, even those who have been loyal to the company for 20 years or more. On the other hand, small business owners, struggling to keep their business afloat, either reduce the number of hours their employees work or eliminate positions altogether. Regardless of the company size, it is not unusual to see corporations or small businesses file for bankruptcy. At the same time, however, other employers, depending on their industry, are scrambling to fill positions.

A concern among some of today's employers is the shrinking pool of qualified applicants, and particularly qualified minorities. Undoubtedly, many em-

Learning for Economic Self-Sufficiency, pages 121–132

ployers would argue that they have jobs, but having the opportunity to choose from a skilled workforce to meet their demands increasingly evades them given the record number of layoffs. Dunkelberg and Wade (2006) found that "the job market is tight, owners have serious intentions to hire, but are frustrated by the lack of qualified applicants" (p. 1). Additionally, "As the population grows, and as minorities constitute an increasing share of the population... the gap between the number of jobs to be filled and the number of people who are qualified to fill those jobs will significantly widen" (Investing in People, n. d., p. 26). Furthermore, by the year 2028, "there will be 19 million more jobs than workers who are adequately prepared to fill them" (Investing in People, p. 14). This results in a preponderance of complaints on both sides. On the one hand, employers express a need to fill job vacancies. On the other, potential employees who lack training and necessary skills cry foul because they are barred from many positions in the job market. This obviously creates an aperture between job vacancies and qualified employees.

Old habits are hard to break. This appears to be the situation for employers seeking to fill positions. Such is the case in employment circles. What was the norm has now become passé. For some potential employees, particularly low-skilled adults, traditional skills training paths may not be suitable for their literacy level, and employers cannot rely on conventional recruiting mechanisms. Thus, typical avenues for job training need reconsideration and new strategies for identifying and selecting new employees must be used.

While many employers have used colleges and universities as well as head hunters to fill positions, non-traditional sites have also prepared adults for the workforce. A review of the literature reveals the "church has made many grassroots efforts at providing career guidance and development since 1960" (Fox, 2003, p. 179). According to Littlefield (2005), "Scholars have cited the Black church as being the most important contributor in the overall economic development of the African American community and the most effective organization in dealing with the problems facing the African American community" (p. 691). Nash and Herring (2006) note that because of the uncertainty of the job market, many Black churches are providing job skills and placement programs. "Many blacks welcome and call on their churches to tackle pressing issues such as . . . joblessness" (Brown & Brown, 2003, p. 618). The purpose of this chapter is to explore the role of the Black church in preparing African Americans for the workforce.

JOBS AND TRAINING

It has been common practice for many young people to enter college, graduate, and, if fortunate, immediately start working. For others, the trend is to attend a trade or technical school to obtain specialized skills training. However, there are many who do not follow either path. Some graduate from high school while others drop out, and later find themselves with little to no employable skills, a low-literacy ability, and are thus relegated to low-paying jobs. This is problematic, because "a large proportion of new jobs—especially jobs that offer competitive salaries and benefits—will demand skills and knowledge far beyond those of a high school graduate" (Investing in People, n.d., p. 14). Unfortunately, the majority of people dropping out of school are minorities (i.e., African Americans and Hispanics). Moreover, within urban areas, which can experience economic decline at greater levels, "social isolation from mainstream ties and institutions is the basis upon which the black urban poor are presumed to lack social capital that facilitates job finding" (Smith, 2005, p. 1). With today's focus on specialized skills and the current economic downturn, adults can no longer rely on basic skills to acquire viable employment. Employers need individuals with skills way beyond high school. Some corporations rely on head hunters and other recruiting agencies to fill key positions. But they, too, have run into a barrier in their attempts to find qualified applicants.

Many full-time employees engage in lifelong learning opportunities through their employer. These include employer-sponsored training and off-site and online seminars. Some employers offer tuition assistance or reimbursement to employees. Other learning activities are provided through employer partnerships. For example, the Workforce Investment Act, established in 1998, encourages collaboration between adult education providers and employers. One of its goals is to "help business and incumbent workers retain their competitiveness in a global economy" (Hopkins, Hansman, & Monaghan, 2009, p. 150). Hopkins, Hansman, and Monaghan (2009) further explain that incumbent workers receive job training through one-stop centers, on-the-job training, employer-based curricula, and/or state funded programs. Corporations and other institutions may further provide professional development opportunities for their employees. Some corporations even have their own specialized training centers. McDonald's Corporation established Hamburger University in 1961 to train employees in a variety of areas related to its operations. For public and private employers, there are programs for managers, administrative staff, and, faculty, to name a few. With technological advances, many employers provide in-house computer training. For example, in academe, there are workshops and seminars to assist professors in the use of instructional techniques for online courses. Others provide diversity training to educate employees on how to interact with people from different socioeconomic and cultural backgrounds. As this discussion suggests, the lifelong learning possibilities for some employees are limitless.

For employees with low-level skills or limited education, employers may provide basic educational training through, for example, the General Education Development (GED) program. In St. Louis, Missouri, a large healthcare system provides educational support to its employees. Employees pursuing a high school diploma online or a GED can receive additional tutoring in basic math skills, history, and science. Employees enrolled in college-level courses can get assistance with research papers and other homework assignments. While company-sponsored educational programs are useful for current employees, employers still need assistance in identifying qualified applicants for job vacancies.

For years, corporations have partnered with local colleges and universities and other agencies to provide skills training in order to fill vacant positions. The U.S. government's Employment and Training Center awards significant grant funding to colleges and universities that provide this training. In 2001, it awarded over $14 million in grants to higher education institutions to develop and train workers for highly-skilled jobs in community areas where companies were facing labor shortages (Employment and Training Administration, 2000). In the Kansas City region, to address the shortage of skilled employees, the National Association of Manufacturers and its Manufacturing Institute piloted a program in conjunction with the Alliance for Innovation in Manufacturing-Kansas City to provide manufacturing jobs and expand training opportunities (OneKC Wired, 2008).

Finding fault for the lack of qualified job applicants is easy to do. Some blame parents for not spending quality time with their children and for not instilling the value of education. Some are quick to hold our elementary and secondary educational system at fault. Regardless of who is held culpable, it is imperative that we improve education. According to *Vocational Training News* (VTN) (2002), "without 'immediate action' to improve education for all Americans, tomorrow's workforce will neither be ready to meet the challenges of a knowledge-intensive workplace, nor be able to take advantage of the 'vast' economic opportunities, warns a new report from a collation of corporate and higher education leaders" (p. 9). VTN also urges America to promote and take advantage of our diversity. Not doing so will cause a major social and economic crisis whereby it is projected that "by 2028 there will be 19 million more jobs than workers who are adequately prepared to fill them" (Investing in People, n.d., p. 14). Additionally, around 40% "of the people available to take the jobs will be members of minority groups" (Investing in People, n.d., p. 14). Thus, we must prepare all U.S. citizens, regardless of their literacy levels, to fill job vacancies if our country is to remain viable globally.

No one institution can meet all the job training needs before us. Therefore, we need to "support and strengthen existing outreach programs" (Investing in People, n.d., p. 16). There are numerous partnerships among community-based organizations, churches, hospitals, universities and colleges, and businesses. Social service agencies have long recognized the benefits to collaborating with non-profit organizations and agencies to disseminate information, conduct research, and enhance the quality of life of adults and children. Employers seeking to fill current and future job vacancies must expand their recruiting efforts to these organizations as well. Additionally, colleges and universities must partner with non-profit institutions to meet the future skills demand. While businesses and higher education institutions have maintained successful unions, they must broaden their purview to train and recruit non-traditionally skilled adults. Hence, they must widen their lens to see the value in working with faith-based organizations. As the following discussion indicates, the Black church has been instrumental in providing job training for African Americans.

JOB TRAINING AND THE BLACK CHURCH

In low-income communities, some residents do lack the necessary skills in order to obtain viable employment. In urban communities, which at times are reflective of economic decline and low levels of social organization (Mason, 2005; Wilson, 1996–97), potential applicants often want to obtain employment, but need assistance in acquiring the appropriate skills to meet employment demands. In urban areas, several factors "have led to the development of a bifurcated system of service delivery of adult education programs targeting learners who are either resource rich or resource poor" (Martin, 2004, p. 1). Hence, those with resources are able to engage in specialized training or are more likely to participate in formal educational programs (i.e., college or university). Those with fewer resources have to rely on other means such as community-based programs like those offered by the church.

Some adults have been successful in acquiring marketable skills when they turned to their local church for support and guidance. In her review of career guidance and development in the church, Fox (2003) determined that the church was a "logical source of career guidance and development" (p. 168). In fact, she found that vocational guidance was one of its many responsibilities. Some churches have provided career awareness and job-seeking skills (Fox, 2003). In a review of the church's role between the 1990s and early 2000s, some of the adult educational activities included resume writing, interviewing skills, and adult group career programs.

History of Black Church and Economic Development

Churches have long been associated with social service activities such as providing food and clothing, temporary shelter, and financial assistance.

Within the African American community, the Black church was a "significant voice" (Moore, 2003, p. 357) that spoke on behalf of its members. Juxtaposed with their social role was a strong belief in education. Therefore, education and subsequently, literacy has been central to the role of the Black church.

Education in the African American community was associated with freedom, advancement, and self-determination (Franklin, 1984). Historically, the Black church has played a significant role in the economic and job skills development of African Americans. It has been the conduit for African Americans to gain basic literacy skills and acquire trades (Isaac, Guy, & Valentine, 2001). Developed in response to racism and other ills (Lincoln & Mamiya, 1990; Littlefield, 2005), the Black church has "played a strong leadership role in communicating social change" and "economic empowerment" (Ford, 2004, p. 6). And, at the institutional level, throughout the twentieth century, the Black church promoted education (Markins, Fox, Taub, & Gilbert, 2002). Therefore, the Black church was not only a place of worship but also a place of teaching, a place where African Americans could develop business and leadership skills (Rowland, 2001). In essence it is a "representation of the African American community because it embodies the beliefs, values, struggles and culture of people of African descent" (Littlefield, 2005, p. 688). Thus, as an extension of the African American community, the Black church often responded to the needs of African Americans. Isaac (2002) found that external factors impacted adult educational activities in the church. In other words, based on the needs of the community, the church responded with appropriate educational programming. Economically, it continues to be a "significant combatant in the struggle by... training individuals to operate the secular world" (Moore, 2003, p. 358).

When African Americans faced limited employment opportunities, it was the church that provided employment, training, and skills. Many African Americans developed leadership skills (Este, 2004; Franklin, 2007) by serving in the church as trustees, deacons, and lay leaders. They also participated in several ministries and activities in the church. There were opportunities to develop entrepreneurial skills through planning and implementing bake sales, fish fries, and other promotional activities that provided many with planning and marketing experiences. These promotional activities advanced the financial stability of the church and promoted leadership skills among African Americans. In addition to leadership skills, many contemporary churches have invested in the economic development of its people, which has not only enhanced the community, but in the case of the Black church has also provided skills training and work experience for African American adults.

Lincoln and Mamiya (1990) studied the role of the Black church on black economic development and reported that "the most severe forms of racial discrimination against black people have been economic in character" (p. 238). However, "the Black church is the most economically independent institutional sector in the black community. It does not depend upon white trustees to raise funds... nor does it depend upon white patronage to pay its pastors or erect its buildings" (Lincoln & Mamiya, 1990, p. 241). Even today, the "church finds itself in a situation where it is the best continuing, organized entity in the black community for the acquisition and redevelopment of land, the building of business enterprises and the employment of people" (Gite, 1993, p. 6). Lincoln and Mamiya (1990) noted the development of various Black businesses that opened as a result of the owners' affiliation of with the Black church. Black farmers and Black insurance companies in the nineteenth and early twentieth centuries, Black banks, funeral parlors, mortuaries, and other Black-owned and -operated businesses all had roots in the Black church. Although the major thrust of Black economic development among the Black churches is aimed at creating businesses and financial stability, undoubtedly, employment and job training are products of it. As with society in general, new businesses mean job growth. Using economic development through non-profit organizations and foundations has allowed African Americans with little to no employable skills (i.e., customer relations, managerial, and technological) to acquire or enhance transferable, specific job skills.

The Black Church and Workforce Training

African Americans have historically used the church to develop their skills (Brown & Brown, 2003). The Black church provided health, civic, and social skills as well as job training. Booker T. Washington and his work with the Bible School at Tuskegee is an early example of the Black church's involvement in economic development. Washington sought to raise the standard of living by working with African American preachers to fight illiteracy and economic dependence (Denton, 1993).

During the early 20th century, the Black church provided job skills training. For example, in 1907, the Berean Presbyterian Church in Philadelphia established a training and industrial school that enabled adults to acquire carpentry, sewing, stenography, and upholstery skills (Franklin, 1990). As early as 1922, New York's Abyssinian Baptist Church had well established itself its educational programs, many of which were sponsored through its Abyssinian Community House (Franklin, 1990). In 1925, the Congregationalist Church of the Good Shepard of Chicago provided employment counseling, health education, and vocational guidance as well as other adult training programs (Franklin, 1990). The Metropolitan Baptist Church in the District of Columbia held leadership training classes (Gandy, 1945). Through educational programs in the community, African Americans were able to engage in learning activities that would have otherwise evaded them.

Contemporary Role of the Black Church and Workforce Development

With the contemporary shift in the economy to the service industry and technology fields, many African Americans are unable to compete for jobs that require specialized training (Pinn, 2001). The Black church has found it more crucial than ever to intercede on behalf of African Americans to provide economic stability through jobs (Isaac, 2005). Many churches, in line with the historical examples mentioned earlier, have established non-profit corporations, such as economic development organizations, to meet the needs in the African American community. Examples of job and skills development training programs abound in the Black church. The Reverend Leon Sullivan and his program of the Opportunities Industrialization Centers (OIC) and the Entrepreneurial Development Training Program was one of the most successful and fastest growing skills training programs in the United States. This self-help program, built on the Sullivan Principles, helped millions of African Americans receive the training they needed for the jobs they were seeking (Sullivan, 1998). The "Principles" originally served as an equal opportunity and human rights guide or code of conduct for businesses operating in South Africa. In 1997, Sullivan expanded the Principles for further use in other communities. In 1998, he noted that "one-half of all the businesses in Philadelphia are run by Blacks who received their management training from that Entrepreneurial Development Training Program in Progress Plaza" (Sullivan, 1998, p. 23). Through working with the Black church and using the social capital of church goers, Sullivan was able to build and staff Black-owned shopping centers, open factories, and rebuild neighborhoods in Philadelphia. Sullivan's work as well as that of other churches established businesses and entrepreneurial endeavors and provided job development and training.

Through development corporations and other non-profit organizations, churches have stabilized a number of local community businesses. According to Pinn (2001), some churches have opened "restaurants, food stores, and gas stations and have invested in high-tech industry and garment production" (p. 46). Others have developed "job banks that allow people to tap into city and state opportunities for employment" (Pinn, 2001, p. 48). First African Methodist Episcopal (A.M.E.) Church of Los Angeles, California, epitomizes how the church works to match jobs with potential employees: "Using primarily volunteers, the church contacts potential employers to tell them about the church's applicant database. By locating and screening potential employees" (Pinn, 2001, p. 48), the church has placed over 1,700 people of color in jobs. Abyssinian Baptist Church in Harlem, NY, created a development corporation that links education and job training (Environmental Protection Agency, 2007). Union Bethel A.M.E. Church in Maryland utilizes its economic development corporation to educate and empower African Americans and other adults and "generates new jobs and career advancement opportunities" (Union Bethel, 2008, p. 1). In Atlanta, Antioch Baptist Church North's Computer Training Center exists as a joint venture between the EDS Corporation and its non-profit organization. This venture allows the church to provide computers and computer training for congregants (Antioch, 2006). These are but a few examples of church initiatives that have created and/or provided of and training.

From its inception, the Black church has responded to the needs of African Americans. It provided spiritual support and inspiration as well as a safe haven from the outside forces which seemingly attacked from every angle (i.e., economics, social, and educational). As a foundation within the African American community, the Black church could not divorce itself from the many struggles in its own community. It had to respond with services and programs that met the various needs of African Americans. To tackle economic and financial matters, the Black church provided entrepreneurial opportunities and skills training, which in turn resulted in jobs for many African Americans who could not participate in formal training and educational programs.

CONCLUSION

The need to find employment and obtain employable skills is more important today than ever before. As it has done in the past, the Black church can play a role in preparing low-income and low-literacy adults with job skills and training. Despite the constant news of downsizing and job layoffs, some employers are seeking qualified applicants. For those employers seeking potential employees with special skills, finding them can be challenging. For years, many employers have relied on colleges, universities, or proprietary schools to train individuals to meet the workforce needs. Many employers have found success in partnering with agencies to provide skills training. Nevertheless, in doing so, low-skill and low-literate adults have more than likely been shut out of the job market. For those willing and able to participate, post-secondary formal educational settings can provide them with the necessary skills and training to acquire jobs. However, low-literate adults sometimes are still unable, embarrassed, or lacking the desire to participate in such public settings. Thus, the church offers another conduit for learning.

In the African American community, the Black church can provide the necessary training and education for low-literate adults. "Without the dedication of 'Black' religious institutions, 'Blacks' would not have achieved their present level of integration, and they would have been prevented from making significant contributions in all spheres of life and society" (Byrd, 2001, p. 90). Indeed, the Black church has contributed to the education and employment skills training of its congregants, and it presents a unique opportunity for adult educators, colleges and universities, as well as businesses to partner with the church to promote economic development among community members.

Some industries (i.e., social work and health) have already realized the value of partnering with the Black church to provide health and social services. The health and social services literature is replete of studies and programs conducted in conjunction with the Black church. Universities and businesses can follow suit. With the projected need for specialized skills, it is important for institutions and programs of higher education and businesses to establish partnerships with local churches. If they can collaborate with the Black church to provide job skills training for adults less likely to participate in formal educational programs, all three parties could mutually benefit. More importantly, however, society as a whole would benefit. The gap between job vacancies and job seekers would close. Employers' pool of qualified applicants would grow. Access to viable employment may cause some adults to determine that attending a formal institution of higher learning is possible.

There are many examples of churches that have been successful in rebuilding communities through various economic development activities. Along with business, industry, and institutions of higher learning, more programs can be developed, creating a higher return on investment for all.

REFERENCES

Antioch Baptist Church North. (2006). *Antioch Urban Ministries, Inc.* Retrieved January 10, 2009, from http://www.antiochnorth.org/aumi.htm

Brown, R. K., & Brown, R. E. (2003). Faith and works: Church-based social capital resources and African American political activism. *Social Forces, 82*(2), 617–641.

Byrd, A. D. (2001). Adult educational efforts of the American Black church, 1600–1900. *Journal of Religious Thought, 44*(22), 83–92.

Denton, V. L. (1993). *Booker T. Washington and the adult education movement.* Gainesville: University Press of Florida.

Dunkelberg, W. C., & Wade, H. (2006). Labor markets. *NFIB Small Business Economic Trends.* Retrieved on September 5, 2008, from http://www.nfib.com/page/sbet

Employment and Training Administration. (2000). *Grants will enable minority colleges and universities to close skill gaps and create job.* U.S. Department of Labor. Retrieved January 10, 2009, from http://www.doleta.gov/sga/awards/00-109award.cfm

Environmental Protection Agency. (2007). *EPA, Boro Prez, and local organization celebrate Harlem's environmental renaissance: Neighborhood projects win national award for smart growth.* Retrieved December 12, 2008, from http://yosemite.epa.gov/OPA/ADMPRESS.NSF/eebfaebc1afd883d85257355005afd19/7c31353edb4387d0852573b800687dde!OpenDocument

Este, D. C. (2004). The Black church as a social welfare institution: Union United Church and the development of Montreal's Black community, 1907–1940. *Journal of Black Studies, 35(1),* 3–22.

Ford, R. (2004). Reaching the *Black church* year-round. *Public Relations Tactics, 1*(2), 6.

Fox, L. A. (2003). The role of the church in career guidance and development: A review of the literature 1960–early 2000s. *Journal of Career Development, 29*(3), 167–182.

Franklin, R. M. (2007). *Crisis in the village: Restoring hope in African American communities.* Minneapolis: Fortress Press.

Franklin, V. P. (1984). *Black self-determination: A cultural history of the faith of the fathers.* Westport: Lawrence Hill.

Franklin, V. P. (1990). Education for life: Adult education programs for African Americans in northern cities, 1900-1942. In H. G. Neufeldt & L. McGee (Eds.), *Education of the African American adult: An historical overview* (pp. 113–134). New York: Greenwood Press.

Gandy, S. L. (1945). The Negro church and the adult education phase of its program. *Journal of Negro Education, 14,* 381–382.

Gite, L. (1993). The new agenda of the Black church. *Black Enterprise, 24*(5), 54–56.

Hopkins, J. L, Hansman, C. A., & Monaghan. C. H. (2009). Conflict and collaboration: Providers and planners implementing the Workforce Investment Act (WIA). In R. Lawrence (Ed.), *Proceedings of the 50th Annual Adult Education Research Conference* (pp. 150–154). National Louis University, Chicago, IL.

Investing in People: Developing all of America's Talent on Campus and in the Workplace. (n.d.). *Business–Higher Education Forum.* Retrieved February 20, 2009, from http://www.acenet.edu/bookstore/pdf/investing_in_people.pdf

Isaac, E. P. (2005). The future of adult education in the urban African American church. *Education and Urban Society, 37*(3), 276–291.

Isaac, E. P., Guy, T., & Valentine, T. (2001). Understanding African American adult learners' motivations to learn in church-based adult education. *Adult Education Quarterly, 52*(1), 23–38.

Isaac, P. (Spring, 2002). The adult education phase of the African American church revisited. *Christian Education Journal, 6*(1), 7–23.

Lincoln, C. E., & Mamiya, L. H. (1990). *The Black church in the African American experience.* Durham: Duke University Press.

Littlefield, M. B. (2005). The Black Church and community development and self-help. The next phase of social equality. *Western Journal of Black Studies, 29*(4), 687–693.

Lohan, M. C. (2000). Environmental inhibitors to informal learning in the workplace: A case study of public school teachers. *Adult Education Quarterly, 50*(2), 83–10.

Markens, S., Fox, S. A., Taub, B., & Gilbert, M. L. (2002). Role of Black churches in health promotion programs: Lessons from the Los Angeles mammography promotion in churches program. *American Journal of Public Health, 92*(5), 805–810.

Martin, L. G. (2004). Adult education in the urban context. In L. G. Martin & E. E. Rogers (Eds.), *Adult education in an urban context: Problems, practices, and programming for inner-city communities* (pp. 3–16). New Directions for Adult and Continuing Education, No. 101. San Francisco: Jossey-Bass.

Mason, B. J. (2005). And I am part of the greatness. Twelve Black elderly women and men decry their urban community's reality. *Journal of Black Studies, 36*(1), 97–115.

Moore, T. (2003). Promoting change through the African American church and social activism. *Journal of Psychology and Christianity, 22*(4), 357–362.

Nash, S., & Herring, C. (2006). The Black church and community economic development. In C. A. Conrad, J. Whitehead, P. Mason, & J. Stewart (Eds.), *African Americans in the U.S. economy* (pp. 363–372). Lanham, MA: Rowman & Littlefield.

OneKC Wired. (2008). *Alliance for Innovation in Manufacturing-Kansas City (AIM-KC).* OneKC Wired. Retrieved December 11, 2008, from http://www.onekcwired.com/partners.cfm

Pinn, A. B. (2001). Of God, money, and earth: The Black Church on economics and environmental racism. *Religious Thought, 56/57*(2), 43–61.

Rowland, M. L. (2001). Lift every voice and sing: Adults' perceptions of learning through religious music in an African American church. *Arts and Learning Research Journal, 17*(1), 176–196.

Smith, S. S. (2005). "Don't put my name on it": Social capital activation and job-finding assistance among the Black urban poor. *American Journal of Sociology, 111*(1), 1–57.

Sullivan, L. (1998). *Moving mountains: The principles and purposes of Leon Sullivan.* Valley Forge: Judson Press.

Union Bethel A.M.E. Church. (2008). *Unity Economic Development Corporation.* Union Bethel A.M.E. Church. Retrieved December 9, 2008, from http://www.ubame.org/UEDC.htm

Vocational Training News. (2002). Improve education for all, or risk economic crisis. *Vocational Training Newsletter, 33*(2), 9. Retrieved January 10, 2009, from http://web.ebscohost.com/ehost/pdf?vid=3&hid=111&sid=83202831-420b-4b39-9e4b5db6768b6b10%40sessionmgr110

Wilson, W. J. (1996–97). When work disappears. *Political Science Quarterly, 111*(4), 567–595.

CHAPTER 9

LEARNING ON THE MOVE

Migrant Workers in Adult Education

Aida A. Nevárez-La Torre
Fordham University

INTRODUCTION

When I decided to migrate to the United States over three decades ago, I was already an experienced teacher. I had a bachelor's and a master's degree, was bilingual in English and Spanish, had friends and family to support me, and some savings in a bank account to assist me financially while I settled down. I chose to move to Massachusetts because, at the time, it was a state with a bilingual education law; thus, I felt I would surely find a job as a bilingual teacher. I first worked as a bilingual teacher in a migrant summer program, teaching children mostly from Mexico in an elementary school. There was a set curriculum I needed to follow, multiple forms to document each child's progress, and many materials and resources available to us. The children were brought in buses to the school grounds every morning where breakfast, lunch, and snacks were provided to them. Each classroom had two teachers and a teacher's aide. That summer, several field trips to museums and water parks were scheduled. I remember wondering about

Learning for Economic Self-Sufficiency, pages 133–153

the parents of these children since none ever came to the school or accompanied them during field trips.

One day a friend took me to see the migrant campsites, and, for me, it was a rude awakening. Until that day, I did not realize that the time the children spend at the school was, perhaps, the only time during the day that they could be just that—children. The campsite looked very desolate. There was nothing there but trailers and some shacks with a door and a small window at each side. As we traveled around the different fields, all I could see were bodies with colorful handkerchiefs and hats on their heads, bent down, moving slowly down rows of crops. On some Sunday afternoons, the members of a church I attended at the time visited some campsites. It was then that I entered some of the shacks to interact in Spanish with the wives and children of the laborers. I noticed that each family only had one medium-sized room where the kitchen was located as well as the space where they ate and slept. There was one bathroom that was shared with another family. The furniture was minimal, and there were no books that I could see.

After a few years, I moved again to a larger city to pursue my doctoral studies at an Ivy League school and did not work with migrant children again. Once I finished my degree, I moved to a different state, got married, and secured a tenure-track position at a large university. The images of migrant workers in the fields were fossilized in my mind; I often contrast their experiences as immigrants in this country with my own.

Today, as in the past century, the agricultural, livestock, forestry, horticulture, and fishing industries in the U.S. are reliant on seasonal migrant labor for their existence and vigor (Pappamihiel, 2004). Consequently, laborers, the majority of whom are from Mexico and Central America, travel to the U.S. seeking employment that oftentimes takes them to secluded parts of the country. Frequently, they come with their families. Overall, they, are very poor, lack any English language fluency or literacy skills, are undocumented with less than seven years of formal schooling, and are unfamiliar with the educational system in the U.S. (Shields, 2002).

In this chapter, I explore the salient issues of providing quality education for migrant workers. I begin by defining migration and describe their presence in the U.S. An identification and analysis of the conflicts of learning on the move follows. Finally, some promising practices are suggested to address the many challenges of educating highly mobile adult students.

MIGRANTS WORKERS: WHO THEY ARE AND WHAT THEY DO

Scholars from a variety of fields including economics, sociology, anthropology, and psychology have studied migration. It has been found that this process involves physical, biological, cultural, and psychological changes (Prewitt-Diaz, 1994). This researcher considers the term migration as "the movement of people across cultures and across geographic boundaries" (p. v). Migration is conceptualized as having four characteristics: (1) it involves the movement of people through space (including establishing real or perceived distance); (2) it recognizes the issue of time or duration—some migrant groups with a long history of work in the U.S. are able to concentrate their labor within the same states, while newer groups find jobs of shorter duration and move more frequently, covering farther distances (Milton & Watson, 1997); (3) it includes some level of disruption (major personal, emotional, social, and economic readjustments); and (4) it reflects an individual as well as a group response (Prewitt-Diaz, 1994). This definition is useful in pointing out the different dimensions of change across time and space as well as the chaotic nature of this type of existence.

Although these definitions serve bureaucratic purposes of identification for delivery of services, they fall short of providing a comprehensive and sensitive picture of migrant laborers in the U.S. Consistent, accurate information about the demographics of this population is hard to obtain. Analysis of the literature revealed that this difficulty is in part a result of migrant workers' high mobility across the nation and also because there is no tracking system that effectively and systematically documents their entry and exit from the migrant jobs within and across states (Kloosterman, Skiffington, Sanchez, & Kiron, 2003; Milton & Watson, 1997; Pappahimiel, 2004;).

Recent estimates suggest that migrant families constitute approximately three to five million people in the U.S. who, each year, relocate to work and improve their financial situations (National Center for Farmworker Health, 2001; U.S. Department of Education, 1994, as cited in Kloosterman et al. 2003). According to Kindler's (n.d.) analysis of U.S. Department of Education data, in 2000, about 800,000 migrant children attended schools in different states (also see Huddle, 2000).

Approximately 97% of migrant workers are native Spanish speakers, the majority of whom are Mexicans and Puerto Ricans, followed by other Central and South American countries (Migrant and Seasonal Head Start Quality Improvement Centers, 2003). These workers are usually between the ages of 25 and 44 years. Many are not literate in their native language, which is typically, but not always, Spanish (Runsten & Kearney, 1994, as cited in Milton & Watson, 1997); they might, for example, speak Mixtec, one of the indigenous languages of the state of Oaxaca in southern rural Mexico. Shields (2002) explains that on average they earn from $5,000 to $6,000 a year (also see Rothenberg, 1998). They are considered to be the most undereducated major subgroup in the country (Ortiz, 1995; Velázquez, 1996; Vocke, 2007). The picture just presented serves to outline the intricate reality of migrant families, which is predictive of difficulties in improving their lives. The following section scrutinizes further one important goal of many migrant families—that is, obtaining quality education for themselves and their children.

HISTORICAL TRAJECTORY OF EDUCATIONAL OPPORTUNITIES

Across centuries, migrant workers have provided *manual capital* to build this nation's economic infrastructure. In 2001, "the labor–intensive work of migrant families helped to harvest more than $28 billion of fruit, vegetables, and horticulture crops in the United States" (U.S. Department of Agriculture, 2002, as cited in Kloosterman et al., 2003).

Regardless of the multiple contributions of migrants over the years, the majority of U.S. society is blind to the difficult daily reality that these workers face and the monumental obstacles they encounter towards obtaining education. I agree with Guerra (1998), who contends:

> We still need to learn as much as we can about the actual lived experience of members of marginalized groups in the U.S., especially those whose limited economic and educational options give them little choice but to make their homes in highly segregated racial and ethnic communities out of which some members rarely venture. (p. 5)

For migrants, in this sense, the contexts of school, workplace, and institutional settings are contested (Nevárez-La Torre, 2010) since it is there that the different cultures in which they live clash and languages collide.

Migrant families and their children have always lived at the margins of society in the U.S. Kozoll, Osborne, and Earnest García (2003) observe that migrants "seem to fall between the cracks of our society because of their life on the road and the low level of interactions they have within the communities in which they work" (p. 568). Their paths rarely cross with families who are better off economically in cities, suburbia, and even in rural parts of the nation. As such, they have been labeled an *invisible minority* in the literature (Salinas & Fránquiz, 2004; Vocke, 2007). Thompson (2002) denounces that the fresh produce we buy in groceries stores disguise labor injustices, as well as other types of injustices within the food industry. He states, "Fewer U.S. citizens in each succeeding generation know someone who makes a living at farming or one who gets his or her hands dirty in the fields" (p. 15). For the world outside of migrant worker campsites, it is very easy to ignore that these families experience the impact of stressful economic conditions surrounded by substandard living conditions. Milton and Watson (1997) explain that the campsites are evidence of extreme poverty with inferior housing, unserviced roads, untreated water, and inadequate basic public services.

These conditions are the background to educational opportunities for migrants before and after the 1960s, when the first migrant educational law was enacted. During most of the 19th and 20th centuries, Chinese, Japanese, Russian, Italian, and Mexican immigrants were among the largest ethnic groups to have participated in agriculture, fishing, and forestry industries (Fránquiz & Loya Hernández, 2004). Before the 1960s, the context of migrant workers' lives was often characterized by meager salaries, with no health or social security benefits, unhealthy living conditions, and being excluded from the educational system (Branz-Spall & Wright, 2004). With no social support networks and lacking any English language skills, they felt trapped by the abuses that went unnoticed or were ignored by authorities and the general public across the states where they resided for short periods of time (Green, 2003; OSPI, n.d.).

Migrant students have always experienced a high incidence of mobility, and thus were viewed by school districts as non-residents, and as such, not their responsibility. They received short spans of instruction, had no continuity of instruction from district to district or from state to state, and suffered academically because resources did not follow students as they moved (Meyertholen, Castro, & Salinas, 2004). Locally, church and community groups might have voiced concern about the unfair and, at times, inhumane treatment of migrants, but nothing really changed until the 1960s. Some religious and political organizations started to open day care centers, supported by private funds, and offered summer programs for migrant children (Branz-Spall & Wright, 2004).

Key events during that decade brought the difficult working conditions for adult migrant workers and the poor education available to them to the forefront of U.S. media channels. For example, Cesar Chavez organized several marches, strikes, and boycotts in California and other western states to protest the unfair treatment of crop laborers (Gonzales, 1996). The famous television documentary *Harvest of Shame* chronicled the low living standards for this population across the nation (Educational Media Collection, 2007). At the same time, different community, religious, and political organizations increased their demands at the state and national levels for a radical change to improve the lives and education of these laborers (Branz-Spall & Wright, 2004).

Among the federal bureaucratic initiatives that were created during that decade to address the educational needs of migrant families was the Office of Migrant Education (OME) within the Office of Elementary and Secondary Education in 1966. This office worked towards providing migrant children, in elementary and secondary schools up to age 21, educational opportunities and resources. Educational policies were based on a compensatory philosophy common during that time. The OSPI website explains this philosophy:

> The goals of the program are to raise each child academically, physically, and socially to a level of opportunity for life at least equal to that of all other children in the United States.... They are designed to compensate for academic, health, social, and/or physical deficiencies caused by migratory work patterns and cultural and linguistic differences of the families. (OSPI, n.d., p. 2)

As specified earlier, while the creation of OME was a positive step toward addressing the educational needs of migrant families, it concentrated on educating migrant children and youth. Some of its programs, however, did offer indirect education services to migrant adult learners (for example, through family literacy programs).

Yet, in many instances, this population still depends on adult basic education programs offered through public adult schools, community colleges, libraries, community and faith-based organizations, and correctional institutions (California Department of Education, n.d.; Milton & Watson, 1997). The federal Adult Education and Family Literacy Act, enacted as Title II of the Workforce Investment Act, provides federal funding to supplement adult education programs in both public and private non-profit institutions. These funds complement Adult Basic Education (ABE), English as a Second Language (ESL), and Adult Secondary Education (ASE) programs. The goal of these programs is to enable adults to become more employable, productive, and responsible citizens through literacy (California Department of Education, n.d). The next section explores the scope of these programs and their struggles in educating migrant adults.

CURRENT REALITIES

Efforts to improve the lifestyle, work conditions, and skills of itinerant laborers fall victim of multiple debilitating forces. Thompson (2002) contends that the U.S. agricultural system does not facilitate routes for farm laborers to improve their skills and their livelihood. His metaphor of the "farm worker treadmill" effectively depicts this as an oppressive system. Thompson (2002) argues that migrant farm workers

> remain unskilled workers who rarely if ever graduate to landownership or to a position of respect in the agricultural community. Though farm workers have farm knowledge and real skills that are invaluable on farms, skills learned from generations of ancestors in Mexico and elsewhere, these skills do not help them advance in the field of agriculture. Thus, farm work as it is organized today is a treadmill of labor that benefits agribusiness and entraps workers in cycles of travel and poverty. (p. 9)

For instance, although several programs at the federal and state levels, under the Office of Migrant Education and the Office of Vocational and Adult Education (OVAE), exist today to support migrant families' quest for better educational opportunities, a survey of the literature reveals that many problems still plague their achievement of this goal. As of 2008, OME administers grant programs to offer education and supportive services, mainly to migrant children and youth. The U.S. Department of Education website identifies a few of the sponsored programs that incorporate services for adult laborers: (1) College Assistance Migrant Program (CAMP), (2) Migrant Education Coordination Support Center, (3) Migrant Education Even Start (MEES), and (4) Migrant Education National Hotline (ESCORT).

Other programs are sponsored through OVAE, including (1) Adult Education, (2) Vocational Education, (3) The America's Career Resource Network, and (4) Tech-Prep Education Community Colleges. While these programs target adults and older youth who have dropped out of school, the available descriptions did not specify many concentrated efforts to specifically reach adult migrant laborers. Many of the limited number of programs even offered today fall short of what migrant learners need.

Collecting data on the effectiveness of these different types of programs is difficult due to the high mobility of the population, different record keeping among states, and the absence of a national tracking system. I did not locate any experimental studies that explore the quality of implementation of these programs and their overall impact in improving educational conditions for migrant workers. Kloosterman and colleagues (2003) point out the lack of outcome studies that document how migrant and seasonal programs perform in achieving the goals for quality migrant schooling set by educational and funding agencies, such as Head Start. Salinas and Reyes (2004) acknowledge the scarcity of research studies that comprehensively explore migrant education and the educational needs of migrant families. However, key scholarly reports that qualitatively describe present educational opportunities for the adult migrant education population are discussed in the following paragraphs. Unfortunately, recent reports confirm that working and living conditions for migrants have remained the same for much of the last 50 years. The educational attainment of migrant students continues to lag behind that of non-migrant students (Fránquiz & Loya Hernández, 2004; Hanley, Wrigley, & Ulewicz, 2007; Kloosterman, et al., 2003; Minarik, Flom, & Williams, 2007; Vocke, 2007).

Family literacy programs, such as Even Start, offer an integrated education approach, which includes adult basic education and literacy, parenting education, and early childhood education. The programs' design is supposed to value and actively use the families' resources, networks, and traditions as well as talents and abilities in the educational offerings for migrant workers.

Despite the best of intentions, Migrant Education Even Start programs have had difficulty accommodating the unique attributes of the migrant lifestyle and addressing the particular literacy needs of family members—for instance, providing bilingual family literacy in English and in Spanish (Ward & Fránquiz, 2004). Also, the task of home visits has proven challenging due to the geographically distant and isolated areas where many camps are located. Another challenge is to sustain the home visits schedule around the migrant parents' schedules. Although migrant adults express a desire to learn English, acquire literacy skills, and obtain a GED, they are impeded in achieving this because of time constraints related to family, work and household responsibilities, frequent and unplanned moves, unreliable transportation, poor health, and inadequate resources for day care (Ward & Fránquiz, 2004).

Even Start calls for adult education to align their curriculum to the adults' educational goals. This presents some difficulties since migrant adults have diverse academic needs, from lack of literacy in their first language (L1) and in their varying-level of skills in a second language (L2) to understanding how to communicate with coworkers, government agencies, teachers, and to help their children with academic work. The programs then need to have resources in more than one language and address social as well as academic communicative skills to serve this population. This in turn, imposes a need to collaborate with educational, social service, community and business groups in the offering of services.

The poor living conditions described in the previous section "pose serious safety and health hazards and undermine efforts to advance education services for migrant families" (Kloosterman et al., 2003, p. 11). The cramp spaces in many migrant camps, with no privacy, no air condition, or adequate lighting do not provide the best physical environment for studying. Even when online educational programs are offered, the students cannot access computers in the camp sites or do not have a working phone line. Meyertholen, Castro, and Salinas (2004) caution that in many camp sites the only phone that exists is a pay phone; computer labs in schools are usually closed during the summer, when migrant students need to use them; and most programs operate out of libraries, migrant labor camps, community centers, and migrant families' residences, all sites where there is a limited access to technology. When taking correspondence courses, they lack the assistance of a teacher, forcing them to work by themselves. Moreover, after they complete the course, they need to wait until they enroll in a school to take the necessary exams for the correspondence course (Solís, 2004).

A different type of challenge is the teachers' and administrators' ongoing lack of awareness and knowledge about the culture, history, values, and worldview of migrant families. For instance, we know that the majority of society in the U.S. might see migrant families as lacking a home since they do not own or even rent a physical structure of residence like a house or apartment. However, the concept of home for migrants is very different than the common understanding imposed by those outside their culture. Kozoll et al. (2003) argue that migrating is a choice these families make in order to maintain their family structure. For them, "homed–homeless" is not a dichotomy; rather, the operative word to define home is "family" (Kozoll et al., 2003, p. 568). Their ethnographic study revealed that for Latina/o migrant agricultural workers,

> home means family . . . and is, in part, detached from space and place and these families often choose to be "homeless," in the sense that we usually think of the term, in order to maintain their "home" or family structure. In particular, choosing to be in the United States (for most are not U.S. nationals) signifies choosing family over "home." (p. 568)

In order to approach migrant families in more culturally sensitive ways, this difference in perception of what constitutes home needs to be made explicit to school teachers and program administrators.

Another problematic perception is that the migrant home environment is linguistically and culturally sterile (Jiménez & Barrera, 1999). Kindler (n.d.) clarifies that even when the literacy rate among migrant adults is very low and their children are less likely to be exposed to rich print environments, "migrant parents, like all parents, see education as a path to a better life and place a high value on their children's education" (para 6).

The negative ways that some educators see migrants have been documented in the literature. Fránquiz and Loya Hernández (2004) note that schools often see migrant families as uninvolved and uncaring about their children's education. These researchers see a connection between the lack of quality services offered to improve the lives of migrants and these misinformed, pervasive attitudes. They instead call for the "reeducation of the educational community" about migrant students and their families to ameliorate the misconceptions.

In general, effective education is not just about methods, standards, and resources; it is also about personal and professional worldviews, ideologies, and philosophies that permeate our thoughts, spoken and written language, and behaviors. Ward and Fránquiz (2004) point out some of the different perspectives on education between mainstream middle-class families and Latino migrant families. Ward and Fránquiz (2004) explain that while for Latinos *educación* refers to all values that shape the character of a person (i.e., academic, moral, emotional, relational), the understanding in the U.S. of *education* for middle class families focuses on the academic (i.e., reading, math, writing). Such a fundamental difference needs to be acknowledged, respected, and understood if we are to meaningfully involve migrant families in education. They reaffirm Guadalupe Valdés' contention that, "family literacy efforts should consider the interplay of social inequalities, educational ideologies, educational structures, and interpersonal interactions" (Ward & Fránquiz, 2004, p. 94).

Practical issues of aligning migration patterns to adult education programs' availability are still a matter of concern. Migration patterns follow an eastern, central, and western stream (Shotland, 1989). Migrants trail the crops from south to north in the spring and then back south in the fall (Baca, 2004). This pattern of migration negatively affects the school attendance of the migrant children, since they have to enroll late in the fall and withdraw from schools in early spring, impeding them from completing even one full term in the same school (Kindler, n.d.).

The lack of schooling and language skills of migrant adults and children pose many challenges for educational agencies professionally unequipped to instruct this highly diverse student body. The majority of migrants lack oracy and literacy skills in English when they enter schools and adult education programs (Kindler, n.d.). Also, although many may come from Mexico, as indicated before, not all speak Spanish as their first language. Many lack literacy skills in their first language (Milton & Watson, 1997). These programs have few resources to offer bilingual education in the indigenous languages that some migrant workers speak.

A lack of translators in the languages spoken and a lack of ESL and bilingual teachers who speak the different native languages combine with a lack of quality educational materials and resources. Many teachers lack training in specialized methods to teach English as a second language (ESL). These conditions echo Nieto's (2000) contention that many teachers today do not have "extensive personal experiences nor professional training in cross-cultural issues, and most would prefer to work in a suburban setting, teaching White, middle-class youth" (p. 181).

Other practical issues become barriers to the participation of migrant workers in education. While the campsites are very isolated and distant from schools, libraries, community centers, and colleges, transportation is not provided by school districts or by the agricultural corporation who hired the laborers (Milton & Watson, 1997). They might decide not to attend ABE or ESL classes because of their work schedule or lack of childcare for their children. Given the anti-immigration sentiments in parts of U.S. (Anti-Defamation League, 2006), they may experience apprehension about unfamiliar settings where classes are held and fear violence against themselves as migrants (Thompson, 2002).

According to Kloosterman et al. (2003), an unequal distribution of resources exists across the states that host migrant workers. States with a high number of migrant workers will have the resources to offer well-coordinated academic programs, whereas educational services in states with a small migrant population may be lacking or nonexistent. There is, therefore, a pronounced lack of consistency in the type and quality of programs made available to migrant adults.

The curricula used in some programs also deserve attention. Programs might just emphasize oral skills, at the expense of literacy, because of demands on migrants' time. ABE and GED classes might segregate adult migrants from the English speaking population and track them away from the college prep courses (Kindler, n.d.; Milton & Watson, 1997). This separation diminishes their exposure to comprehensible language use and opportunities to interact with members of the majority culture. Both of these are important variables in second language development and cultural understanding (Krashen, 1985; Swain, 1993).

Another dimension of migrant education is to decipher the opportunities offered to adult laborers to access postsecondary education. These students are not exposed to the rigorous curriculum that will prepare them for college and to the knowledge needed to fill out college applications, entrance essays, financial forms, college admissions tests, and placement tests; this knowledge is a de facto *hidden curriculum* for them (Salinas & Reyes, 2004). The final section of this chapter provides some suggestions to improve the educational opportunities of adult migrant workers.

A CRITICAL VIEW OF THE FUTURE: CONCLUSIONS AND IMPLICATIONS

Learning on the move becomes a way of life for migrant workers whose mobile existence demands creative alternatives to obtain an education and break the cycle of travel and poverty. The layering of obstacles discussed in the previous sections of this chapter calls for multifaceted and resourceful measures to surmount them. This last section offers innovative strategies towards achieving this goal and discusses key implications for the exploration of education on the move. The discussion addresses five key areas of need outlined earlier: (1) development of a cohesive system for information gathering and sharing, (2) design of educational supports that cater to a mobile life style, (3) creation of relevant curriculum, (4) restructure of programs to make adult migrants visible, and (5) intensification of investigative efforts.

Development of a Cohesive System of Information Gathering and Sharing

The collaboration among and coordination of programs within and across states and across nations are still thorny issues and in need of critical attention. Still today, there is a need for a nationwide system of tracking migrant student records and educational progress that is feasible, competent, and secure (Salinas & Franquíz, 2004a). Such a system would create information files that can be accessed from a centralized location and programs and agencies that work with adults from different states. Kindler (n.d.) explains that the electronic availability of this information would strengthen the continuity of migrant students' education and facilitate the analysis of outcome data to trace the educational development of migrant learners. Although the No Child Left Behind Act called for the federal government to play an increased role in the reestablishment of a national system of records transfer (Kindler, n.d.), very little progress has been observed on this issue.

Increasingly, the use of technology is presented as an innovative tool to manage the documentation and exchange of migrant students' records across educational agencies and states (Salinas & Franquiz, 2004b; Shields, 2002;). Technology can be use to improve professional collaboration in the areas of family literacy by sharing instructional resources and curriculum across states. An encouraging step is that in the absence of a nationwide tracking system, some states have taken the initiative to create intrastate and regional interstate electronic databases for these purposes (Kindler, n.d.).

The use of technological advances, although necessary, is not sufficient. Branz-Sprall and Wright (2004) explain that while communication venues like phone, email, and/or fax as well as the use of translators and interpreters might be available, in many cases a disposition to work cooperatively to share information might be lacking.

Increased and more sophisticated training and professional development could ameliorate deficiencies in information sharing, program coordination, and delivery of services across multiple programs and agencies. Topics to address should include: servicing multicultural and mobile students; negotiating different educational programs and requirements; implementing cooperative skills and strategies; and adaptation of curricular requirements based on individual needs.

Ward and Franquiz (2004) suggest that it is also imperative to open collaboration across nations. Researchers (Jiménez & Barrera, 1999; Smith & Martínez-León, 2003) have further written about the need to make biliteracy in English and Spanish part of instructional curricula to benefit transnational students (shuttle migrants who cyclically move across borders). Thus, international collaborative efforts that create educational networks to extend learning opportunities across the country's borders need to be closely explored. In this regard, efforts have been directed toward the creation of the Binational Migrant Education Program between the U.S. and Mexico (Kindler, n.d.). Currently few states participate, and the information shared is about school-age migrant students. Again, such a system needs to broaden its scope to include information about adult migrants who wish to continue their education in their place of origin. International models of programs for the reintegration of migrants into their native countries exist (i.e., the Philippines' Alternative Investments for Community Development and Reintegration, MSAI-CDR) and should be explored for implementation in the U.S. (Villalba, 2007).

The many needs of migrant education demand creative and comprehensive intervention strategies that can break the cycle of not reaching this mobile population. The recommendations posed above demand a unified, cohesive, and comprehensive approach to migrant education. For this purpose, a modern, more flexible, and technologically resourceful infrastructure is required to sustain long-term and long-distance cooperative initiatives, information gathering, and program implementation. The burden to support such an integrated approach needs a mentality of "collective responsibility" (Branz-Sprall & Wright, 2004), from corporations, and local, state, and federal entities so that in this resourceful and technologically advanced nation, adult migrants do not go without appropriate education.

Design of Educational Supports that Cater to a Mobile Life Style

As the previous discussion illustrates, migrant families are among the neediest and most difficult to identify and recruit for educational services. The itinerant nature of migrant labor makes these families very difficult to reach. Durón (2004) clarifies that the hardest migrants to identify and recruit are usually active laborers who are constantly on the move, who live in campsites far away from towns and schools, those who are alone without other relatives, older youth, those who are out of school, and those who are undocumented. Some current trends in addressing these unique conditions are (1) increased communication and interstate and intrastate resource sharing, (2) flexibility in applying and reporting, (3) streamlined processes to target students most at risk of not achieving content and performance standards, and (4) increased technical assistance and training for educators.

Recruitment efforts should be made where the migrant families live and work, and in the language that they speak. In this vein, some grassroots strategies to make the recruitment approach more personable and accessible include

- Establishing the trust of the family through reliable and helpful assistance

- Asking about older youth in the family and having information about services ready
- Leaving packets of information about ESL and GED classes with families
- Recruiting in groups so families and out-of-school youth do not feel singled out
- Seeking information from community sources to determine places frequented by migrant families (i.e., service agencies, faith-based institutions, businesses)
- Seeking information at employment sites (i.e., from crew leaders, growers, and shift managers) (Durón, 2004)

New efforts for retention and drop-out prevention mechanisms targeting the specific realities of migrant learners should be developed. One alternative program format suggested by Milton and Watson (1997) is worth mentioning. Implementing work experience and work-study programs to help migrants develop new and marketable job skills and earn a salary might ameliorate the dropout rate of migrant laborers while providing financial support for families.

The living conditions of migrants and their families need to be upgraded to improve their quality of life and provide adequate physical spaces where they can successfully study and use technology. Agricultural corporations need to be held accountable for improving the housing of migrant laborers (i.e., assuring the availability of running water and that adequate ventilation and lighting are available). State and federal monies could be used for connecting the campsites to the outside world through technology. In sum, when trying to incorporate technology into the education of migrants, both their oppressive lifestyle and lack of resources need to be considered.

Creation of Relevant Curriculum

The literature discussed earlier suggests that most programs today follow a traditional format of educational delivery and curriculum, expecting migrant families to accommodate to them. However, alternative designs have been implemented across the nation, ranging from residential instruction to video and correspondence courses to computer-based programs of study. Some of the programs targeting adult migrant learners are described below.

Two categories of programs offer some form of distant education to itinerant students. Milton and Watson (1997) identify the PASS program (Portable Assisted Study Sequence) as one of the remaining correspondence types of programs still available in some states. It allows students to complete partial credits by providing text-based study modules (workbooks and reading assignments) to be completed by the student, and assessed by migrant student counselors. One issue discussed by these authors is that often times it is difficult to find qualified professionals to proctor the tests in a timely manner.

In the late 1990s, some migrant education programs received federal funds to develop projects that integrate technology as a long-distance education alternative to traditional schools for migrant learners. Available information suggests that most of the projects were for migrant children and youth (i.e., Texas' Project *SMART*—Summer Migrants Access Resources through Technology; and Florida's Project *MECHA*—Migrant Education Consortium for Higher Achievement) (ED.gov, 2005; also see Llanos, 1999; Meyertholen, Castro, & Salinas, 2004). Yet some might offer GED materials, ESL courses, and ABE resources for migrant adults by accessing NovaNET online resources (Shields, 2002).

Although few studies have explored how electronic delivery of programs serves migrant learners, Milton and Watson (1997) articulate the potential benefits of distance education for this mobile population. They argue that through distance learning programs the challenges of delivering educational programs to this group because of their high rate of mobility are addressed. Distance learning programs that move with the students and allow them to access their coursework from anywhere they live could provide the greatest potential for academic success. According to them, such a program would integrate a variety of media, including print, radio, television, telephone, and the Internet.

While Milton and Watson's vision is provocative and worthy of exploration, as mentioned earlier, it is imperative to face the obstacles that exist when trying to apply education through technology to the migrant lifestyle. Moreover, attention should be directed to help adult migrants transition to technology. Given the different backgrounds and low educational levels of adult laborers, adult education must provide some educational interventions to ease their embrace of living in a technological sophisticated world (Kinzel, 2008).

There is no doubt that adult education must teach the migrant to read, write and speak the host country language in which they reside. Yet, the content as well as the methods used to achieve this instruction need to be revisited. Some argue for the integration of migrant families funds of knowledge (González, Moll, & Amanti, 2005) related to various content areas. First, understanding the literacies adult learners bring to the classroom would make literacy learning germane to their everyday lives and therefore more compelling and motivating (Au & Raphael, 2000). To reach this deeper understanding, Guerra (1998) argues that research on the language and literacy of marginalized groups must look at practices where migrants interact with one another as well as contexts where they commune with the majority group. Ward and Franquiz (2004) suggest that

> literacy needs of such families will be served best through strategies that help families achieve specific literacy skill that are additive and can serve as foundation blocks for the attainment of other skills; are considered important by families and can reasonably be achieved within limited time constraints; are important in and of themselves, and when achieved, will enhance the family's situation, and are sustainable, and once developed, are not likely to need redevelopment at a later time. (p. 107)

Second, incorporating the unique strategies and skills developed from the migrant way of life into the educational process is critical. The job of migrant workers provides a harsh life for families that requires moral strength and cognitive power. Cardenás (2004) clarifies that this type of strength and power is ignored by traditional schools or eludes their realm of effective instruction and relevant curricular offerings.

Jiménez and Barrera (1999) advocate for a meaningful educational curriculum that addresses issues relevant to migrant reality, such as:

- Brokering: translation and explanations of both oral and literate forms of language. Both require great language skill, but are not recognized in formal education; its use is absent from curricular materials and teacher education programs.
- Transnational character of literacy: preparing students for oral and literacy demands of moving back and forth across countries (i.e., Mexico and the U.S.)
- Interrelation between oracy and literacy: the way migrants understand language and communication
- Migrants' knowledge capital: using the linguistic, cultural, social, and education resources migrants bring
- Valuing multiple literacies: acknowledging ways in which literacy is enacted and lived by members of the Latina/o communities.

Third, the education of teachers and administrators is another dimension that requires creative and sensible changes. Teachers who work with adult learners need to develop a new and improved set of skills to work with a diverse (and transient) student population including teaching ESL and developing a second language across content areas. Administrators should be equipped to design fair practices for the distribution of resources among states and local schools, districts, and faith-based and community centers to promote educational equity (Branz-Sprall & Wright, 2004).

Nieto's (2000) vision of teacher education for the 21st century offers some vital approaches for teacher preparation in adult education. The education of teachers should offer specializations in multicultural and multilingual (bilingual and ESL) education or a combination of these to better confront the current demands of working with a highly diverse and transient student population. Teacher education should stress the development of strategies for creating just learning environments that validate learners' voices, that critically examine oppressive policies and curricular practices, and that uphold a transformative vision of education.

Restructure of Programs to Make Migrants Visible

The previous discussion suggested that although federal and state programs target adult learners as well as migrant education, adult migrant learners are often left outside the circle of services. It is imperative that concerted efforts are made to design programs that specifically serve adult migrants in both the Office of Migrant Education and the Office of Vocational and Adult Education. The review of the literature suggests that most of the programs in place favor migrant children and youth or adult learners in the general society. This double invisibility makes it even harder for adult migrant laborers to be educated and aspire to advance their social and economical mobility.

Gathering more precise information on the programs in place and who is (and is not) being served should be a priority for these agencies. OME and OVAE should coordinate efforts so that there is no duplication of services and they can efficiently support one another in addressing the unique educational needs of the adult mobile population.

Intensification of Investigative Efforts

Although a few educational programs exist for adult migrant learners, very little is known about their short- and long-term effectiveness. Future efforts should explore the success of systematic implementation of recruitment and retention initiatives throughout programs in and across states. It is important to document what happens when hard-to-identify adult migrants are reached. Information needs to be collected about the types of educational services offered to them and if and how they thrive in assisting adult migrants learn English and pursue education.

It is encouraging that some innovative educational programs are available to address the unique learning needs imposed by the nomadic lifestyle of adult migrant laborers. Currently, more is needed to establish and disseminate knowledge about their effectiveness, the factors that contribute to their successful execution, and what is needed to multiply their implementation in ways that are relevant to the different settings migrants work and live. The availability and implementation of this knowledge will assure that effective ways of educating adult migrants on the move become the rule and not the exception.

REFERENCES

Anti-Defamation League. (2006). *Extremists declare 'Open Season' on immigrants: Hispanics target of incitement and violence.* Retrieved July 9, 2009 from http://www.adl.org.

Au, K. H., & Raphael, T. E. (2000). Equity and literacy in the next millennium. *Reading Research Quarterly, 35*(1), 170–189.

Baca, L. (2004). Foreword. In C. Salinas & M.E. Fránquiz (Eds.), *Scholars in the field: The challenges of migrant education* (pp. 9–10). Charleston, WV: ERIC CLearinghouse on Rural Education and Small Schools.

Branz-Spall, A., & Wright, A. (2004). A history of advocacy for migrant children and their families: More than 30 years in the fields. In C. Salinas & M. E. Fránquiz (Eds.), *Scholars in the field: The challenges of migrant education* (pp. 3–11). Charleston, WV: ERIC Clearinghouse on Rural Education and Small Schools.

California Department of Education. (n.d.). *Adult Education—Specialized programs.* Retrieved July 18, 2009 from http://www.cde.ca.gov/sp/ae.

Cardenás, B. (2004). Breaking through in migrant education. In C. Salinas & M. E. Fránquiz (Eds.), *Scholars in the field: The challenges of migrant education* (pp. 241–250). Charleston, WV: ERIC Clearinghouse on Rural Education and Small Schools.

Durón, S. (2004). Identification and recruitment: Trends and issues. In C. Salinas & M. E. Fránquiz (Eds.), *Scholars in the field: The challenges of migrant education* (pp. 31–44). Charleston, WV: ERIC Clearinghouse on Rural Education and Small Schools.

ED.gov. (2005). *Technology grants for coordinating teaching and learning in the migrant community.* Retrieved June 6, 2009, from http://www.ed.gov/print/programs/migranttechgrants/awards.html

Educational Media Collection. (2007). *EMC Abstract: Harvest of Shame.* University of Washington. Retrieved June 1, 2009 from http://www.CSS.Washington.edu/emc/title/7396?abstracts

Fránquiz, M. E., & Loya Hernández, C. (2004). Casa de la Esperanza: A case study of service coordination at work in Colorado. In C. Salinas & M. E. Fránquiz (Eds.), *Scholars in the field: The challenges of migrant education* (pp. 77–89). Charleston, WV: ERIC Clearinghouse on Rural Education and Small Schools.

Gonzáles, D. (1996). *Cesar Chavez: Leader for migrant farm workers.* Springfield, NJ: Enslow Publishers, Inc.

González, N., Moll, L. C., & Amanti, C. (Eds.). (2005). *Funds of knowledge: Theorizing practices in households, communities, and classrooms.* Mahwah, NJ: Erlbaum.

Green, P. E. (2003). The undocumented: Children of migrant workers in America. *Bilingual Research Journal, 27*(1), 51–71.

Guerra, J. C. (1998). *Close to home: Oral and literate practices in a transnational Mexicano community.* New York, NY: Teachers College Press.

Hanley, T., Wrigley, P., & Ulewicz, M. (2007). *Final report: Pennsylvania comprehensive needs assessment.* Harrisburg: Migrant Education Program, Pennsylvania Department of Education.

Huddle, D. (2000). *Fiscal impacts of undocumented aliens.* Washington, DC: Urban Institute Press.

Jiménez, R. T., Barrera, R. B. (1999). Review of Close to home: Oral and literate practices in a transnational Mexicano community, by Juan Guerra. *Journal of Literacy Research, 31*(4), 483–490.

Kindler, A. (n.d.). *Education of migrants: Migrant families, school programs for migrant students.* Retrieved May 5, 2009, from http://education.stateuniversity.com/pages/2231/Migrants-Education.html

Kinzel, T. (2008). *Integrating technology with traditional classroom pedagogy to increase level gains of English as a second language adult students.* Unpublished master's thesis, Heritage College, Gatineau, Quebec, Canada.

Kloosterman, V. I., Skiffington, S., Sanchez, Y., & Kiron, E. (2003). *Migrant and seasonal Head Start and child care partnerships: A report from the field.* Newton, MA: Education Development Center, Inc.

Kozoll, R. H., Osborne, M. D., & Earnest García, G. (2003). Migrant worker children: Conceptions of homelessness and implications for education. *Qualitative Studies in Education, 16*(4), 567–585.

Krashen, S. (1985). *The input hypothesis: Issues and implications.* London: Longman.

Llanos, M. (1999). Migrant teens get online schooling. Posted on ZDNet News. Retrieved June 6, 2009, from http://news.sdnet.com/2100-9595_22-102109.html?legacy=zdnn+

Meyertholen, P., Castro, S. V., & Salinas, C. (2004). Project SMART: Using technology to provide educational continuity for migrant children. In C. Salinas & M. E. Fránquiz (Eds.), *Scholars in the field: The challenges of migrant education* (pp. 181–191). Charleston, WV: ERIC Clearinghouse on Rural Education and Small Schools.

Migrant and Seasonal Head Start Quality Improvement Centers. (2003). Operations Profile. Retrieved July 1, 2009 from www.mhsqic.org/

Milton, K., & Watson, J. E. (1997). Distance education for Mexican-American migrant farmworkers. Retrieved June 5, 2009, from http://seamonkey.ed.asu.edu/~mcisaac/emc598/Spring97/6/watson6.htm

Minarik, P., Flom, E., & Williams, J. (2007). *Migrant students: Resources for migrant children similar to other students but achievement still lags.* Florida State Advisory Committee to the U.S. Commission on Civil Rights. Retrieved September 20, 2009, from http://www.law.umaryland.edu/marshall/usccr/documents/122707_Flmigrant.pdf

National Center for Farmworker Health. (2001). *About America's farmworkers.* Retrieved June 6, 2009 from http://www. ncth.org

Nevárez-La Torre, A. (2010). *The power of learning through inquiry: Teacher research as a professional development tool in multilingual schools.* Charlotte, NC: Information Age Publishing.

Nieto, S. (2000). Placing equity front and center: Some thoughts on transforming teacher education for a new century. *Journal of Teacher Education, 51*(3), 180–187.

Ortiz, F. I. (1995). *Mexican American women: Schooling, work, and family.* (ERIC Document Reproduction Service No. ED388490. Retrieved June 5, 2009, from http://aelliot.ael.org/~eric/digests/edorc959.html

OSPI (Office of the Superintendent of Public Instruction in the State of Washington). (n.d.). *Migrant and bilingual education: Historical perspective.* Retrieved June 5, 2009, from http://www.k12.wa.us/MigrantBilingual/history.aspx

Pappamihiel, E. (2004). The legislation of migrancy: Migrant education in our courts and government. In C. Salinas & M. E. Fránquiz (Eds.), *Scholars in the field: The challenges of migrant education* (pp. 13–27). Charleston, WV: ERIC Clearinghouse on Rural Education and Small Schools.

Prewitt-Diaz, J. O. (1994). *The psychology of Puerto Rican migration.* Lancaster, PA: Author.

Rothenberg, D. (1998). *With these hands: The hidden world of migrant farmworkers today.* Berkeley: University of California Press.

Runsten, D., & Kearney, M. (1994). *A survey of Oaxacan village networks in California agriculture.* Davis, CA: California Institute for Rural Studies.

Salinas, C., & Fránquiz, M. E. (2004). Making migrant children and migrant education visible. In C. Salinas & M. E. Fránquiz (Eds.), *Scholars in the field: The challenges of migrant education* (pp. 11–18). Charleston, WV: ERIC Clearinghouse on Rural Education and Small Schools.

Salinas, C., & Reyes, R. (2004). Graduation enhancement and postsecondary opportunities for migrant students: Issues and approaches. In C. Salinas & M. E. Franquiz (Eds.). *Scholars in the field: The challenges of migrant education* (pp. 119–134). Charleston, WV: ERIC Clearinghouse on Rural Education and Small Schools.

Shields, C. J. (2002). *Harvest time.* Retrieved June 6, 2009, from http://www.districtadministration.com/viewarticlepf.aspx?articleid=813

Shotland, J. (1989). *Full fields, empty cupboard: The nutritional status of migrant farmworkers in America.* Washington, DC: Public Voices for Food and Health Policy.

Smith, P., & Martínez-León, N. (2003). Transnationalism and language-in-education planning in Mexico. *Applied Language Learning, 13*(1), 57–60.

Solís, J. J. (2004). Scholastic demands on intrastate and interstate migrant secondary students. In C. Salinas & M. E. Fránquiz (Eds.), *Scholars in the field: The challenges of migrant education* (pp. 113–117). Charleston, WV: ERIC Clearinghouse on Rural Education and Small Schools.

Swain, M. (1993). The output hypothesis: Just speaking and writing aren't enough. *Canadian Modern Language Review, 50,* 158–164.

Thompson, C. D. (2002). Introduction. In C. D. Thompson, Jr. & M. F. Wiggins (Eds.), *The human cost of food: Farmworkers' lives, labor, and advocacy.* Austin, TX: University of Texas Press.

U.S. Department of Agriculture. (2002). *Statistical bulletin. Statistical highlights 2001 and 2002.* Washington, DC: Author.

U.S. Department of Education. (1994). Improving America's schools act, 103–382 statute, Title I, Part C, (Migrant Education) Program purpose, Section 1301–(4). Washington, DC: Author.

Velázquez, L. C. (1996). Voices from the fields: Community-based migrant education. In P. A. Sissel (Ed.), *A community-based approach to literacy programs: Taking learners' lives into account* (pp. 27–35). New Directions for Adult and Continuing Education, No. 70. San Francisco, CA: Jossey-Bass Publishers.

Villalba, M. A. C. (2007). *Migration and integration from an international perspective—Challenges and opportunities.* German Adult Education Association, DVV International, vol. 70. Retrieved July 11, 2009 from http://www.iiz-dvv.de

Vocke, K. S. (2007). *Where do I go from here? Meeting the unique needs of Migrant students.* Portsmouth, NH: Heineman.

Ward, P. A., & Fránquiz, M. E. (2004). An integrated approach: Even Start family literacy model for migrant families. In C. Salinas & M. E. Fránquiz (Eds.), *Scholars in the field: The challenges of migrant education* (pp. 93–109). Charleston, WV: ERIC Clearinghouse on Rural Education and Small Schools.

CHAPTER 10

CONSUMPTION, GENDERED STEREOTYPES, AND THE STRUGGLE FOR RESPECT

Controlling Images of Poor Women as Consumers in Popular, Political, and Adult Education Courses

Jennifer A. Sandlin
Arizona State University

In this chapter, I focus on how shopping and consumption have been constructed as "feminine" domains and explore how historically negative perceptions of women as consumers are still targeting and affecting women, particularly poor women. Drawing from academic literature, as well as from my own examinations of popular accounts of poor women—and especially poor women who are African American, who seem to be a particularly harshly targeted group in popular culture—and also women on welfare as

Learning for Economic Self-Sufficiency, pages 155–174

consumers, I use what I am calling "critical description" to examine the racism, classism, and sexism in these discourses. I argue that these dominant discourses of poor women as consumers operate as master narratives (Mishler, 1995), or what Solórzano and Yosso (2002) call "majoritarian stories" (p. 29), creating "controlling images" (Collins, 2000) that perpetuate a "politics of disgust" (Hancock, 2004) that demeans and oppresses poor women, and in particular poor African American women and women on welfare. These master narratives express "the values of dominant social and political groups. Their unexamined taken-for-granted assumptions about how the world is and ought to be conceal patterns of domination and submission. Like all narratives, these are selective representations, excluding experiences and views of some sectors of society while including and privileging others" (Mishler, 1995, p. 114).

Andrews (2002) argues that the power of such dominant discourses "derives from their internalization. Wittingly or unwittingly, we become the stories we know, and the master narrative is reproduced" (p. 1). Narratives embody certain ideologies and ways of acting in the world, shape how groups in society are perceived, and influence social policy, which has both ideological and material consequences (Gring-Pemble, 2003; Sandlin & Clark, 2009). These dominant discourses "create a particular kind of social world, with specified heroes and villains, deserving and undeserving people, and a set of public policies that are rationalized by the construction of social problems for which they become solutions" (Bennett & Edelman, 1985, p. 159). As I show in this chapter, dominant discourses of poor women as consumers overwhelmingly cast them in the role of "villains," to put it mildly. Through critical description, I, in the spirit of critical race methodology, hope to reveal and challenge the deficit, racist, classist, and sexist perspectives in these majoritarian stories, in order to expose White, male, and middle-class privilege (Solórzano & Yosso, 2002).

After examining dominant discourses about poor women as consumers in public culture, I turn to a discussion of how these stereotypes have infiltrated adult basic education programs and have infused "life skills" education and consumer education within these programs with deficit perspectives that blame poor, low-literate women for their economic situations. Researchers have argued that master narratives influence adult literacy classroom practices, as they influence how we (consciously *and* unconsciously) perceive adult learners, which has a direct impact on how we treat them and what we expect from them in the classroom (Gowen, 1992; Sandlin & Clark, 2009; Sparks, 1999; St.Clair, 2004). This research has focused on how master narratives provide particular frameworks on the world and templates of what it means to be a good "student," "worker," "parent," "family member," and "citizen." In this chapter, I focus specifically on how these discourses construct what it means to be a good "consumer." I argue that the negative discourses circulating within adult education programs about poor women as consumers create yet another barrier poor women must fight against in their struggle for economic self-sufficiency.

I offer this examination to illuminate how these perspectives are upheld in adult literacy education, to help adult educators critically reflect on their role in perpetuating these perspectives, and to move them to resist these dominant narratives. I end with a call for adult education programs to challenge these negative discourses of poor women as consumers through counter-storying (Solórzano & Yosso, 2002) and re-storying (Barone, 2000), and to enact more critical consumer education in adult literacy programs.

CONSUMPTION AS A "FEMALE REALM"

The "consumer revolution" began in the eighteenth century, first in England and later in the United States, and was marked by increased numbers of more affordable, available, and desirable consumer goods (Lubar, 1998). Indeed, while consumer culture exploded in the 1900s, even by the 1830s contemporary American commentators such as Ann Smart Martin were stating that America had become a country "obsessed with economic gain, consumerism, and materialism" (Lubar, 1998, p. 9). From the beginning of this revolution, shopping and consumption have been historically constructed as "female" domains, and consumer culture has been generally associated with feminization (Slater, 1997; see also Bocock, 1993; Bowlby, 1987, 2001; Scanlon, 2000). Marketers and popular and political discourses have created and perpetuated gendered stereotypes, positioning women as shoppers and men as producers; in so doing, production has come to be "masculinised and valorized" while consumption has been "feminised" (Belk, 1995, p. 61). Bocock (1993) further explains the consequences of this gender division: "Production was active, led to men earning money and provided them with some form of power exercised through newly created trade unions.... .Consumption was more passive, involved spending money, and did not lead to any publicly recognizable forms of power" (p. 95).

At times this feminization of consumption has crafted women in a positive light, as when it positions women as "purchaser consumers" (Cohen, 2003) who enact their duties to family and country through shopping. At other times this feminization has resulted in women being "denigrated" (Belk, 1995, p. 61) and portrayed as mentally ill, dupes of advertising, or reckless.

The association of consumption with the feminine is grounded in capitalism's ideology of the sexual division of labor, which assumes that "society is divided into two separate spheres of home and outside work and that these are women's and men's spheres, respectively" (Fraser, 1989, p. 149; see also

Slater, 1997, pp. 56–57). This sexual division of labor divides public (male) and private (female), production (male) and reproduction (female), and production (male) and consumption (female). Slater (1997) explains how women were increasingly associated with domestic reproduction, and how this association became linked to (domestic) consumption:

> Woman's responsibility for domestic reproduction is increasingly defined, through advertising, home economics and other educational discourses, state policy and media portrayals, as a responsibility to manage consumption. As domestic reproduction increasingly comes to mean building a home by buying commodities, women are increasingly defined as 'experts in consumption'. The man brings home the pay packet that the woman spends (either in good domestic management or, in a popular image, impulsively and irrationally). (pp. 56–57)

Women thus became associated with the home and were seen to be in charge of the domestic sphere, which included caretaking, raising children, and attending to their husbands and families. Shopping and consumption became integral parts of the domestic realm—that is, "buying and arranging domestic objects was women's work" (Lubar, 1998, p. 9).

In the midst of these gendered relations of production and consumption, beginning in the mid-nineteenth century in the United States and slightly later in Britain and Germany, women began being urged by a burgeoning advertising industry to "go out and buy" (Bocock, 1993, p. 95); during this same period department stores, such as the Paris Bon Marché, opened in Europe and in North America. By the 1880s, shopping in department stores—which were decidedly gendered spaces that appealed specifically to women, and were associated with women—had become a popular activity outside of the home "for middle-class women in the main cities of western capitalism" (Bocock, 1993, p. 95). The Paris Bon Marché, for instance, gave away instructions specifically to women, explaining how to reach the store by public transportation (Bocock, 1993). Bowlby (1987) explains how the act of women venturing outside the home by themselves marked a break with the past, and argues that department stores offered women a way to escape the boundary of the home, as department stores were "the first public places—other than churches or cathedrals—which were considered respectable for her to visit without a male companion. But this also signaled, at another level, a stepping out from domestic bounds" (p. 189). Popular discourse at the time crafted women as incompetent and unknowledgeable when dealing with the public sphere, so department stores were "safe" public spaces designed specifically for women, to bring "order to the potential chaos of women customers"—department stores "opened 'the public' safely to women without threatening men's public power" (Glennie, 1995, p. 186).

FEMALE SHOPPERS: DOMESTIC MANAGERS OR IMPULSIVE AND IRRATIONAL?

While women were increasingly associated with shopping, two main stereotypes emerged that positioned women as *particular types* of shoppers. The more "benign" association of consumption with the feminine draws upon notions of caretaking, as women have been crafted as "purchaser consumers" (Cohen, 2003), acting out their duties to family and country through shopping—what Slater (1997) refers to above as "good domestic management." Cohen (2003), for instance, states that during World War II, male citizens "were defined in productivist ways, 'serving their country' by laboring in the military or, if not possible, in defense industries" (p. 75). Women, on the other hand, "were defined in consumerist ways, as keepers of the homefront fires through their own disciplined patriotic market behavior" (p. 75). While this perspective appears more "benign" than the one I will discuss below, even this "benign" perspective has negatively affected both women and shopping, as it positions women as emotional rather than rational (Jubas, 2008).

There has also been a competing, blatantly negative discourse that positions women as irrational, "flighty" (Bowlby, 2001, p. 119), dupes, excessive shoppers, and even mentally ill. By the mid-nineteenth century, the culture of consumption had become widespread and engrained as part of everyday life in many Western countries; consumption's association with women was also well established by this point. During this time period, popular discourse began expressing misogynistic and moralistic views about women as out of control, mentally ill, and suffering from shopping "diseases." Slater (1997) explains that these fears arose because women, through moving into the public spaces of department stores, were no longer under the patriarchal gaze of the home—shopping spaces were unregulated, places that stirred up fantasy, desire, and "insatiable need" (p. 76). Slater (1997) explains how this fear manifested itself as moral panic about hysterical female shoppers overcome with desire:

> Moral panics arose about women, addicted to shopping, abandoning husbands and children. This pathology of desire was medicalized from mid-century onwards through the notion of 'kleptomania', which was unsurprisingly classified as a form of hysteria—a disease of the womb—and therefore as a sexual disorder. Just as in Hogarth's time, it is feared that the freedom of the money economy leads directly to the madness of lust through the loss of moral regulation. (p. 76)

A similar misogynistic tone emerges in this commentary on female shoppers from the *Australian Worker* in 1906:

> Women sweating, struggling, swarming round the damaged gloves; snarling, gesticulating over the eighteen-penny muslins. Scratch a bargain-hunter and you get a Tartar every time.... Their fat, bulging, gloating eyes are twinkling with greed. Their hands lovingly fondle the prizes they are losing their self-respect to win. Never once do they pause to realize that someone must go short that their insatiable greed may be satisfied. (Reekie, 1993, as cited in Jackson & Thrift, 1995, p. 219)

Jackson and Thrift (1995) comment on how this passage betrays the writer's "disgust," "horror," and "moral indignation" about women, and how this commentator links women's perceived promiscuity for sex with their lust for luxury items (p. 219).

In the 1920s, advertisers focused much of their work on the female audience, believing them to be the primary shoppers. Advertisers assumed women were overly emotional, and described them in terms of "capriciousness, irrationality, passivity, and conformism" (Marchand, 1986, p. 69). Marchand (1986) explains that advertisers "became increasingly committed to a view of 'consumer citizens' as an emotional, feminized mass, characterized by mental lethargy, bad taste, and ignorance" (p. 65). These negative stereotypes of women have remained throughout history, as Slater (1997) argues that the popular conception of "consumer as dupe" was and is typically associated with women. Women have been described in popular culture since the beginning of the 1900s as "whimsical and inconstant, flighty, narcissistic; they can be seduced, or their resistance overcome, by stimuli or persuasion in order to achieve market penetration" (Slater, 1997, p. 57). This weak, ill, out of control female figure stands in sharp contrast to the rational, autonomous, calculating "economic man" that emerged in the early 1900s in neoclassical economics and that remains the masculine foil to the flighty female consumer (Sassatelli, 2007).

Some argue that this negative stereotype of women as impulsive, out of control shoppers has largely disappeared from academic discourse. Bowlby (2001), for instance, argues that through the 1960s and 1970s, consumerism was associated with women, who were seen as "the unresisting victims of manipulative advertising and vulgar, alluring displays," who wasted too much time shopping. She goes on to argue that since that time, the consumer has "lost her sex"—meaning that the consumer is now viewed as gender neutral—and has come to be seen as "no longer a fool, but the model of modern individuality... who... demands and gets the deal" (Bowlby, 2001, p. 6). While, in academic discourse, perceptions of consumers might have shifted in a more positive, gender-neutral direction, I posit that negative stereotypes of female shoppers as ill, overly materialistic, and flighty are still widely propagated in public discourse and popular culture. For instance, this image is alive and well in Sophie Kinsella's (2001) wildly popular *Confessions of a Shopaholic* book series, which was recently made into a Hollywood movie that has earned over one hundred million dollars at box offices worldwide (Box Office Mojo, 2009). As I highlight in the next section, I argue that these negative stereotypes are also present in public and political discourses of poor women, poor African American women, and women on welfare, and also appear in educational programs for adults.

MATERIALISTIC, IRRESPONSIBLE, UNCONTROLLABLE?: CONTROLLING IMAGES OF POOR WOMEN

The shopaholic in Sophie Kinsella's novels, Becky Bloomwood, is a white, college-educated, upper middle class woman who has high cultural capital but who lacks sufficient monetary capital to maintain her extravagant lifestyle. Becky "has a fabulous flat in London's trendiest neighborhood, a troupe of glamorous socialite friends, and a closet brimming with the season's must-haves. The only trouble is that she can't actually afford it" (Random House, 2008, para 2). While there is no doubt that this book presents a negative stereotype of women as materialistic and out of control shoppers, the lead character is also somewhat sympathetic, as, in the end, "even she recognizes that shopping and acquisition are insufficient" (Jubas, 2007, p. 327) for happiness. By the end of the book, Becky gets the man of her dreams, solves her debt problems, and comes to be seen by the other characters as a "person of intelligence and integrity—as well as feminine beauty and style" (Jubas, p. 327).

Poor female consumers and, in particular, poor African American female consumers, rarely get even a marginally sympathetic treatment in popular, political, and even educational discourses. Collins (2000) presents the concept of "controlling images"—which are stereotypical images of Black women that serve to justify racist, sexist, and classist oppression. I believe this concept of "controlling images" is helpful in understanding how poor women, and particularly poor African American women as well as women on welfare, are still plagued by incredibly negative perceptions of their consumption behaviors. Collins (2000) explains that "because the authority to define societal values is a major instrument of power, elite groups, in exercising power, manipulate ideas about Black womanhood," through perpetuating negative stereotypical images; these images "are designed to make racism, sexism, poverty, and other forms of social injustice appear to be natural, normal, and inevitable parts of everyday life" (p. 69).

Closely related to this notion of "controlling images" is Hancock's (2004) concept of the "politics of disgust"—which is an "emotion-laden response to long-standing beliefs about single, poor African American mothers" (p. 9) that has spread to other poor women and recipients of welfare programs. It consists of a "strong repugnance, aversion, or repulsion excited by that which is loathsome or offensive" (Hancock, 2004, p. 9). Controlling images help create and perpetuate this politics of disgust, which negatively affect the objects of such scorn by reinforcing "silence and invisibility among those brought into the public sphere as part of another citizen's ideological arguments" (Hancock, 2004, p. 15). In this section, I outline some of the "controlling images" related to poor women, poor African American women, and women on welfare as shoppers or consumers that circulate through popular and political discourses.

Some of the "controlling images" of poor African American women that Collins (2000) identifies are the "welfare queen," the "Jezebel," and the "gold-digging hoochie." Negative stereotypes about Black women are not new, however—they go back as far as slavery. After the American abolition, Victorian era social welfare policies and educational programs championed by elite and middle-class women—both White and Black—targeted poor Black (as well as Eastern and Southern European immigrant) women, and focused on instilling in them middle-class values such as "thrift" and "discipline," with the accompanying assumption that poor women lacked such values. Hancock (2004) also argues that the specific "welfare queen" stereotype has remained persistent for the past 70 years, citing President Franklin D. Roosevelt's New Deal policies from the 1930s that sought to regulate the behavior of poor Black women. This stereotype became widely and wildly popular—and permanently entrenched in the American collective psyche—in the 1980s with Ronald Reagan's (unfounded) proclamations about "welfare queens" who "milked the system." This negative, unfair, and degrading stereotype is most often discussed in terms of how it portrays poor African American women as sexually promiscuous and as "using the welfare system." Less often discussed is how this stereotype (and other similar controlling images) perpetuates negative assumptions about poor women's shopping or consumption behavior, which is the focus of this chapter. While these negative images are typically stereotyped as "Black," similar negative stereotypes—specifically focusing on the lack of personal responsibility and materialistic tendencies—are also applied to poor women of any race or ethnicity.

In terms of their consumption, these negative stereotypes portray poor, and poor African American women in particular, as materialistic, gluttonous, lacking self-control, unable to make responsible choices and live on a budget, and ultimately responsible for their own poverty because of poor consumption choices and irresponsible consumer behavior. One of the most prevalent negative stereotypes concerning the consumption behavior of poor women is that they are materialistic. According to this discourse, poor women, and specifically women on welfare, live lavishly, waste money on unnecessary luxury items, and have insatiable appetites for expensive commodities. Several of the controlling images that Collins (2000) discusses focus on this supposed materialism. For instance, Collins (2000) presents the "gold-digging hoochies," who are portrayed in popular discourse as craving material goods and, to satisfy these cravings, as trying to establish "a long-term relationship with a man with money. These gold-digging hoochies often aim to snare a highly paid athlete and can do so by becoming pregnant" (p. 82). Collins also discusses the "Jezebel" or "whore," who is portrayed as a "sly, conniving, manipulative, materialistic, sexually aggressive African-American woman whose appetites are subject to very little self-control" (Neubeck & Cazenave, 2001, p. 35). Collins (2000) also shows how the "welfare queen" stereotype is portrayed as a "highly materialistic, domineering, and manless working-class Black woman" (p. 80), who "live[s] lavishly" (Neubeck & Cazenave, 2001, p. 127). Zucchino (1997) explains that the stereotype of a "welfare queen" is that of a "Cadillac-driving, champagne-sipping, penthouse-living" woman on welfare (p. 13)—however, Zucchino, a journalist, sought out but could not find any real life examples of these so-called "welfare queens," thus exposing the myth as false, racist, and oppressive.

These stereotypes of materialism are alive and well in current popular discourses about the consumption behavior of poor women. Christopher J. Priest (2007), a Southern Baptist preacher and internet blogger in Colorado Springs, for instance, attributes social issues such as "crime, addiction, teen pregnancy, [and] violence" to the "materialistic communal dementia" from which he claims poor African Americans are suffering (para 8). Priest states that young African Americans "assess the value or 'hip'-ness of most any given item by its retail price" (para 2). Priest goes on to warn parents that "every time you abandon your nine year-old kid in front of the tube and let him or her ingest this garbage, you are committing them to a career path more likely to lead to Welfare Queen and Lowlife than Doctor and lawyer" (para 6). A recent news article by WWAY, a Wilmington, North Carolina television news channel, highlighted how the number of individuals applying for food stamps has increased recently due to the economic recession (WWAY, 2008). When this article was posted on WWAY's website, many readers left comments that represent the racist, sexist, and classist "majoritarian" (Solórzano & Yosso, 2002) discourse focused on the supposed wastefulness and materialism of women on welfare. One commentator, "cintrek," reveals the disgust with which women on welfare are viewed by White, middle-class society:

> Before handing out food stamps require the recipients to cancel cable/satellite, cell phones, internet service, sell their computer, if they drive a gas guzzler require them to trade it in for a small, fuel efficient car, smoke, drink alcohol—quit, drug test, electronic toys, expensive jewelry, big screen tv—sell. Require them to do everything they can to eliminate the accesses [sic] and when they are living only on the basics then pass out the food stamps. But

> they have to prove it. That goes for every other social service in this nation. I believe that if you can afford to smoke or drink or watch cable tv then you can afford to buy food.

Similar sentiments are expressed by "Dalaimama," who posted a question about "welfare fraud" on the Internet site "answerology.com." She asks, "If someone in your immediate family was committing welfare fraud, would you report them?" She goes on to explain the consumer habits of these family members, portraying them (and, by association, all poor women on welfare) as materialistic and selfish:

> The cash and food stamps are being used to buy liquor and furnish food for the parties the parents are holding and the food stamps are being sold for cash to buy Xbox video games and a big screen television. (The parent's [sic] of the children recently came to me and asked me to purchase their children school clothes because they had spent all the welfare money on frivolous items for themselves). (Dalaimama, 2009)

Another anonymous commentator on a recent post by blogger Kyle Krannebitter (2008) also perpetuates this stereotype that women on welfare are materialistic and wasteful:

> I know a family that are on welfare and they have high speed internet, big plasma screen TVs and fancy cars.

It is not just bloggers who perpetuate these stereotypes; they also abound in more formal, established news outlets. In a critical analysis of the portrayal of African American women in popular culture, Adair (2000) recounts one news story in the *Washington Post* that read, "young black 'welfare pimps' drive their girls to state offices in limos" (p. 1) and another that "exposed" a "group of female welfare recipients who 'clad in leather and shopping network faux pearls,' spent their days taking taxis from one welfare office to the next, collecting welfare checks under fraudulent names" (p. 1).

Closely related to the majoritarian stereotype of poor women, poor African American women, and women on welfare as materialistic are the stereotyped assumptions that these women lack self-control, are gluttonous, are unable to make wise and thrifty consumption decisions, are unable to live on a budget, lack middle class values such as "thrift" and "discipline" (Hancock, 2004, p. 32), and lack any sense of personal responsibility regarding managing (or not managing) their money (Hancock, 2004). These stereotypes abound in popular discourse. For example, in an online blog entry called "Regulate the Welfare Abuse," Kyle Krannebitter (2008) perpetuates this myth of lack of self-control and gluttony, when he states that "Welfare has become a target for gluttonous mothers and others who have no values or willingness to obtain a job" (para 1) and argues that women on welfare are "greedy, lazy Americans that are able to work, but do not choose to" (para 6). Similarly, in the comments section of an online article on the media-focused website G4TV (Padilla, 2008) about the Black Friday, 2008 stampede that killed a Wal-Mart employee in Valley Stream, NY, one reader, echoing racist majoritarian discourses, called the women who shopped at Wal-Mart "stupid dirty fat ghetto dwellers," while another upheld sexist and classist controlling images, as he stated that "these white trash housewives kill people every year in a blind rage for sales." In another sickeningly offensive statement, another reader commented, "it would've been nice if the store workers all had baseball bats and they can swing at the fat welfare queen ghetto gorillas." And commenting on Krannebitter's (2008) blog, a reader calling himself "Sick of Welfare" reveals how deeply steeped he is in racism, classism, and sexist majoritarian discourses that perpetuate a politics of disgust, as he argues that women on welfare engage in gluttonous consumption, not just of material commodities, but also of food. He describes women on welfare in degrading terms that are reminiscent of the 1906 *Australian Worker* newspaper description of women in department stores, cited earlier in this chapter. He states:

> They sit on the couch all day eating snack cakes and potato chips, (which they bought with their food stamps), watching soap operas on their 50" plasma TV (that was paid for by their welfare check) and wonder why their ass has ballooned to 500 pounds.

Again, these stereotypes are not confined to blogs and online rants, but are also embraced by journalists and politicians. Feeding a politics of disgust and perpetuating unfair and unjust stereotypes about poor women's supposed lack of responsibility, journalist Kathleen Sylvester wrote in the *Washington Post* that, "welfare women have refused to sacrifice," and suggests that we need to monitor their behavior and teach them how to "manage household money" (quoted in Adair, 2000, p. 26). And in a *Seattle Times* article, Washington State Congressman Steve Quigly wrote a piece called "Wean Parents from Dependency," in which he argues that we should put poor women in group homes where "we could watch the way they spend their money" and "where they could be watched and where their behavior could be modified with constant supervision" (quoted in Adair, 2000, p. 17).

The conclusion that is often drawn in popular and political discourse, which is closely linked with these negative stereotypes, is that poor women, poor African American women, and women on welfare are ultimately responsible for their own poverty because of their lamentable consumption choices and irresponsible consumer behavior. In Hancock's (2004) content analysis of the mainstream news media and the congressional record, in which she examined how news media and politicians portrayed and discussed welfare, the idea of "personal responsibility for one's predicament" (p. 181)—that is, the notion that "welfare mothers did not deserve government assistance, largely because they were responsible for their own poverty" (p. 55)—arose repeatedly and consistently. This notion, that poor people create their own poverty because they supposedly lack the so-called "middle class values" of thrift and financial responsibility, is deeply engrained in our society, and has become a taken-for-granted public myth that serves the interests of those in power, while "normalizing" the unequal racist, sexist, and classist economic structures that allow some to grow rich while dooming others to permanent poverty.

While academics such as Bowlby (1987, 2001) have announced the end of the "gendered" shopper, and praise the ways in which consumers are viewed as rational and savvy, my analysis of popular and political discourses that make wildly unfounded assumptions about the consumption behaviors of poor women, poor African American women, and women on welfare has revealed a starkly different picture. It is appallingly clear that these women are the recipients of massive amounts of rage and disgust, and are subject to incredibly unfair, demeaning, racist, sexist, and classist perceptions about their supposed consumptive behaviors. This vilification is a far cry from how middle-class shopaholic Becky Bloomwood is portrayed in Kinsella's (2001) *Confessions of a Shopaholic*, and is vastly different from the kinds of academic accounts of consumers referenced by Bowlby (1987, 2001). Researchers, including myself, who have examined how low-income consumers and consumers belonging to other historically oppressed groups make consumer decisions (Edin & Lein, 1997; Hancock, 2004; Sandlin, 2001; Seccombe, 1999) have outlined how these stereotypes are misleading, false, unfair, racist, sexist, degrading, and overwhelmingly *not* grounded in fact. Employed as controlling images (Collins, 2000), they create and reinforce a "politics of disgust" (Hancock, 2004), and ultimately serve to reinforce a hegemonic worldview that blames the poor for their own poverty, ignoring the social structures that create and perpetuate a system that works against those who are not already White and middle class. Despite their lack of grounding in reality, however, these stereotypes continue to flourish in popular, political, and even educational contexts, as I discuss below.

IMAGES OF POOR WOMEN AS CONSUMERS IN ADULT EDUCATION PROGRAMS

It is important to also examine how these majoritarian discourses appear in adult basic education programs because while certainly not all adult learners in these programs are poor or on welfare, adult literacy education and job training are increasingly being viewed as essential to moving people off welfare and out of poverty. Dirkx (1999) argues that adult education is touted as a critical process that can provide poor women and women on welfare with "a chance to become economically self-sufficient as well as to be able to fully participate politically in civil society" (p. 84). Along with academic skills, many adult education programs also offer "life skills" and "consumer education" to women on welfare, with the implicit assumption that through teaching more "responsible" ways of handling money and making consumer decisions, adult education can help bring people out of poverty and help them achieve individual social mobility, an assumption that sees consumer problems as an individual deficit, grounded in individual behaviors. A more critical approach views the problem not primarily as an inability to make smart consumer decisions, but as a problem of resource scarcity in an increasingly unstable economic climate.

Similar stereotypes as those discussed above in public discourses—although somewhat "toned down"—about poor women as consumers are also prevalent in adult education programs. They appear, for instance, in consumer education textbooks that are used in adult literacy programs (Sandlin, 2000, 2001), and also in professional development programs—specifically Ruby Payne's (2005) *Framework for Understanding Poverty*—that adult education teachers and administrators participate in and that are designed to teach educators how to understand the so-called "culture of poverty" that Payne claims affects poor learners. In previous research (Sandlin, 2000), for example, I examined a number of consumer education texts that are used in adult literacy education, and found that these texts focus on learners' deficits, wastefulness, and inability to make good consumer decisions. They present an ideology of victim blaming, where learners are assumed to lack control, crave material goods, and need guidance, lest they spend more than they have, go into debt, and make unwise consumer decisions. The texts make the assumption, much like the stereotypes in popular culture that I discussed above, that the adult learners (many of whom are poor and female, and many of whom are receiving welfare benefits) reading the texts have insatiable consumer appetites. This theme is especially clear in many of the lessons on credit, in which the texts imply that if adult literacy learners obtain a credit card, they are likely to overspend and get in trouble.

A particularly glaring example of how these majoritarian controlling images appear in adult education programs is provided by the phenomenon of Payne's (2005) *Framework for Understanding Poverty*. The book was first published in 1996 and has since sold over one million copies (Schafft & Prins, 2008). Payne and her colleagues at the for-profit, self-publishing and consulting company aha! Process, Inc. (Bohn, 2006) have developed books, workshops, workbooks, and other materials for teachers and administrators—which are wildly popular among K–12 teachers and administrators, adult educators, employment preparation teachers who work with women on welfare, and family literacy educators—focused on how to understand students who are steeped in the so-called "culture of poverty." Payne and her colleagues conduct over 200 seminars each year and have trained over 25,000 teachers and administrators since 1996 (Bohn, 2006). Payne regularly speaks at adult literacy and family literacy conferences. I first encountered her work when I was doing my dissertation work in Georgia in the late 1990s. While collecting my data, the teachers with whom I was working in an employment preparation, life skills, and adult literacy program for women on welfare went to a Ruby Payne workshop and came back raving about how much they had enjoyed it. They talked about all of the information they had gathered about the "hidden rules" of poverty, and shared the insights they had learned about why the poor women in their classes behaved the way they did.

Payne draws upon the "culture of poverty" thesis that was created in 1961 by Oscar Lewis. This perspective argues that people who live in poverty share a particular "culture" (Gorski, 2008a, p. 32) consisting of "rules, values, and knowledge" that are passed down from one generation to the next (Bohn, 2006, para 5) and that are markedly different than middle-class and upper-class cultures. Payne argues that in order for poor people to succeed and move out of poverty, they must be taught the "hidden rules" of the middle-class. However, what Payne does not realize or acknowledge is that the "culture of poverty" thesis has been overwhelmingly, resoundingly rejected and debunked for decades by social scientists. Years of empirical research have shown that in fact "there is no such thing *as a culture of poverty*" (Gorsky, 2008a, p. 33, emphasis in original). That is, the "differences in values and behaviors among poor people are just as great as those between poor and wealthy people. In actuality, the culture of poverty concept is constructed from a collection of smaller stereotypes which, however false, seem to have crept into mainstream thinking as unquestioned fact" (Gorski, 2008a, p. 33).

Other researchers have debunked Payne's so-called "hidden rules" of the poor—specifically as they relate to poor people's supposed inferior cognitive ability, present time orientation, undeveloped work ethic, lack of motivation, lack of interest in education, deficient parenting skills, linguistic deficiencies, and proclivities towards alcohol and drugs—pointing out that Payne's work is based on anecdotal evidence, which means that it is not grounded in empirical research and is not "verifiable, reproducible, valid, or reliable," (Bohn, 2006, para 11). I want to, instead, briefly focus on how Payne describes poor people's consumer behaviors and attitudes towards money. What follows are several statements from the *Framework* that reinforce the deficit perspectives of the dominant discourses I discussed earlier. Describing various attitudes and behaviors that make up the "hidden rules" of poverty, Payne (2005) states:

- "The bottom line in generational poverty is entertainment and relationships" (p. 41).
- In poverty, money is "to be used, spent" (p. 42).
- "One of the biggest difficulties in getting out of poverty is managing money and just the general information base around money. How can you manage something you've never had? Money is seen in poverty as an expression of personality and is used for entertainment and relationships" (p. 44).
- "Often the attitude in generational poverty is that society owes one a living" (p. 47).
- In poverty, individuals lack any sense of order or organization: "Many of the homes/apartments of people in poverty are unkempt and cluttered. Devices for organization (files, planners, etc.) don't exist" (p. 53).
- People in poverty are impulsive and have an inability to self-govern their behavior. Someone in poverty "lives in the moment—does not consider future ramification: Being proactive, setting goals, and planning ahead are not a part of generational poverty. Most of what occurs is reactive and in the moment. Future implications of present actions are seldom considered" (p. 53).
- People living in poverty are "extremely disorganized." They do not possess "planning, scheduling, or prioritizing skills. Not taught in poverty" (p. 80).
- People living in poverty "cheat or steal: indicative of weak support system, work role models/emotional resources" (p. 80).

As Bohn (2006) argues, Payne's *Framework* presents a "superficial and insulting" portrait of individuals living in poverty, one that upholds many of the negative assumptions about poor women as consumers that circulate in public discourse—that they cannot manage money, make unwise consumer decisions focusing on entertainment, are disorganized and impulsive, steal, and cannot prioritize financial decisions. In essence, as in the majoritarian stories I outlined above, in Payne's world, women living in poverty are responsible for their own situations because of their poor consumer values and choices.

COUNTER-STORYING AND RE-STORYING NEW VISIONS OF WOMEN AS CONSUMERS

Contrary to the assumptions of the consumer education texts described above, and those in Ruby Payne's framework, a strong body of research that has explored how poor consumers navigate the economic worlds around them has determined that they possess a great deal of consumer information, can successfully navigate in the consumer world, and make careful decisions about how to spend their limited money (Edin & Lein, 1997; Mogelonsky, 1994; Newton, 1977; Roberts, 1991). For instance, Newton (1977) uses ethnographic data on how the poor make consumer decisions to support her argument that, despite the public rhetoric asserting that the culture of poverty creates consumers with irrational and wasteful consumer behaviors and values, poor people "make the most of what they have" (p. 58). And, Caskey (1994) states strongly that "despite the widespread notion that lower-income households tend to be more shortsighted and wasteful in their spending behavior, this has not been demonstrated in statistical studies" (p. 82). My own research (Sandlin, 2001) with poor women in adult literacy programs also shows that they defy the negative stereotypes that circulate in public culture. The women I interviewed lived within their means, made do with the amount of money they had, responsibly spent money to meet their needs, and were smart shoppers. They also tried their best to save money for the future. Newton (1977) concludes, and I agree, that poor women "are not in need of programs designed to increase their efficiency; what they need are more resources" (p. 50).

These dominant discourses of poor women, poor African American women, and women on welfare as consumers serve the ideological purpose of selecting for us one way of looking at the world, while hiding or distracting us from other possible ways of viewing the world. These stories vilify poor women and their supposed consumer behaviors. Dominant discourses lambaste poor women for not making responsible consumer decisions, thus blaming them for their own poverty; these discourses serve as forces of domination because they legitimate a social system that is systematically dismantling a social safety net. Increasingly, individuals are called upon to be "personally responsible" for their own welfare; current political discourse calls for "self-reliance," which Giroux (2004) argues betrays "an eviscerated and refigured state" that fails to provide "adequate safety nets for its populace, especially those who are young, poor, or racially marginalized" (p. 496). These dominant discourses thus work against the best interests of poor women, poor African American women, and women on welfare.

If adult literacy education wants to truly serve adult learners, adult literacy educators, curriculum developers, program planners, and researchers need to be aware of how adult literacy programs are perpetuating the majoritarian, controlling images about poor women as consumers that are so prevalent in public and political discourse. Quigley (1997) argues that while adult literacy educators have a deep sense of caring about learners, they have often been complicit in the perpetuation of the negative images of adult literacy learners; thus literacy educators need to pay closer attention to how learners are perceived in society and how they help shape that perception. One of the biggest challenges for the field of adult literacy, then, is how to create counter-narratives (Andrews, 2002) or counter-stories (Solórzano & Yosso, 2002) that work in the interest of adult learners. We must re-story (Barone, 2000) the experiences of poor women so that they defy the majoritarian narratives that are so engrained in society. We must create consumer education and life skills lessons in adult literacy programs that embrace critical pedagogies instead of dominant ideologies. Gorski (2008b) argues that helping women move out of poverty and towards economic independence will not happen by embracing the kinds of deficit perspectives and negative stereotypes about poor women as consumers that are so prevalent in popular discourse and in adult educational programs. Instead, Gorski (2008b) posits that we need to engage in serious critique and analysis of "corporate capitalism and corporate welfare, globalization, the corporatization of schools, consumer culture, the ongoing war against the poor, and how all of these systems contribute to perpetuating class structures in the U.S. and around the world" (p. 145). That is, we need to foster a critical pedagogy of consumption in adult education programs. Instead of unquestioningly accepting "common sense" explanations of consumer culture and poverty, we need to explore with learners the social and political contexts of consumerism and focus on how power, gender, race, and class are related to both consumption practices and consumption's pedagogy—the ways we are socialized into the ideology of consumerism through advertising, store layout, and so on. We must encourage learners to explore their own attitudes about consumption and engage in reflecting on how these attitudes are not natural but are, rather, produced and negotiated. We should also explore with learners the global, regional, and local economic and environmental effects of consumption. Finally, we must focus on exposing and critiquing the kinds of myths about poor women as consumers I have discussed above, and encourage learners to write and speak their own consumption stories—to talk back to those dominant and repressive discourses.

REFERENCES

Adair, V. (2000). *From good ma to welfare queen: A genealogy of the poor woman in American literature, photography, and culture.* New York: Garland Publishing, Inc.

Andrews, M. (2002). Introduction: Counter-narratives and the power to oppose. *Narrative Inquiry, 12*(1), 1–6.

Barone, T. F. (2000). *Aesthetics, politics, and educational inquiry: Essays and examples.* New York: Peter Lang.

Belk, R. W. (1995). Studies in the new consumer behaviour. In D. Miller (Ed.), *Acknowledging consumption* (pp. 53–94). New York: Routledge.

Bennett, W. L., & Edelman, M. (1985). Toward a new political narrative. *Journal of Communication, 35*(4), 15–171.

Bocock, R. (1993). *Consumption.* London: Routledge.

Bohn, A. (2006). A framework for understanding Ruby Payne. *Rethinking Schools Online, 21*(2). Retrieved August 12, 2009 from http://www.rethinkingschools.org/archive/21_02/fram212.shtml

Bowlby, R. (1987). Modes of modern shopping: Mallarmé at the Bon Marché. In N. Armstrong & L. Tennenhouse (Eds.), *The ideology of conduct: Essays in literature and the history of sexuality* (pp. 185–205). New York: Routledge.

Bowlby, R. (2001). *Carried away: The invention of modern shopping.* New York: Columbia University Press.

Box Office Mojo (2009). *Confessions of a shopaholic.* Retrieved August 12, 2009 from http://www.boxofficemojo.com/movies/?id=confessionsofashopaholic.htm

Caskey, J. P. (1994). *Fringe banking: Check-cashing outlets, pawnshops, and the poor.* New York: Russell Sage Foundation.

Cohen, L. (2003). *A consumer's republic: The politics of mass consumption in postwar America.* New York: Knopf.

Collins, P. H. (2000). *Black feminist thought* (2nd ed.). New York: Routledge.

Dalaimama. (April 15, 2009). *If someone in your immediate family was committing welfare fraud, would you report them?* Posted on Answerology.com. Retrieved July 7, 2009 from http://www.answerology.com/index.aspx/question/2644566_If-someone-in-your-immediate-family-was-committing-welfare-fraud-would-you-report-them.html

Dirkx, J. M. (1999). New skills for literacy educators. In L. G. Martin & J. C. Fisher (Eds.), *The welfare-to-work challenge for adult literacy educators.* New Directions for Adult and Continuing Education, *83.* (pp. 83–94). San Francisco: Jossey-Bass.

Edin, K., & Lein, L. (1997). *Making ends meet: How single mothers survive welfare and low-wage work.* New York: Russell Sage.

Fraser, N. (1989). *Unruly practices: Power, discourse, and gender in contemporary social theory.* Minneapolis: University of Minnesota Press.

Giroux, H. A. (2004). Public pedagogy and the politics of neo-liberalism: Making the political more pedagogical. *Policy Futures in Education, 2*(3&4), 494–503.

Glennie, P. (1995). Consumption within historical studies. In D. Miller (Ed.), *Acknowledging consumption* (pp. 163–202). New York: Routledge.

Gowen, S. G. (1992). *The politics of workplace literacy.* New York: Teachers College Press.

Gorski, P. C. (2008a). The myth of the "culture of poverty." *Educational Leadership, 65*(7), 32–37.

Gorski, P. C. (2008b). Peddling poverty for profit: Elements of oppression in Ruby Payne's framework. *Equity & Excellence in Education, 41*(1), 130–148.

Gring-Pemble, L. M. (2003). *Grim fairy tales: The rhetorical construction of American welfare policy.* Westport, CT: Praeger.

Hancock, A. M. (2004). *The politics of disgust: The public identity of the welfare queen.* New York: New York University.

Jackson, P., & Thrift, N. (1995). Geographies of consumption. In D. Miller (Ed.), *Acknowledging consumption* (pp. 203–236). New York: Routledge.

Jubas, K. (2007). Consuming fiction: Stories about consumerism, shopping and consumption. In L. Servage & T. Fenwick (Eds.), *Learning in community: Pro-*

ceedings of the joint international conference of the Adult Education Research Conference (AERC) and the Canadian Association for the Study of Adult Education (CASAE) (pp. 325–330) Halifax, Nova Scotia, Canada: Mount St. Vincent University.

Jubas, K. (2008). *Promise and trouble, desire and critique: Shopping as a site of learning about globalization, identity and the potential for change.* Unpublished doctoral dissertation, Department of Educational Studies, University of British Columbia.

Kinsella, S. (2001). *Confessions of a shopaholic.* New York: Dell.

Krannebitter, K. (October 6, 2008). *Regulate the welfare abuse.* Retrieved July 7, 2009, from http://searchwarp.com/swa382257.htm

Lubar, S. (1998). Men/women/production/consumption. In R. Horowitz & A. Mohun (Eds.), *His and hers: Gender, consumption, and technology* (pp. 7–38). Charlottesville: University Press of Virginia.

Marchand, R. (1986). *Advertising the American dream: Making way for modernity, 1920–1940.* Berkeley: University of California Press.

Mishler, E. G. (1995). Models of narrative analysis: A typology. *Journal of Narrative and Life History, 5,* 87–123.

Mogelonsky, M. (1994). Poor and unschooled, but a smart shopper. *American Demographics, 16,* 14–15.

Neubeck, K. J., & Cazenave, N. A. (2001). *Welfare racism: Playing the race card against America's poor.* New York: Routledge.

Newton, J. M. (1977). Economic rationality of the poor. *Human Organization, 36*(1), 50–61.

Padilla, R. (2008). *Wal-Mart employee killed in Black Friday stampede.* G4TV.com. Retrieved July 7, 2009, from http://74.125.47.132/search?q=cache:9dkrRFo8l4cJ:g4tv.com/attackoftheshow/blog/post/691364/WalMart_Employee_Killed_In_Black_Friday_Stampede.html%3Futm_source%3Dg4tv%26utm_medium%3Drssfeeds%26utm_campaign%3DAOTB+%22attack+of+the+blog!+wal-mart+employee%22&hl=en&client=safari&gl=us&strip=1

Payne, R. K. (2005). *A framework for understanding poverty.* Highlands, TX: aha! Process, Inc.

Priest, C. J. (2007). *The gospel of impotence: The crises of values in the Black church.* Retrieved July 7, 2009, from http://www.digital-priest.com/riv/frames/impotence.htm

Quigley, B. A. (1997). *Rethinking literacy education.* San Francisco: Jossey-Bass.

Random House. (2008). *Confessions of a shopaholic.* Retrieved July 7, 2009, from http://www.randomhouse.com/bantamdell/kinsella/books/display.pperl?isbn=9780440241416

Roberts, S. D. (1991). Effects of sudden income loss on consumption and related aspects of life: A study of unemployed steel workers. *Research in Consumer Behavior, 5,* 181–214.

Sandlin, J. A. (2000). The politics of consumer education materials used in adult literacy classrooms. *Adult Education Quarterly, 50*(4), 289–307.

Sandlin, J. A. (2001). Out of balance: Contradictory depictions of adult literacy learners as consumers. *Adult Basic Education, 11*(1), 17–39.

Sandlin, J. A. & Clark, M. C. (2009). From opportunity to responsibility: Political master narratives, social policy, and success stories in adult literacy education. *Teachers College Record, 111*(4), 999–1029.

Sassatelli, R. (2007). *Consumer culture: History, theory and politics.* London: Sage.

Scanlon, J. (Ed.). (2000). *The gender and consumer culture reader.* New York: New York University Press.

Schafft, K. A. & Prins, E. S. (2008, Fall/Winter). Rural poverty, educational reform, and the Ruby Payne phenomenon. *CREC Works, 3*(1), 1–2. Center on Rural Education and Communities. Retrieved August 12, 2009 from http://www.ed.psu.edu/CREC/PDF/CRECWorks_v3n1.pdf

Seccombe, K. (1999). *"So you think I drive a Cadillac?": Welfare recipients' perspectives on the system and its reform.* Boston: Allyn and Bacon.

Slater, D. (1997). *Consumer culture and modernity.* Cambridge, UK: Polity Press.

Solórzano, D. G., & Yosso, T. J. (2002). Critical race methodology: Counter-storytelling as an analytical framework for education research. *Qualitative Inquiry, 8*(1), 23–44.

Sparks, B. (1999). Critical issues and dilemmas for adult literacy programs under welfare reform. In J. C. Fisher & L. G. Martin (Eds.), *The welfare-to-work challenge for adult literacy eduators* (Number 83 ed., pp. 25–28). San Francisco: Jossey-Bass.

St. Clair, R. (2004). Success stories: Aspirational myth in the education of adults. *International Journal of Lifelong Education, 23*(1), 81–94.

WWAY (December 18, 2008). *Number of people applying for food stamps is on the rise.* Retrieved July 7, 2009, from http://www.wwaytv3.com/node/12398

Zucchino, D. (1997). *Myth of the welfare queen.* New York: Scribner.

CHAPTER 11

LEARNING FOR SELF-SUFFICIENCY AMONG IMMIGRANTS IN CANADA

The Role of Community-Based Adult Education

Shibao Guo
University of Calgary

INTRODUCTION

As an immigrant society, Canada has been successful in attracting an increasing number of immigrants in recent years to help the country ameliorate its aging population and labor shortages in a booming economy. According to the 2006 Census of Canada (Statistics Canada, 2007), from 2001 to 2006, 1.1 million immigrants, many of whom were from Asia (58%), Africa (11%), and the Caribbean and Central and South America (11%) came to reside in Canada. Furthermore, the census also revealed that among recent immigrants to Canada, 57% were in the prime working age group of 25 to 54. In the process of adapting to a new life in Canada, these new immi-

Learning for Economic Self-Sufficiency, pages 175–192

grants face a number of barriers, including language and cultural barriers, integrating into the labor force, lack of social networks, devaluation of their prior learning and work experience, racism, and other systemic barriers. With the erosion of the welfare state and the subsequent downsizing of its settlement programs, community organizations took on greater responsibility for the development of programs to assist immigrants with their settlement and in achieving self-sufficiency.

Drawing from case study research, this chapter examines the role of community-based adult education in providing effective, responsive, and equitable learning programs to immigrants at a grassroots organization in Vancouver, called SUCCESS (United Chinese Community Enrichment Services Society). The study focuses on the historical development of SUCCESS, the provision of programs and services, major changes in SUCCESS, and its social contributions. The study reveals that SUCCESS was founded in 1973 in response to the failure of government agencies and mainstream organizations to provide accessible social services and adult education programs for newly arrived Chinese immigrants from Hong Kong. During its first 35 years, SUCCESS helped build a community for adult immigrants where they felt they belonged. It played multiple roles with a three-pronged focus: (1) providing adult education programs and professional services, (2) advocating on behalf of immigrants, and (3) facilitating citizenship education and community development. This study exemplifies the role of community-based adult education for social change in helping immigrants achieve self-sufficiency. It demonstrates that grassroots organizations are important sites for emancipatory learning and social action.

The chapter is organized into four parts. It starts with an overview of barriers facing new immigrants in adapting to a society, followed by an examination of the role of community-based adult education. Next, the chapter explores the history of SUCCESS and continues with the examination of its educational programs and services. Finally, it ends by assessing the experience of SUCCESS.

IMMIGRATION, ADAPTATION AND BARRIERS FACING IMMIGRANTS

Canada admits immigrants under three major categories: economic class, family class, and refugee. Immigrants under "economic class" refer to skilled workers and business immigrants. Skilled workers are admitted under a point system using prescribed selection criteria based on education, occupation, language skills, and work experience. Canada has three classes of business immigrants: investors, entrepreneurs, and self-employed persons, each with separate eligibility criteria. Immigration under "family class" reunites close family members of an adult resident or citizen of the hosting country, such as children, parents, spouse, and common-law partner. Refugee protection is usually offered to those who fear returning to their country of nationality or habitual residence because of war, fear of persecution, torture, or cruel and unusual treatment or punishment.

Since the mid-1990s, under Canada's knowledge-based economy, immigrant selection practices have given more weight to education and skills, favoring economic class immigrants over family class immigrants and refugees. According to Li (2003), this new shift was based on the assumption that economic class immigrants brought more human capital than family class immigrants and refugees and, therefore, were more valuable and desirable. According to Li, economic class immigrants made up more than half of all immigrants admitted to Canada throughout the late 1990s. This number peaked in the new millennium, reaching 62% in 2001 (Citizenship and Immigration Canada, 2008). A considerable number of these recent immigrants are highly educated professionals, particularly scientists and engineers. Also in the year 2001, 23.5% (58,910 individuals) of the total 250,638 immigrants and refugees admitted were admitted as skilled workers (Citizenship and Immigration Canada, 2008).

Current immigration policies under Canada's new economy have primarily focused on the country's interests, including labor force shortages, and have ignored the barriers immigrants may face while adapting to Canadian life. Research shows immigrants moving to a new country are likely to encounter multiple barriers in the process of adapting to a new society. They need assistance with language acquisition, employment, housing, education, daycare, health, counseling, and legal and social services. Reitz (1995) reviewed nearly 400 international publications and concluded that recent immigrants very often underutilize many important social and education services, despite evidence of significant need. Reitz further found that immigrants contribute more to the economy through taxation than they use in services. Immigrants' low utilization can be attributed to a number of barriers, including language and cultural difficulties. Others, such as Henry, Tator, Mattis, and Rees (2006), argue that the persistence of racial inequality in immigrant settlement and adaptation can be attributed to the existing ideologies of democratic racism. Although Canadians commit to democratic principles such as justice, equality, and fairness, individuals still retain their negative attitudes and behaviors towards minority groups or any differential treatment that is aimed at improving the low status of these groups. The ideology in which these two sets of conflicting values coexist is referred to by Henry and colleagues (2006) as "democratic racism."

Recent studies identify employment barriers as new challenges facing immigrants. Despite Canada's preference for highly skilled immigrants, and despite the fact that immigrant professionals bring significant human capital resources to the Canadian labor force, a number of studies have shown that many highly educated immigrant professionals experience unemployment and underemployment as a result of the deskilling and devaluation of their prior learning and work experience after immigrating to Canada (Grant & Nadin, 2007; Henry et al., 2006; Krahn, Derwing, Mulder, & Wilkinson, 2000; Mojab, 1999). In a study on skilled immigrants from Asia and Africa, Grant and Nadin (2007) found high levels of underemployment as participants took casual and part-time work for which they felt overqualified. Although almost all of the participants (97.5%) in Grant and Nadin's (2007) study held post-secondary degrees from their country of origin, they were surprised by their inability to find suitable Canadian employment. Highly skilled immigrants were forced to take jobs that underutilized their skills, which consequently resulted in a considerable waste of valuable human capital and triggered a myriad of strong emotions among immigrant professionals, including disappointment, sadness, and anger.

Highly educated refugees also encounter similar barriers in Canada. In comparison with Canadian-born individuals, refugee professionals are more likely to experience unemployment and underemployment, such as part-time and temporary employment (Krahn et al., 2000). A lack of recognition of prior learning and work experience was identified as the top contributing factor to this phenomenon. Other factors include a shortage of Canadian references and work experience, English language difficulties, and employer discrimination. With respect to the process of recognizing foreign credentials, it is important to note that professional associations often play a significant part in the labor market. By retaining strict control over the adjudication of foreign credentials, these associations restrict competition for well-paying professional jobs and assure their lucrative nature (Krahn et al., 2000). As Henry et al. (2006) note, there is little recognition in Canada of the professional qualifications, credentials, and experiences of immigrants. Some immigrants experience major shifts from prior occupations in sciences, engineering, business, and management to occupations in sales, services, and manufacturing. As a result, they suffer from wage loss and downward social mobility.

ADULT EDUCATION FOR SOCIAL CHANGE

The role of adult education for social change and community development has been addressed by a number of adult educators (Cunningham, 2000; Freire, 1970; Lindeman, 1926). As early as the 1920s, Lindeman (1926) deliberated on the social role of adult education. Lindeman (1926) viewed adult education as an agency of social progress and the most reliable instrument for social actionists. An early Canadian example of community development was the Antigonish Movement led by Moses Coady and Jimmy Tompkins (Welton, 2001). After Lindeman and Coady, pivotal adult educators such as Freire (1970) and Cunningham (2000) further advanced the role of adult education for social transformation and emancipatory learning. Freire (1970) believed that adult education is an important tool to raise people's critical consciousness through action and critical reflection, or praxis. Cunningham (2000) regards social movements and social learning as a major source of alternative knowledge production. Community development is an important site where such learning can take place.

As part of its social role, adult education is also deemed an important forum for building inclusive citizenship. Citizenship can be defined as membership in a socio-political community, which comprises four dimensions: legal status, rights, identity, and participation (Bloemraad, 2000). The past decade has witnessed a revitalized debate regarding the concept of citizenship. Part of this debate has been focused on the membership of immigrants in the national community, or the identity dimension of citizenship. Traditional liberals advocate a culturally neutral state (Rawls, 1971). Critics of such paradigm claim, however, that the ideal of a culturally neutral state embodies an oppressive illusion (Kymlicka, 1995; Tamir, 1995; Taylor, 1994). Cultural neutrality promotes a universal citizenship that ignores differences and perpetuates oppression and inequality. Consequently they propose "differentiated citizenship" as an alternative model (Young, 1995). As to the best approach of promoting citizenship, Derwing (1992) suggests a community-based, learner-centered approach in which members of the cultural and linguistic communities concerned are involved in every aspect of the programs.

In a new era of immigration, the changing demographics in Canada have posed both challenges and new opportunities for adult education in developing inclusive educational programs to help newcomers overcome barriers to participation. This research attempts to examine the role of community-based adult education in bringing about social change through providing accessible and responsive community-based adult education programs at SUCCESS (United Chinese Community Enrichment Services Society)—an immigrant community organization in Vancouver, Canada. The study focuses on: (1) the historical development of SUCCESS, (2) the provision of educational programs and services for adult immigrants, and (3) social contributions.

BRIDGING THE GAP: THE HISTORY OF SUCCESS

The central guiding question for this research was: How did a community-initiated voluntary organization such as SUCCESS respond to the changing needs of an ethnic community in a multicultural society? The qualitative research methods of document analysis and personal interviewing were used to conduct this study. Document analysis included SUCCESS annual reports, newsletters, minutes of annual general meetings, important speeches, and program brochures. Twenty interviews were conducted with the top executive, board members, and program directors. Time and resources did not permit interviews with clientele, so their views of this organization are not represented here. In addition to the two major methods, site visits and participant observation were used as complementary methods to help contextualize what was read and heard about the organization. A four-stage process of analysis was developed:

1. Identifying main points
2. Searching for salient themes and recurring patterns
3. Grouping common themes and patterns into related categories, and
4. Comparing all major categories with reference to selected theoretical constructs to form new perspectives.

This four-stage process assured frequent interplay between the data and theory.

An analysis of the organizational history reveals that SUCCESS was founded in response to the failure of government agencies and mainstream organizations to provide accessible social services and adult education programs for Chinese immigrants. The development of SUCCESS from its founding in 1973 can be best organized into three stages: Stage One (1973–1979), the founding and establishing stage; Stage Two (1979–1989), the developing and maturing stage; Stage Three (1989–2008), the expanding and transforming stage.

Stage One

In 1967, an increasing number of Chinese immigrants arrived in Canada from Hong Kong following the introduction of a "point system" that selected immigrants based on their "education, skills, and resources" rather than on their racial and religious background (Whitaker, 1991, p. 19). According to Li (1998), between 1968 and 1976, about 90,000 Chinese immigrants came to Canada; and between 1977 and 1984, an additional 80,000 arrived. Many of those who came through family reunification programs had a limited grasp of English and found it difficult to gain access to mainstream social services and education programs. In 1973, SUCCESS started with the Chinese Connection Project, a demonstration project funded by Health and Welfare Canada, aiming to bridge the gap between social service agencies and the needs of newly arrived Chinese immigrants, primarily from Hong Kong. During this first stage, the organization mainly provided basic settlement services and language programs for adult immigrants. Services included English as a Second Language (ESL) classes and providing information on Canada's education and health care system. This project also involved making direct referrals of immigrants to other service providers and providing translation services to help them navigate unfamiliar bureaucracies and organizations. This became the founding and establishing stage of SUCCESS.

Stage Two

Stage Two witnessed a large increase in Chinese immigrants from Hong Kong because its residents were worried about their future due to the Sino–British Agreement in 1984 (Wong, 1992). A large number of these immigrants found home in Vancouver. This led to substantial increases both in the volume of services and budget. Another change that occurred during this period was that immigrants were settling in a broader geographic area beyond the Chinatown area (Hiebert, 1999), and this led to establishing two branch offices outside Chinatown, one in South Vancouver in 1984 and a second in Richmond in 1989. The Richmond Office, located in a suburb to the south of Vancouver and close to the airport, offered career consultation and job referrals as well as traditional services. It met the "service needs of local residents" and established "bridges and linkages" for them (To, 1989, p. 8). During this maturing stage, SUCCESS won a number of awards from the Chinese community and mainstream organizations in recognition of its contributions to community development. A noteworthy development during this period was a growing advocacy role in response to instances of discrimination in national and local media. Two major incidents occurred when the Chinese were slighted in the media. In the first incident, a national TV news magazine portrayed second- and third-generation Canadian citizens of Chinese descent as foreign students taking educational opportunities away from white Canadians at taxpayers' expense. In the second, CBC Radio broadcast the "Dim Sum Diaries," which satirized the accents of new Chinese immigrants and stereotypes of their behavior. SUCCESS participated in a national campaign against the first and led a protest against the second, resulting in apologies and withdrawal of programs.

Stage Three

Stage Three of the development of SUCCESS was characterized by expansion and transformation. By the time it celebrated its 25th anniversary in 1998, SUCCESS had become a well-established multi-level service agency providing a wide range of programs and services to both Chinese and non-Chinese immigrants. During this period, the make-up of the immigrant population shifted. Increasing numbers of immigrants came from other regions of China including Taiwan and mainland China. In 1998, immigrants from mainland China outnumbered those from Hong Kong, and China became the top source country of immigrants to Canada (Guo & DeVoretz, 2006a). Furthermore, the years preceding the handover of Hong Kong to China in 1997 produced a substantial influx of immigrants from Hong Kong. The changing composition of immigrants required SUCCESS to alter its program offerings to include, for example, more programs suited to professional and business immigrants and the growing numbers of Mandarin-speaking immigrants. To further meet the needs of Mandarin speakers, SUCCESS opened one Mandarin Service Centre in Vancouver's Oakridge area in 1994 and a second in Chinatown in 1996.

In all three stages of development between 1973 and 2008, SUCCESS experienced tremendous changes that were evident in the fiscal growth of the organization. When SUCCESS was founded in 1973, the organization only employed four full-time professional social workers. By 2008, it had a professional team consisting of over 400 people. SUCCESS effectively bridged gaps left by government and mainstream organizations that were not developing programs for this group. It has, indeed, successfully played multiple roles as a service provider, advocate, and facilitator for citizenship education. The remaining chapter will focus on the role of SUCCESS in providing educational programs and professional services for adult immigrants.

LEARNING FOR SELF-SUFFICIENCY: CONSTRUCTING EDUCATIONAL PROGRAMS FOR IMMIGRANTS

The Chinese name for SUCCESS is the Chinese Immigrant Mutual-Help Society. The founding and development of SUCCESS was supported by the philosophy of mutual help, self-help and voluntarism. The Chinese community in Canada had a long tradition of mutual-help and self-help. As Willmott (1969) pointed out over 40 years ago, the Chinese are unique among immigrant groups in Canada "in the extent to which they organize voluntary associations within their community" (p. 30). According to Willmott (1969), the Chinese produced proportionately more mutual-aid associations than any other immigrant group in Canada. SUCCESS inherited this tradition. With the help of staff and a numerous volunteers, SUCCESS provided educational programs and professional services to help immigrants help themselves and achieve self-sufficiency.

When SUCCESS began in the 1970s, a lack of resources limited its ability to provide basic settlement services such as language interpretation and information services to immigrants. By the time SUCCESS celebrated its 25th anniversary, its programs and services had expanded into seven areas:

1. Immigrant airport reception
2. Settlement services
3. Language training
4. Employment program and services
5. Small business development and training
6. Counseling services
7. Advocacy and community development.

SUCCESS was no longer a single-focus organization providing only settlement services; it had become a well-established multi-service community organization. Some of these programs have remained constant throughout this 35-year period because the needs have remained more or less unchanged. ESL programs within the Language Training and Settlement Services area have remained important for all non-English speaking immigrants to help them acquire the language skills necessary for full participation in society. This section will further examine the programs in the seven areas with a focus on the purpose of the programs, the scope of services, its social contributions, and challenges.

Community Airport Newcomers Network (CANN)

SUCCESS provided immigrant reception services from the moment they landed in the Vancouver airport. The Community Airport Newcomers Network (CANN) was set up in 1992 to help newly arrived immigrants and refugees with their landing procedures and pre-settlement through the provision of a welcome reception, resource orientation, and referral services, all at the Vancouver airport. The orientation was often conducted by a multilingual team, first in English, and then followed by another language that most of the immigrants of that particular group spoke. While newly arrived immigrants were waiting to be interviewed by immigrant officers at the airport, CANN staff members distributed materials that contained useful settlement information. During the waiting time, they would also provide orientation to the new immigrants and answer any questions that they may have, in the immigrants' native language if they found it useful. Finally, CANN staff would help orient immigrants about the customs inspection. Because of limited time at the airport, CANN staff could only provide basic introduction to the services, and they would refer newcomers to local immigrant service agencies for specific programs and services, depending on where they planned to stay, the kinds of services they required, and the language they spoke. CANN was also mandated to receive government refugees or privately sponsored refugees. Unlike receiving regular landing immigrants, CANN staff members had to receive all refugees at the Vancouver Airport, despite the time of arrival. Francis Chan, then Program Director of CANN, stressed in an interview that it is important to provide immigrants and refugees with proper information at the earliest time possible to help them with the settlement process. Many immigrants who received this service found that it was useful to have people who spoke their own languages greet them and help them go through the landing procedures and get necessary settlement information upon arrival.

Settlement Services

Settlement services have always been the core of SUCCESS programs and services to help immigrants ease their daily struggle with the process of settlement and achieve a better understanding of Canadian society. This division provided direct information and referral services, workshops, new immigrant orientation, and citizenship classes. Direct information and referral services are referred to as the core or first step toward achieving integration for immigrants. Ansar Cheung, Program Director of Language Training and Settlement Services, explained during the interview, "People come with different kinds of questions. They ask anything about immigration, about medical services plan, about the social benefits, about education, about customs, citizenship, anything." That's why her staff had to be equipped with a lot of information, "like a walking dictionary." In addition, they provided workshops and orientation classes that also covered a wide range of topics from public transit to education. Cheung also mentioned that they tried to use immigrants' native languages where possible at new immigrant orientations. It seems clear that settlement was not only about providing necessary information and services for new arrivals; more importantly, it has become a process of lifelong learning: learning to live, to know, and to become, as stated by Jarvis (2008). Through the process of settlement and adaptation in a new socio-cultural environment, immigrants acquired the necessary knowledge and information as new citizens and learned to navigate an unfamiliar culture and a bureaucratic system.

Language Training Program

Language is a significant barrier for many immigrants. In a Vancouver-based study with recent Chinese immigrants, Guo and DeVoretz (2006b) reported that among many barriers facing immigrants, employment and language were the two most frequently cited barriers inhibiting their integration into the Canadian social and economic spheres.

Among all programs and services, language training has always been at the center of SUCCESS. SUCCESS offered two kinds of language training programs to help immigrants overcome this barrier: government-sponsored as well as fee-charging language programs. For the government-sponsored programs, only five levels of English, far from enough particularly for job seekers, were funded. Before 1999, the program was funded by Citizenship and Immigration Canada through a program called Language Instructions for Newcomers to Canada (LINC). In 1999, there was a redistribution of funding from the federal government to the Province of British Columbia. As a result of this restructuring, the program is now called English Language Services for Adults (ELSA), under the Ministry of Attorney General, Settlement and Multiculturalism. For those who were not eligible for government-funded programs, and for those who wish to continue improving their English after they have taken the government-sponsored program, the ELSA program was now available. Meanwhile, Ansar Cheung and her colleagues were lobbying the government to provide more English classes, particularly classes at a higher level and focusing on workplace-oriented English. A lack of secured funding was a major issue facing the ELSA program as well as the whole organization. Cheung commented that lack of funding and the nature of short-term funding caused "tremendous instability and frustrations among staff members."

Employment Training and Service

Securing a job is an important step toward achieving economic self-sufficiency for immigrants. The SUCCESS Employment Training and Services was originally set up in the mid-1980s to assist immigrants with upgrading their English skills, learning job searching skills, preparing resumes, and preparing for job interviews. Thomas Yeung, Program Director of that division during the interview, commented that "without getting a job we won't be able to help immigrants to settle here in Canada." Since then, the program has gone through several stages of development. According to Yeung, when resource-based industries were closing down in British Columbia, the focus shifted to skills training in order to equip people with specific skills to find other jobs. In more recent years, employment training had moved away from specific skills training to learning broader skills in order to prepare people with flexible skills for the rest of their lives. Another change was the delegation of federal responsibilities to the provincial government. With the restructuring of government funding policies, funding of its programs became provincial responsibilities starting in July, 1999. Yet the most challenging shift involves government fee-charging policies. Yeung noted that employment training programs used to be free based on the needs of individuals. Now participants had to pay. In addition, these programs had to be opened up to non-immigrants. Without any doubt, this change had a great impact on the programs and services at SUCCESS, and SUCCESS had to make adjustments accordingly. Yeung stated that they were using all their resources to help immigrants realize their goal.

Since the mid-1990s, Canada has been successful in attracting well-educated immigrant professionals, but many of them have had difficulties finding a job (Li, 2003). It had become a top priority for SUCCESS to strengthen its employment programs. In 1999, SUCCESS consolidated all employment-related programs and services and formed the SUCCESS Training Institute, which oversaw three program areas: language training, employment services, and small business development. According to Yeung, with the restructuring, employment programs are more coordinated than before. Now this program has gone through an accreditation process by the Council on Accreditation (COA) and has met the highest national standards of professional performance. In fact, its employment training and services have grown into one of the largest not-for-profit training service providers in Canada, employing approximately 100 staff members. It has also become the driving force behind SUCCESS' growth and expansion in the past few years.

Small Business Development and Training

In the 1980s, the Canadian government introduced the "business immigrant" category, which consisted of self-employed entrepreneurs and investors. This program attracted immigrants predominantly from Asia and the Middle East. By 1986, 40% of all business immigrants came from Hong Kong (Whitaker, 1991). In response to the needs of proliferating business immigrants, SUCCESS launched its Small Business Development and Training in 1995. It offered three major programs and services, including (1) information and referral services for immigrants who were interested in setting up their own business, (2) setting up joint business ventures with corporations (such as IBM Canada, Royal Bank of Canada), and (3) the Youth Entrepreneurial Development Program. While the first two were primarily for recent immigrants, the last program was for both immigrants and non-immigrants. The objective of these programs was to help participants become self-sufficient economically through setting up their own businesses, with the long-term benefits of economic integration. Thomas Tam, Program Director of Small Business Development and Training, explained that expanding SUCCESS beyond the scope of helping immigrants overcome language and cultural barriers to now include programs and services for small business training was regarded as an extension of SUCCESS' original mandate, not a contradiction. This program has won a number of awards, including one from the Human Resources and Social Development Canada (HRSDC).

Family and Youth Counseling

Family and Youth Counseling first started in early 1980s as a family program and later expanded to include counseling services. This component served two major purposes: to help immigrants with family and relational issues and to advocate on behalf of immigrants in the areas of family services. Family and youth counseling was the core program of this division. The program handled around 600 cases per year and also provided public education through workshops, library resources, and the media. In addition, they produced 13 episodes of a family life education series in collaboration with a local TV station. Frequently, they partnered with schools to help bridge gaps between students, parents, and the school. They adopted an effective and innovative approach to provide group programs, using theatrical techniques. According to Kelly Ng, Program Director of Family and Youth Counseling, immigrant families usually needed support in the following three areas: marital issues, parent–child relationships, and family violence, such as spousal assault and child abuse. All these issues are beyond the scope of an immigrant's actual settlement, but they can hamper or slow down immigrants' integration process. Ng believed SUCCESS could play an important role in providing culturally and linguistically appropriate professional family and counseling services. He noted the significance of providing counseling in the clients' native languages. All of his 14 staff members were bilingual in English and Cantonese or Mandarin Chinese. Ng also shared the same frustration with other colleagues in terms of shortages of funding. The funding for Family and Youth Counseling programs was not stable. It kept changing from one year to the next and frequently they had to find new sponsorship. In most recent years their programs were sponsored by the municipal and provincial governments. He also expressed other issues facing the organization, which included overwork, lack of job security, and low pay. Ng explained:

> One of the things is the situation of burn-out. People are overworked. We can't help the situation. Everybody is using their commitment. The need is huge, and we are under pressure to fulfill. The other is unstable working environment. They are not sure when they will be without a job. The other one is salary. We are below market price, comparing to the major therapy organiza-

tions. We are about 1/3 below them. (Kelly Ng, Program Director of Family and Youth Counseling, SUCCESS)

Indeed, these problems create hardships on the organization in its attempts to continue to meet the needs of newcomers as they acculturate in the new society.

Advocacy and Community Development

Advocacy and Community Development focuses on advocacy, community development, and public education. This area encompassed a wide range of programs, including seniors' programs, womens' programs, and civic education. Community outreach is another component of this division in the form of collaborating with the mainstream and Chinese media and reaching out to neighborhoods and community centers to promote immigrants' access to their services. This division also organized many events (such as the Chinese New Year celebration and the Mid-Autumn Festival), coordinating with other organizations within the Chinese community, including clan organizations, the Chinese Cultural Centre, the Chinese Benevolent Association, and the Chinese Merchants' Association. Over the past years, SUCCESS has built partnerships with 150 mainstream organizations such as hospitals, health boards, police, school boards, and the media. This division fulfilled its major goal of building bridges on both sides.

In addition, Advocacy and Community Development was also responsible for facilitating volunteer and membership development. Volunteers helped SUCCESS with its daily operation and different tasks in various areas. In the 1980s, most of the volunteers were mainly involved in interpretation services. They also contributed by helping Vietnamese refugees settle in Vancouver. The number of volunteers increased from 150 in 1980 to over 2,000 in 2008. In 2008, volunteers contributed a total of 127,400 service hours to SUCCESS, equivalent to 70 full-time staff working for one year (SUCCESS, 2008). In addition, volunteers contributed 1,400 service hours to other agencies. Shirley Leung, Program Director of Advocacy and Community Development, called volunteers "the backbone of SUCCESS." She maintained that, without the help of volunteers, "SUCCESS could not survive." By the size of its membership, perhaps SUCCESS was the largest immigrant community organization in Canada. As of March 2008, SUCCESS had a membership of 3,862 people. Many members were once their clients who had joined SUCCESS as members because they wanted to express their appreciation by supporting its cause. Leung stated that the large membership was an important vehicle to maintain its grassroots base. Through its members, SUCCESS was kept well informed of the needs and trends of the community. The contributions of volunteers and members exemplified the spirit of mutual help and self-help in achieving self-sufficiency.

ASSESSING THE EXPERIENCE OF SUCCESS

This study reveals that SUCCESS experienced tremendous changes between 1973 and 2008. These changes were manifested in the growth of the organization and in the expansion of its programs and services. Changes touched many aspects of the organization. SUCCESS has grown exponentially and is strong enough to be noticeable not just in the Chinese community but also in mainstream society. It has played multiple roles with a three-pronged focus: (1) providing adult education programs and professional services, (2) advocating on behalf of immigrants, and (3) facilitating citizenship education and community development. It is evident that three major social forces have contributed to the evolvement of SUCCESS, including responding to changing community needs, community support, and a community-based holistic approach.

First, SUCCESS was successful in responding to the changing needs of immigrants. The profile of recent immigrants changed in light of modified Canadian immigration policies, such as the adoption of the "point system," the introduction of the business immigrant category, and the opening of the immigration division in the Canadian Embassy in Beijing. The needs of newly arrived immigrants differed from their early counterparts, and SUCCESS responded to meet these changing needs. For example, to make its programs and services more accessible to new immigrants, especially those from Taiwan and mainland China, SUCCESS established Mandarin service centres and hired Mandarin-speaking staff members in each office. In the 1990s, many new arrivals were professional and business immigrants, and SUCCESS introduced employment and small business training programs and established the SUCCESS Training Institute to consolidate its employment programs.

Second, SUCCESS has built a strong community support network. The organization has a relatively large membership and an immense volunteer base. These aspects promote the strength of the organization. When these numbers were converted into political and economic resources, its voice cannot be ignored by politicians and policymakers. It is evident that Chinese immigrants benefited immensely from this network. At the same time, this study has demonstrated the importance of a mutual help society in building facilities like this to help immigrants achieve self-sufficiency at a time when the welfare state has eroded. As a transitional organization, SUCCESS was a stepping stone toward integration into mainstream society. Meanwhile, it is also an important entrance for government agencies and mainstream organizations to approach a hard-to-reach ethnic community. The experience of SUCCESS provided a means to investigate the dynamic between individual immigrants' agency and the structural or institutional constraints they face in exercising that agency.

Furthermore, from its past experience, SUCCESS developed a community-based holistic approach in helping immigrants become self-sufficient, socially, culturally, linguistically, and economically. This approach treats settlement, adaptation, and learning as a holistic process requiring integrated educational programs and social services, including landing reception, settlement services, language programs, employment training, counseling, business programs, and community development. All these programs and services are interrelated and interdependent. The holistic approach required a collaborative endeavor among all sections of SUCCESS programs and services. It also involved people from outside SUCCESS, such as business partners, community organizations, and government agencies. As part of the SUCCESS holistic approach, SUCCESS accomplished the effective combination of the three roles: providing professional services, advocating on behalf of immigrants, and facilitating community education and development. Only providing integrated educational programs and services can enhance the full integration of immigrants. The community-based holistic approach has proven most effective because they are more closely connected with and responsive to ethnic community needs.

This study has several implications for adult education. In illustrating how SUCCESS emerged as a key adult education provider for new immigrants and how its programs and services evolved in responding to changing needs of immigrants, the study reveals how its educational programs and services helped immigrants to navigate the complex paths that citizenship entails and to upgrade their language, knowledge, and skills to achieve self-sufficiency in Canadian society. The experience of SUCCESS exemplifies the role of adult education for social change by providing accessible and culturally appropriate and linguistically appropriate educational programs and services, which immigrants were entitled to but often deprived of, owing to the failure of the state and mainstream social service agencies. The study shows that community organizations can be a more effective alternative other than mainstream organizations, because they are more closely connected with and responsive to community needs. Its advocacy role demonstrates that communities are important sites for emancipatory learning and social action. The study also shows the important role that community organizations can play in building an inclusive citizenship organization where previously marginalized citizens now feel they belong. In the context of SUCCESS, its role in citizenship education was twofold: building a facility where adult immigrants can acquire necessary skills and knowledge in order to become an active citizen and alerting mainstream organizations about their service approaches and changing public attitudes towards immigrants. One of the most important contributions was that SUCCESS helped build a home and a learning community for adult immigrants where they felt they belonged.

REFERENCES

Bloemraad, I. (2000). Citizenship and immigration: A current review. *Journal of International Migration and Integration, 1*(1), 9–37.

Citizenship and Immigration Canada. (2008). *Facts and figures: Immigration overview permanent and temporary residents.* Ottawa: Author.

Cunningham, P. (2000). A sociology of adult education. In A. Wilson and E. Hayes (Eds.), *Handbook of adult and continuing education* (pp. 573–591). San Francisco: Jossey-Bass.

Derwing, T. (1992). Instilling a passive voice: Citizenship instruction in Canada. In B. Burnaby & A. Cumming (Eds.), *Socio-political aspect of ESL* (pp. 19–202). Toronto: The Ontario Institute for Studies in Education.

Freire, P. (1970). *Pedagogy of the oppressed.* New York: Continuum.

Grant, P., & Nadin, S. (2007). The credentialing problems of foreign trained personnel from Asia and Africa intending to make their home in Canada: A social psychological perspective. *Journal of International Migration and Integration, 8*(2), 141–162.

Guo, S., & DeVoretz, D. (2006a). The changing face of Chinese immigrants in Canada. *Journal of International Migration and Integration, 7*(3), 275–300.

Guo, S., & DeVoretz, D. (2006b). Chinese immigrants in Vancouver: Quo vadis? *Journal of International Migration and Integration, 7*(4), 425–447.

Henry, F., Tator, C., Mattis, W., & Rees, T. (2006). *The colour of democracy: Racism in Canadian society.* Toronto: Thompson Nelson.

Hiebert, D. (1999). Immigration and the changing social geography of Greater Vancouver. *BC Studies, 121*, 35–82.

Jarvis, P. (2008). *Democracy, lifelong learning and the learning society.* London: Routledge.

Krahn, H., Derwing, T., Mulder, M., & Wilkinson, L. (2000). Educated and underemployed: Refugee integration into the Canadian labour market. *Journal of International Migration and Integration, 1*(1), 59–84.

Kymlicka, W. (1995). *Multicultural citizenship: A liberal theory of minority rights.* Oxford: Clarendon Press.

Li, P. S. (1998). *The Chinese in Canada.* Toronto: Oxford University Press.

Li, P. S. (2003). *Destination Canada: Immigration debates and issues.* Don Mills: Oxford University Press.

Lindeman, E. C. (1926). *The meaning of adult education.* Montreal: Harvest House.

Mojab, S. (1999). De-skilling immigrant women. *Canadian Woman Studies, 19*(3), 123–128.

Rawls, J. (1971). *A theory of justice.* London: Oxford University Press.

Reitz, J. (1995). A review of the literature on aspects of ethno-racial access, utilization and delivery of social services. Retrieved January 15, 2009, from http://ceris.metropolis.net/virtual%20library/other/reitz1/reitz1.html

Statistics Canada. (2007). *Immigration in Canada: A portrait of the foreign-born population, 2006 census.* Ottawa: Statistics Canada. Retrieved September 20, 2009, from http://www12.statcan.ca/English/census06/analysis/immcit/pdf/97-557-XIE2006001.pdf

SUCCESS. (2008). *Opening new frontiers: SUCCESS annual report 2007–2008.* Vancouver: SUCCESS.

Tamir, Y. (1995). Two concepts of multiculturalism. In Y. Tamir (Ed.), *Democratic education in a multicultural state* (pp. 3–14). Oxford: Blackwell Publishers.

Taylor, C. (1994). The politics of recognition. In A. Gutmann (Ed.), *Multiculturalism: Examining the politics of recognition* (pp. 25–73). Princeton, NJ: Princeton University Press.

To, L. (1989). Executive Director's Report. In *S.U.C.C.E.S.S. Annual Report 1989* (p. 8). Vancouver: SUCCESS.

Welton, M. (2001). *Little Mosie from the Margaree: A biography of Moses Michael Coady.* Toronto: Thompson Educational.

Whitaker, R. (1991). *Canadian immigration policy since confederation.* Ottawa: Canadian Historical Association.

Willmott, W. E. (1969). Some aspects of Chinese communities in British Columbia towns. *BC Studies, 1,* 27–36.

Wong, S. L. (1992). *Emigration and stability in Hong Kong.* Hong Kong: The University of Hong Kong.

Young, I. M. (1995). Polity and group difference: A critique of the ideal of universal citizenship. In R. Beiner (Ed.), *Theorizing citizenship* (pp. 175–207). Albany: State University of New York.

CHAPTER 12

LITERACIES FROM THE INSIDE

Learning from and Within a Culture of Corrections

Dominique T. Chlup
Texas A&M University

Irene C. Baird
Pennsylvania State University

It costs the government half a million bucks to keep me in jail and $450 to teach me to read and write.

—former inmate, cited in Porporino & Robinson, 1992, p. 92

In 1905, when the first prison schools in the United States began to operate systematically and comprehensively, the superintendent of prisons made the significant statement, "Hitherto, the prisons have been run in the interests of the industries; hereafter, they will be run in the interests of inmates" (quoted in Hill, 1924, p. 2). In its earliest inception, the idea of schools in prisons was not fundamentally for economic gains. In fact, A. C. Hill, the New York State Department of Education's Chief of Special Schools Bureau, in his report on *Schools for Adults in Prisons* (1924) argued, "The chief function of an ideal prison school is to salvage lives that have drifted or been driven ashore along the

Learning for Economic Self-Sufficiency, pages 193–211

stream of social influences.... To accomplish their task prison schools must be special schools of character rather than schools of economic efficiency" (p. 7). Education for the purpose of economic self-sufficiency, while valued, was not seen as the overriding factor in a prisoner's reformation. Hill argued in the same report that "work as a factor in promoting reformation should not be exaggerated" (p. 6). The trade instruction, introduced in some prisons, advocated for habits of industry, efficiency, and labor training in the hopes that prisoners would return to society as "self-reliant." This instruction, however, was not sufficient. Hill further emphasized the need for a higher purpose to prison trades than the economic rehabilitation of prisoners.

Prison reformers in the early twentieth century saw the need for a wide range of educational programming. Work, as a means of promoting change in a prisoner's life, was just one of several values promoted within the scope of broader educational prison reform programming. The rhetoric of the period, which included the terms "self-mastery," "self-respect," and "consciousness of power," demonstrated the reformers' emphasis on a multi-prong approach to prison reform. The authors of this chapter believe that approaching the education of prisoners from a multi-prong perspective is a legacy from the twentieth century worth pursuing in the twenty-first century.

Unfortunately, as we get further into the twenty-first century, we are also reminded that the tide has ebbed, and conceptualizing prisons as schools either for economic or educational purposes is becoming more of a metaphorical description than a literal one. For many corrections institutions, the formal work of prison education, due to budgetary cuts, remains on the endangered species list. These budgetary cuts can be explained by changes in the level of federal support for corrections programs. Prior to 1998, the federal government required states to spend *no less than* 10% of their Basic State Grant for Adult Education in state institutions, including corrections institutions. The same law now requires them to spend *no more* than 10% (Coley & Barton, 2006). Prior to 1998, under the Carl D. Perkins Vocational and Technical Act, states were required to spend *at least* 1% of their grants in state institutions, including corrections, but the 1998 amendments specify that *no more* than 1% may be spent (Coley & Barton, 2006). Additionally, in 1994, Pell grant funding for inmates was eliminated, which resulted in the closing of hundreds of college education programs in prisons.

Despite the reality of budget cuts and a declining investment in corrections education, scores of volunteers, outreach programs, faith-based, and community re-entry programs continue to build bridges from the outside in. Another group of prison educators that are often overlooked are the inmates themselves who offer instruction, both formally and informally.

The co-authors of this chapter, who together have a combined thirty years of practice and deep interest in prison education, offer a bridge from "behind bars" to the outside. This chapter uses U.S.-based case examples to provide illustrations of literacy education programs established in adult correctional facilities. The goal of the chapter is to explain how writing and literacy education practices are connected to the pursuit of economic self-sufficiency among low-literate and low-income prisoners. While we provide some surprising statistics on the current prison population and correctional education system, we want to emphasize that addressing prison literacy education from a statistical perspective can be disproportionately negative because numbers may reflect deficits devoid of context. It generalizes the prison population without the essential awareness or understanding of the many personal and community-related factors that tell the story behind the dehumanizing numbers. Further, if contributing factors are not explored and addressed, the prison doors become revolving ones.

This chapter will also discuss the constraints of working in a culture of corrections. Having students confined in their cells, sometimes for up to twenty-three hours per day, provides its own unique set of pedagogical restraints for educators and educational systems. Therefore, we focus this chapter on what works as opposed to what does not work. We frame programs that work as "pockets of hope" (de los Reyes & Gozemba, 2002). We are borrowing this term from de los Reyes and Gozemba (2002) who in their book entitled *Pockets of Hope: How Students and Teachers Change the World,* "celebrate liberatory teachers and their emancipatory pedagogies that engage students in what Freire and Macedo (1987) call 'reading the word and the world' " (p. 2). We believe that even if corrections educators and their students do not claim the terms "emancipatory pedagogies" or "liberatory," by the very act of providing education in a culture of corrections and, by extension, a culture of confinement, they are positioning themselves as agents and advocates of literacy. By providing case examples that demonstrate "pockets of hope," we aim to give recommendations to educators and trainers of adults on how to create programs and environments that facilitate the development of literate and potentially economically stable inmates equipped to re-enter the civilian community.

While we explore prisons as sites for literacy education, we also want to acknowledge that training and development in the basic skills of print literacy should only be a first step for inmates on a long path of educational opportunities. It is central to our thesis that correctional education literacy programs can be both productive and tenuous. Jacobi (2004) noted, "these programs need a bit of 'troubling' if we are to improve the ways we engage in service learning work with writers inside" (p. 3). If we are to improve the ways we work *with* and *for* inmates, these programs need to be critically examined.

A UNESCO report (1966) argued, "Literacy programs should preferably be linked with economic priorities. [They] must impart not only reading and writing, but also professional and technical knowledge, thereby leading to a fuller participation of adults in economic life" (p. 97 quoted in Macedo,

2006, p. 18). Although there is merit in this argument, when we reduce teaching literacy to a capital function of economic self-sufficiency, we lose notions of critical thinking, culture, and power (Giroux, 1983). Given current neoliberal policies that result in crime control policies that favor mass incarceration, focusing solely on the pragmatics of capital and economics results in what Freire (1985) termed the *anesthetization of students' critical abilities* in order to "domesticate social order for its self-preservation" (p. 116). Education for prisoners must, therefore, be more than functional literacy.

In the last section of this chapter, we make the case for educational structures that encourage students to move above and beyond literacy learning for the sake of economic mobility. We place literacy and workplace skills as partial components rather than the only components in the equation for prison education. Effective prison education programs also recognize this distinction.

Access to educational programming is as necessary today as it was a century ago. Firm literacy skills are essential, and yet today's prisoners often represent a population with low-level literacy rates and low educational attainment levels. While highlighting the complexities and nuances of working within a culture of corrections, we envision an educational pyramid (see Figure 12.1) to describe the way of learning in a prison. We envision the acquisition of literacy skills as the base of an educational pyramid on

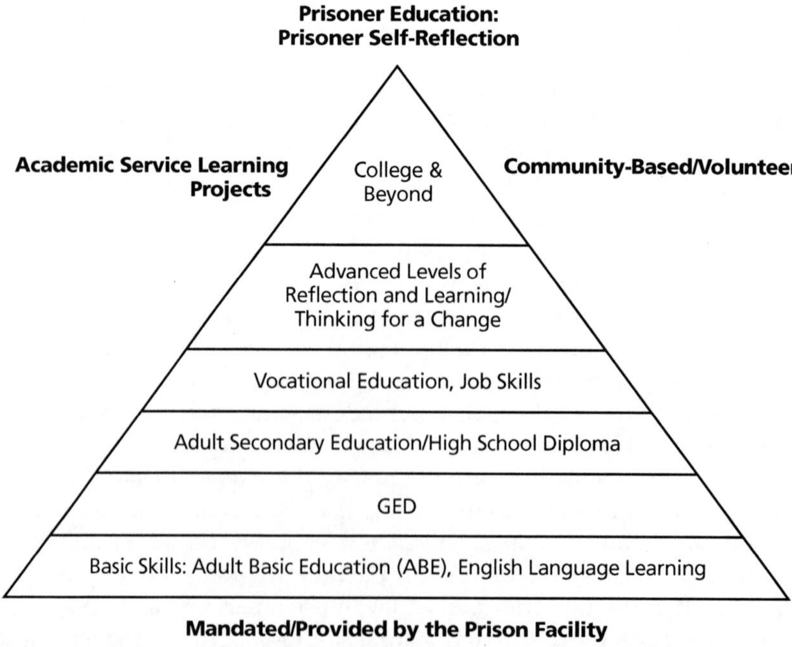

Figure 12.1 Educational pyramid of prison education programs.

which one builds the kind of skills that will prepare inmates for realizing self-worth and self-sufficiency. This raises the question not only of how to acquire the basic skills but how to advance up the pyramid. We continue the discussion by defining the people, places, and politics present in a culture of confinement.

THE CULTURE OF CONFINEMENT: PEOPLE, PLACE, AND POLITICS

The current vision for change, for creating "pockets of hope," must extend to the corrections system. As prison populations continue to increase, it becomes apparent that current corrections facilities cannot handle the ever growing numbers. The "outside" world fears this population and begrudges the financial burden of housing them. As adult educators, we must initially educate ourselves about the corrections system in order to be effective and educate the outside world of the benefits accrued for providing the kind of learning that meets individual needs, ranging from basic literacy to post secondary programs.

Literacy Levels of Prisoners

When prison schools first became a reality in the United States, prisoner illiteracy rates were surprisingly low. Figures indicate it was as low as 5.6% (Hill, 1924). According to a recent report from the United States Department of Justice Bureau Statistics (Harlow, 2003), 40% of inmates in state prisons, 27% of federal inmates, 47% of inmates in local jails, and 31% of those serving probation sentences had neither completed high school nor obtained a GED (Harlow, 2003). This is roughly twice the average for the non-incarcerated population; approximately 18% of the general population did not achieve high school graduation. Even more disturbing, the educational attainment figures for today's prisoners are closer to the national averages for non-incarcerated Americans in 1940. The educational attainment of today's inmates is closer to where the rest of the country was seventy years ago (Chlup, 2004, 2005).

While numbers only begin to tell part of the story, we mention the literacy levels of prisoners here to provide readers with a context for the need for literacy programming within the corrections system. To obtain these statistics we draw from the report *Literacy Behind Bars: Results from the 2003 National Assessment of Adult Literacy Prison Survey* (Greenberg, Dunleavy, & Kutner, 2007). The 2003 National Assessment of Adult Literacy (NAAL) assessed the English-language literacy of incarcerated adults and was administered to 1,200 inmates ages 16 and older in both state and federal prisons. The literacy rates of prisons had previously been assessed in 1992 by the National Adult Literacy Survey (NALS). The 2003 sample was representative of the 1,380,000 adults then imprisoned within the U.S. corrections system. According to the most recent figures, available year-end 2008, the number of incarcerated individuals has grown to 1,610,446 (Sabol, West, & Cooper, 2009). At the end of 2008, over 7.3 million people were either on probation, in jail or prison, or on parole (Bureau of Justice Statistics, 2009).

Rather than relying on indirect measures of literacy such as self-reports, the NAAL measured literacy directly through a series of tasks completed by the adults. The tasks were representative of a range of literacy activities that adults encounter on a daily basis. These tasks were organized into three categories: (1) prose literacy—examples of this type of literacy include editorials, news stories, brochures, instructional materials; (2) document literacy—examples of this type of literacy include job applications, payroll forms, maps, drug or food labels; and (3) quantitative literacy—examples of this type of literacy include balancing a check book, computing a tip, completing an order form, determining the amount of interest on a loan.

According to the assessment, 9% of incarcerated women perform below basic level when assessed on prose literacy. Fifteen percent perform below the basic level on document literacy, and an alarming 47% perform below the basic level on quantitative literacy assessments. The findings for male inmates were similar. Seventeen percent of males perform at below the basic level on prose literacy. Fifteen percent perform below the basic level on document literacy, and 39% perform below the basic level on quantitative literacy questions.

Incarcerated adults, in every age group examined (16 to 24, 25 to 39, and 40 or older), had lower average prose, document, and quantitative literacy than adults in the same age group living in U.S. households (Greenberg, Dunleavy, & Kutner, 2007). Those inmates who had obtained a high school diploma or a high school equivalency certificate had higher average prose, document, and quantitative literacy than prison inmates with lower levels of education (Greenberg et al., 2007).

The NAAL report also indicated that "29 percent of prison inmates had participated in some sort of vocational training. However, more inmates reported being on waiting lists for these programs than were enrolled" (Greenberg et al., 2007, p. 80). According to Greenberg et al. (2007), an overwhelming majority of prisoners in 2003 did have work assignments, 68%. Encouragingly, those with work assignments had higher average prose and quantitative literacy than inmates who did not have work assignments.

According to the NAAL:

> The relationship between literacy and participation in prison activities is complex. Inmates who enter prison with higher literacy may be more likely to engage in some activities, such as using the library and computers, reading, or even getting certain work assignments. Participating in any of these activities may help inmates improve their literacy. (Greenberg et al., 2007, p. 9)

If the research indicates that prisoners who participated in activities that required the use of literacy skills have higher average literacy scores than prisoners who did not, then why don't more prisoners participate in programming that use reading, writing, and numeracy activities? James, Witte, and Tal-Mason (1996) illustrate the distinction between participants in educational programming and non-participants when they refer to two classes of prisoners—convicts and inmates:

> Although inmates are likely to find literacy programs attractive, convicts regard them with contempt. Going to school just because 'they' say you should is an act of treason or cowardice.... Social pressures from convicts are much stronger than those from correctional educators.... The key to enhancing prisoners' participation in literacy programs, then, lies in getting to the convict. (p. 41)

Furthermore, they suggest that by making them each other's "accomplices in literacy," ultimately prisoners will be taking responsibility for their own education (p. 41). This is the difference between prisoner education, initiated by the prisoner, and prison education, initiated by the prison system.

Since prison is often a world where prisoners have no say, allowing prisoners to have responsibility in their own education opens the door for participatory literary practices. In the case of participatory literacy, students' input is used in the formation of the curriculum and the selection of relevant texts. The students work alongside teachers to determine what education is best for themselves and their classmates. Collins (1995) argues that participatory literacy practices counteract functionalist orientations by allowing participants in a prison setting to express themselves. Their voices and life stories become the primary learning materials and the reason for learning centers focusing less on learning to read and more on the needs of the individual learners who happen not to read.

By focusing on the needs of those incarcerated, we may learn from them just how desperately they wish to learn skills that will ease the transition back into life beyond the barbed fences. Simply gaining literacy and workforce skills may not be enough. Desired skills may include the set that assists with economic sustainability and employability.

THE COMPLEX RELATIONSHIP BETWEEN CRIME AND EMPLOYMENT

The relationship between employment and crime is complicated. A portrait of the challenges facing the employability of inmates begins to emerge when one considers that in addition to low literacy and the low educational attainment rate of prisoners, research indicates that 31% of state inmates have a physical impairment or mental condition, and 57% report they used drugs in the month prior to their arrest (Solomon, Johnson, Travis, & McBride, 2004). Additionally, convicted felons are legally barred from many sectors of the work world. It is no surprise that employment rates for ex-prisoners remain low.

Several surveys of ex-offenders provide evidence that their employment rates remain low or sporadic during their first critical months of release from prison. For instance, a survey of male prisoners returning to Chicago indicated that only 44% worked for at least a week in the first four to eight months following their prison release. This same survey found that much of the prisoners' post-release work was part-time (Kachnowski, 2005). In Baltimore, 64% worked within six months after their release, but again the majority of this work was sporadic or part-time (Visher, Kachnowski, La Vigne, & Travis, 2004). In the state of Florida, an analysis of unemployment insurance data found that only about 40% of former state prisoners were working at a job with unemployment insurance benefits one year after release (Tyler & Kling, 2004, cited in Bloom, 2006). Additionally Western, Kling, and Weiman (2001) found that earning rates of ex-prisoners are lower than those of similar individuals who have not spent time in prison.

In a labor market that offers fewer and fewer well-paying, stable work opportunities to individuals without a prison record, it is not surprising that people enter the corrections system hard to employ and leave it harder to employ. As employment prospects in the United States worsen, even for those with a postsecondary education, the aggregate effects of low-level literacy skills, incarceration, and low employment possibility increase for ex-inmates. The accumulation of these disadvantages is startling and underscores the need for educational programming for prisoners. Therefore, we introduce at this point some of the current prison literacy efforts.

LESSONS LEARNED: CURRENT PRISON LITERACY EFFORTS

The diversity of prison literacy work is evident in the various types of educational programming available for inmates. A sampling of categories include:

- service learning academic programs
- college-based programming

- inmates as peer–tutors
- critical literacy instruction
- family literacy programs
- vocational, prison-to-work programs
- arts-based education: writing, drama, photography, visual arts, music
- General Educational Development (GED), Adult Basic Education (ABE), Adult Secondary Education (ASE), and English as a Second Language (ESL) classes

Investment in educational programs has been declining and the percentages of inmates participating in federal and state programs have likewise declined. Findings indicate that 52% of inmates participate in educational programming: only 3% of inmates participate in an ABE class, 23% in GED/high school, 32% in vocational training, 10% in college coursework, 1% in ESL, and 3% in an "other" category (Stephan & Karberg, 2003). These figures are indicative of the constraints that educational programs in correctional facilities face. As White (2004) reports, "On some level, there is an inherent conflict between the philosophy of incarceration and the philosophy of education. The goal of education, a free-thinking mind, encounters opposition in a setting where basic freedoms have been stripped away" (p. 56).

Correctional institutions hold at their core institutionalizing individuals. Inmates are expected to ask permission to do anything and everything. It follows that education for personal transformation, especially when formalized by prison instructors, would be viewed as going against the system. In addition to low levels of participation, declining funding, and resources for educational programming, other constraints include correctional educators with little preparation specific to the needs of incarcerated learners, interruptions from lock downs, visits that cut into class time, court dates that keep students from participating, restrictions that limit materials that can be brought into and out of the prison, and lack of support from correctional staff who see providing inmates with an education as unnecessary and secondary to the purpose of prisons (Kerka, 1995). Prison educators often have long-running programs disbanded or arbitrarily changed with little discussion or direction provided by prison administrators. The changes and disruptions leave educators frustrated, or worse, ready to quit. It is no wonder that prison education is also political education as there are so many barriers and contexts to consider in the process of educating this population of adult learners.

The co-authors of this chapter, prison educators who are continually evolving in our own thinking, recommend keeping in mind that, "We must meet the prisoner as a person, and listen to [their stories]. As [they] speak about [their] lives and experiences... a human face is suddenly superimposed over the mind-numbing numbers" (Chesney-Lind, 1997, p. 8). As adult educators, it is imperative to stay attuned to that voice, to listen to the stories—the lived experiences—in order to assess and address the needs, learning abilities, and styles. This also means being conscious of our own teacher complicity with the very structures we critique while we reap benefits and privileges that are denied to most if not all of our students. In choosing to work with our students, we must continually unpack our own race, class, gender, sexual orientation privileges and avoid what Macedo (2006) terms "benevolent oppression" or a "do-gooder posture [that] smacks of the false generosity of paternalism" (p. 216). At times, we realize we may fall guilty of adhering to good intentions that are a form of "compassionate racism" or classism or sexism or any other -ism (Macedo, 2006, p. 217). The challenge remains in recognizing these moments, acknowledging them with humility, and moving forward, having learned from the experience.

Prisons, similar to society on the outside, experience the same levels of biases, prejudices, and discrimination. Politically speaking, in addition to race and class biases, the corrections system is deeply entrenched in patriarchy, a red flag with respect to the status of incarcerated women. As Baird noted in Sheared and Sissel's *Making Space* (2001), incarcerated women are silenced and invisible. Talvi (2007) confirmed that nothing had changed in the many prisons she visited. She recorded, "...most of the [current females] feel they are a nearly invisible group that has been dehumanized, forgotten and locked away... [their] realities have simply been reduced to their offenses and prison numbers (Talvi, 2007, p. 14). If women feel this way on the inside of prisons, imagine how they feel when trying to re-enter society, a society that often shuns them. It is no secret that towns and communities do not want former inmates living in them. Community members would prefer to believe the adage that all prisoners have been locked up and the key has been thrown away. This is not the reality as 97% of prisoners currently serving sentences will be released and returned to our communities. In the next section, we detail a few of the programs that have been put in place to ease with their transition home.

Re-Entry Programs

Although statistical reports indicate that 97% of prisoners will re-enter our communities, most employment-focused educational programs do not begin until just weeks prior to an inmate's release. Two such programs are the Offender Re-entry Program (ORP) in Suffolk County, Massachusetts and the Texas Project RIO (Reintegration of Offenders).

The ORP offers soon-to-be-released inmates an intensive 6-hours-per-day course of study over a six-week period provided by Bunker Hill Community

College. Inmates receive job assistance at a one-stop career center. Upon re-entry, the inmates continue to receive support from mentors from the faith-based Ella J. Baker House and case work management provided by Community Resources for Justice. They may receive support for six months or longer if they so choose. Similarly, Texas' Project RIO provides incarcerated prisoners with a variety of resources, the goal of which is to match released prisoners with jobs. These services include a week-long job search workshop and job placement assistance before and after they are released.

While we applaud the efforts of these programs, a program of one week or even six weeks is simply too short a period of time to raise one's educational attainment level or job skills to the level required in a demanding labor market. If inmates are to succeed in the re-entry process, then education, job training, career development, and useful work experience must take place over the entire period of incarceration, not simply in the last few days or weeks. Better programming would include employee match programs where corrections institutions work specifically with employers who offer well-paying jobs with benefits and career advancement opportunities to give inmates skills that will be used in jobs lined up and waiting for them once they are released. We would also encourage former inmates to turn around and offer assistance to the men and women coming behind them. Inmates helping inmates is a real possibility and offers incredible potential for everyone involved. Below we describe how Jimmy Santiago Baca, a former inmate himself, is attempting to make a difference in the lives of inmates.

Inmates Helping Inmates

Jimmy Santiago Baca's New Mexico prison literacy project, Cedar Tree, Inc., attempts to make books, reading, and writing very real and necessary components of inmates' lives. Baca is an award-winning poet and author who learned to read and write while incarcerated in the Arizona prison system on drug charges from 1973–1978. He began Cedar Tree, Inc. in 2004 to support his vision of giving the opportunity to all incarcerated people to become educated. The goal of the project is to provide inmates throughout the term of their incarceration with the tools they need to enrich and elevate their spirit so they may attain goals that are grounded, responsible, and contributory. The motto of the non-profit organization is "creating a new life through writing." As an adult with low-literacy skills, Baca can bear witness to the power of writing and literature. He believes that by providing workshops to people in prisons, detention centers, and schools for at-risk youth, his organization can help individuals "gain self-knowledge and instill self-reliance as they explore issues such as race, culture, addiction, community, and responsibility" (Cedar Tree, Inc., 2009b).

Cedar Tree, Inc., as an organization, goes beyond just assisting inmates and adjudicated youth while they are behind bars. The organization employs ex-offenders as interns to assist with the production of documentaries and the development of curricula for incarcerated populations. Self-reliance in this way becomes not just a theoretical component but a lived component for the men and women who come into contact with Cedar Tree, Inc. In a real sense, these former inmates are true service providers. Lori Pompa, in her education program, hopes to provide service learning. Her interesting and inspiring technique follows in the next section.

Service Learning: Becoming Literate

Temple University's Professor Lori Pompa's "The Inside-Out Prison Exchange Program Exploring Issues of Crime and Justice Behind the Walls" takes a unique approach to literacy. She aims to make her "outside" college students literate about prisons while simultaneously making her "inside" inmate-students learn to read their lives in relation to the context of the criminal justice system. Both sets of students meet together weekly for two and a half hours inside the prison. The course, while designed as a service course, aims to do more for both sets of students. "The course is arranged in such a way that we all teach and we all learn together, in a true partnership. The service, therefore, is less a question of 'doing for' than 'being with,' a mutual exchange" (Pompa, 2004, p. 27). The students write a series of reflection papers and a final paper, and read five to six criminal justice texts. Throughout the class, Pompa asks her students to reflect upon "what prisons are for; why people get involved in crime; the myths and realities of prison life; victims and victimization; and the distinction between punishment and rehabilitation" (Pompa, 2004, p. 26).

Pompa (2004) believes there is a liberating quality to becoming literate. She warns that too often we are unaware of what keeps us imprisoned. She explains, "The inability to read—whether the writing in a book or 'the writing on the wall,' or even the writing on our own hearts—can keep anyone of us trapped in a narrow, limited world" (p. 31). Through discovering this level of personal literacy, student inmates gain "the power to turn things inside-out and upside down" (Pompa, 2004, p. 33). In this way, inmates and the college students are given the skills to take action and make change. This is, indeed, a "pocket of hope," an example of teachers and students changing their worlds together.

AN ALTERNATIVE LEARNING MODEL: A CASE EXAMPLE FROM PENNSYLVANIA

We turn the focus now to the program of Irene Baird, one of the co-authors of this chapter. In doing so, we offer here one of our own examples of a "pocket of hope." Baird's "academic" entrance into the culture of corrections happened through an evolutionary process. She spent years facilitating discussion groups for women, using books as the medium for developing positive identity formation and empowerment at a time when women's issues began to be highlighted. During that time, she was also facilitating programs for single welfare mothers who were struggling primarily with economic issues and learning simultaneously that their perspectives/perceptions and choices as women made a difference in the outcomes of their preparation. Those two roads converged with a Pennsylvania Humanities Council grant in 1992 to pilot a project with homeless women at the local YWCA, in collaboration with the then head of the Pennsylvania Women's Commission. A group of the women agreed to participate in the eight-week study, which was designed to assess the efficacy of a book-oriented program as a process for exploring and addressing the crises in their lives. A non-threatening model, the process involved reading, reflection, and discussion of the parable-like nature of the words of authors of similar race, class, and experience. A creative expression component affirmed the insights from the book discussion and reflection. These newly acquired voices subsequently appeared in booklet format, which contributed to the participants' identity and esteem formation and empowerment. Actually, it was a Freirean-like exercise in that the participants' "object" status evolved into that of "subject" as they were learning to acknowledge, accept, and confront their issues in order to take charge of their lives.

Its success generated a larger grant that led to the creation, in 1994, of a program for incarcerated women. At that time, basic education was one of the few programs available to them. The cognitive-based, humanities-oriented model, validated at the YWCA project, seemed paradoxical given the issues the inmates were facing until it became apparent that exploring their crises and searching for resolution served an unmet need. The program annually provided four ten-week sessions to participants, regardless of academic background. Those who could not read could listen and discuss. Those whose writing skills were negligible could tell their stories to a facilitator who would write down the story; the typed version served a dual purpose in strengthening basic skills while sharing a story. In addition, the Latinas could write their story in Spanish and have it translated into English. The efficacy of this process was evident in the experience of a young inmate with marginal literacy skills. After listening to Maya Angelou's personal story of having been raped as a child and choosing to remain mute for several years, the inmate chose to break her silence by dictating a violent rape experience, committed by a group of males. She learned to read the typed copy to her counselor and the healing began.

Based on the selection of books, the program's flexibility lends itself to explore a variety of themes such as esteem, identity, parenting, incarceration, and relationships. In the discussion and writing, however, stories such as the one above predominated. As a result, in 1999, a program based on the same format as the women's began for the males; the only addition to the men's books was the inclusion of the women's writing about their abuse. Vanzant's book for men, *Up From Here* (2002) served to address this pervasive problem. Her theory is that men had ingrained the concept of "how to *do*" and were recognized for their physical performance; neglected or absent was the concept of how to *be* a man, how to behave in a considerate, non-abusive manner. Given the prison's patriarchal environment, it was amazing that the use of this book, with this concept, was explored and accepted. It was, however, an important and necessary perspective to introduce, given the status of women in general and within the prison culture, in particular.

The prevailing societal attitude seems to be that, for survival, inmates must learn basic skills for successful reentry into the community. Hill (1924) argued, however, that this should not be the overriding factor, that there should be a higher purpose, one of achieving "self-respect," "consciousness of power," a sense of balance as noted in the preceding paragraphs. This falls into a complementary kind of learning, the cognitive-based, Freirean orientation that emboldens the "objects" to evolve into "subjects," who, as a result, are ready to successfully acquire the skills as they take control of their lives. In the next section, we describe the educational pyramid we believe prison programmers can make available for prisoners to gain these skills.

WAYS OF LEARNING: AN EDUCATIONAL PYRAMID

Given the central focus of this book on learning "to earn" to achieve self-sufficiency, we envision a path to prisoner self-sufficiency to be a pyramid with the acquisition of literacy skills as the base. While we recognize that no figure would definitively capture our vision, we believe the pyramid is a start. We believe that learning to think about what one is doing and learning to do is essential at all levels of the pyramid. For instance, one can robotically learn the mechanics of doing A, B, C, but without cognition and higher-order thinking skills, the positive, healthy aspects integral to development and growth, what does any of it mean?

Both the incarcerated females and males indicate a preference for "hands-on" learning, "tell me or show me a few times, and I'll learn to do it." This is consistent with Baird's (1994a,b) research with single welfare mothers on how they learn how to make a successful transition from welfare to work. They rejected book learning, which they classified as boring school book learning, but they accepted manuals designed to teach practical skills. As one woman said, "Just by following the manual and some directions from my boyfriend, I learned to change the transmission in my car!" Such messages reject regimented school practices that do not consider or value alternative learning styles and abilities. When only one kind of learning is emphasized, a learner is lost and the desire for education is suppressed.

The inmates also reject theories about the purported reason for their incarceration. Again, theorizing is perceived as a useless academic exercise that fails to understand that this is learned behavior. As one male inmate explained, "When my father died my uncle took over my learning, to change me from a cub to a lion or bear." This inmate's learning experiences represented a form of modeling, and in this case, resulting in a negative outcome.

Superimposed or complementary to the literacy preparation on the educational pyramid is the process that engages the inmate in taking the reflective inward journey—a practical, non-threatening first step toward self-awareness, self-acceptance, and ultimately, self-empowerment.

This process is implemented in a variety of ways that are not training, the "*doing*-centered" process. It speaks to Vanzant's (2002) focus on "*being*." The process is also implicit in Thinking for a Change (T4C, n.d.), an intervention initiated nationally by the National Institute of Corrections (NIC) in 1997. It is a cognitive-based format directed towards thinking, learning to *be* (see Vanzant, 2002). Within the series of 22 lessons, participants are expected to identify and examine the behaviors that led to incarceration. The purpose is to recognize that there is a thinking problem that needs to be explored and addressed. Stressed, also, is the imperative that there are consequences to actions. To date, NIC has trained more than 6,000 corrections staff as facilitators in a program that can be used with juveniles and adults, with males and females in settings such as jails, prisons, probation, and parole supervision sites (T4C, n.d.). This kind of learning serves as another preparatory step up the pyramid towards job skills acquisition.

Near the middle of the pyramid are programs at the high school level (see Figure 12.1). Most prisons and some jails require basic adult education and GED participation. A community college counselor offers sessions on the availability of vocational and academic courses upon release along with the availability of counseling and study technique support. Despite the demise of Pell Grants for prison college courses (Baird, 2009), several academic institutions are reaching out to prisons, recognizing that an educated released prisoner can be an asset and not a deficit to the community. Models/benchmarks to inspire and strive for are the programs at San Quentin (n.d.) in California and Bard College in New York. Both are privately funded and are successful. Bard's course catalog for prisoners rivals that of any liberal arts institution and there is a correlation of all course offerings across the states' sites so that if an inmate is moved there is no gap in the educational process. Bard College (2009) is also in the process of establishing a liberal arts program for females at Bayview Women's Prison in New York City.

The preceding ways of learning speak to an evolutionary process from the basics to the top of the pyramid. Adjuncts to this process, however, are support and advocacy groups such as Women Work! The National Network for Women's Employment (n.d.). This Washington, DC-based organization, which has offices nationwide, began as a support system for displaced homemakers, women with negligible or no work skills who were forced to provide for themselves because they had been displaced or deserted by their husbands. The organization does impressive advocacy on equity in workplace issues and provides counseling and programs dealing with budgeting/financial management, skills acquisition, and education to enhance esteem and economic security. It strongly promotes education as a step towards a career with benefits and opportunities for advancement and self-sufficiency rather than an hourly-paid job in fast food services or cosmetology as examples. At the organization's 2008 conference, the topics included, "Meeting the Employment Needs of Incarcerated and Formerly Incarcerated Women" and "Issues of Post-Secondary Access for Underrepresented Populations." Nationwide, there is a uniformity of program offerings to provide continuity for clients who relocate to another city or state. One of the inmates in Baird's prison group has taken advantage of this kind of service and recommends it highly for its services, which include support groups.

In the preceding sections, we detailed several types of prison education programs that work. In our concluding section, we trouble the waters by reminding educators that education for prisoners needs to go beyond adult basic education and literacy. We argue for multi-layered education that takes into account all of the barriers that prisoners face.

UNLOCKING THE CELL: MOVING BEYOND BASIC LITERACY EDUCATION

While prison literacy efforts are to be applauded, the time has come to move beyond basic literacy education for inmates. As Baird (2001) noted nearly a decade ago:

> Literacy classes are now being offered; however, they do not go far enough in terms of addressing inmates' problems. Even though these classes stress basic reading and writing skills, these skills are approached in a technical [mechanical] 'school book learning' way. Given that these women's [and men's] lives and the reality of their imprisonment are interconnected with who they are in terms of their race, class and gender, it is imperative that adult education classes reflect that reality. (p. 177)

Similarly, O'Connor (2004) has reflected on varying literacy work to encourage moving beyond passing the GED test to educational programs that encourage self-expression and self-development. If we are to move forward helping inmates to become self-reliant and self-sufficient upon their release, then we need to embrace, support, and encourage more programs to become "pockets of hope." Freire articulated the pedagogy of hope as something that "teaches us that the significance of dreaming, of imagining what could be as opposed to remaining paralyzed in what is. Dreaming keeps these pockets of hope energized and focused. Hope keeps them from despair" (as cited in de Los Reyes & Gozemba, 2002, p. xii). If we are to embrace a pedagogy of hope, we need to engage in the ongoing practice of critical education and continue to have the courage as intellectuals and academics to use our resources to address the pressing social issues of the time. The education of prisoners is one of these pressing issues. We need to continue to consider that the complexity of the issue as the plight of prisoners cannot be summed up in a single chapter or statement. Structural, societal, and institutional policies all need to be examined and reexamined if we are to make advancements in unlocking the cell. Author Iyanla Vanzant (1998) wrote that there are many kinds of jails; she reminds us that we are all doing some kind of time, and it is our responsibility to unlock the personal cell. Under the umbrella of Education of Prisoners, increasing educational opportunities and caring adult educators is the recognition that education does unlock the cell.

REFERENCES

Baird, I. C. (1994a). The humanities for homeless women: A paradox in learning. *Adult Learning, 5*(3), 13, 15.

Baird, I. C. (1994b). *Learning to earn 'the right way': Single welfare mothers in mandated education.* Unpublished Doctoral Dissertation, Pennsylvania State University.

Baird, I. C. (2001). Education, incarceration and the marginalization of women. In V. Sheared & P. Sissel (Eds.), *Making space: Merging theory and practice in adult education* (pp. 168–181). Westport, CT: Bergin & Garvey.

Baird, I. C. (2009). The education of prisoners: A holistic perspective. *Pennsylvania Association for Adult and Continuing Education (PAACE). Journal of Lifelong Learning, 18,* 1–12.

Bard College. (2009). *Bard Prison Initiative.* Retrieved January 16, 2009, from http://www.bard.edu/bpi/

Bloom, D. (2006). *Employment-focused programs for ex-prisoners: What have we learned, what are we learning, and where should we go from here?* New York: Manpower Demonstration Research Corporation (MDRC).

Bureau of Justice Statistics. (2009). *Key facts at a glance: Correctional populations.* Retrieved February 10, 2010, from http://bjs.ojp.usdoj.gov/content/glance/tables/corr2tab.cfm

Cedar Tree, Inc. (2009a). *Goals.* Retrieved January 25, 2009, from http://www.jimmysantiagobaca.com/projects.html

Cedar Tree, Inc. (2009b). *Mission.* Retrieved January 25, 2009, from http://cedartreeinc.org/

Chesney-Lind, M. (1997). *The female offender: Girls, women, and crime.* Thousand Oaks, CA: Sage Publications.

Chlup, D. T. (2004). *Educative justice: The history of the educational programs and practices at the Massachusetts Reformatory for women, 1930–1960.* Unpublished doctoral dissertation, Harvard University Graduate School of Education.

Chlup, D. T. (2005). Tides of change: The last 70 years of correctional education. *Focus on Basics, 7D,* 21–24.

Coley, R. J., & Barton, P. E. (2006). *Locked up and locked out: An educational perspective on the U. S. prison population.* Policy Information Report. Princeton, NJ: Educational Testing Service.

Collins, M. (1995). Adult literacy and the correctional ethos. In Davidson, H. S. (Ed.). *Schooling in a "total institution"* (pp. 49–63). Westport, CT: Bergin & Garvey.

De Los Reyes, E., & Gozemba, P. A. (2002). *Pockets of hope: How students and teachers change the world.* Westport, CT: Bergin & Garvey.

Freire, P. (1985). *The politics of education.* South Hadley, MA: Bergin & Garvey.

Freire, P., & Macedo, D. (1987). *Literacy: Reading the word and the world.* South Hadley, MA: Bergin & Garvey.

Giroux, H. A. (1983). *Theory and resistance in education: A pedagogy for the opposition.* South Hadley, MA: Bergin and Garvey.

Greenberg, E., Dunleavy, E., & Kutner, M. (2007). *Literacy behind bars: Results from the 2003 National Assessment of Adult Literacy prison survey* (NCES 2007–473). Washington, DC: U.S. Department of Education Institute of Education Sciences.

Harlow, C. W. (2003). *Education and correctional populations.* Bureau of Justice Statistics Special Report. Washington, DC: U.S. Department of Justice, Office of Justice Programs.

Hill, A. C. (1924). *Schools for adults in prisons, 1923.* Washington, DC: Department of the Interior Bureau of Education.

James, W. B., Witte, J. E., & Tal-Mason, D. (1996). Prisons as communities: Needs and challenges. *New Directions for Adult and Continuing Education, 70,* 37–46.

Jacobi, T. (2004). 'I'm just gonna let you know how it is:' Situating writing and literacy education in prison. [Forward] *Reflections, 4*(1), 1–11.

Kachnowski, V. (2005). *Returning home Illinois policy brief: Employment and prisoner reentry.* Washington, DC: The Urban Institute.

Kerka, S. (1995). *Prison literacy programs.* Eric Digest No. 159. Columbus, OH: ERIC Clearinghouse on Adult Career and Vocational Education.

Macedo, D. (2006). *Literacies of power: What Americans are not allowed to know.* Boulder, CO: Westview Press.

O'Connor, P. E. (2004). Afterword: Rewriting the story of prison literacies. *Reflections, 4*(1), 199–208.

Pompa, L. (2004). Disturbing where we are comfortable: Notes from behind the walls. *Reflections, 4*(1), 24–34.

Porporino, F. J., & Robinson, D. (1992). The correctional benefits of education. *Journal of Correctional Education, 43*(2), 92–98.

Sabol, W. J., West, H. C., & Cooper, M. (2009). *Bureau of Justice statistics bulletin: Prisoners in 2008.* Washington, DC: Department of Justice.

San Quentin (n.d.). Retrieved January 16, 2009, from http://www.prisonuniversity-project.org/pages/about/about-us.html

Solomon, A., Johnson, K., Travis, J., & McBride, E. (2004). *From prison to work: The employment dimensions of prisoner reentry.* Washington, DC: The Urban Institute.

Stephan, J. J. & Karberg, J. C. (2003). *Census of state and federal correctional facilities, 2000.* Washington, DC: U.S. Department of Justice, Bureau of Justice Statistics.

Thinking for a Change. (n.d.). Retrieved January 16, 2009, from http://community.ncic.org/forums/p 1857/1212.aspx+12129?15/2008

Tyler, J. & Kling, J. (2004). *Prison-based education and re-entry into the mainstream labor market.* Brown University Department of Economics working paper.

UNESCO. (1966). *An Asian model of educational development.* Paris: UNESCO.

Vanzant, I. (1998). *Yesterday, I cried.* New York: Simon & Schuster.

Vanzant, I. (2002). *Up from here.* New York: Harper Collins Publishers.

Visher, C., Kachnowski, V., La Vigne, N., & Travis, J. (2004). *Baltimore prisoners' experiences returning home.* Washington, DC: The Urban Institute.

Western, K., Kling, J. & Weiman, D. (2001). *The labor market consequences of incarceration.*

Working paper #450. Princeton, NJ: Princeton University Industrial Relations Section. Retrieved January 16, 2009, from http://www.irs.princeton.edu/pubs/working_papers.html

White, T. (2004). Learning disabilities among the incarcerated. *Reflections, 4*(1), 51–60.

Women Work! (n.d.). Retrieved January 16, 2009, from www.womenwork.org

CHAPTER 13

THE ROLE OF SOCIAL CAPITAL IN DEVELOPING ECONOMIC SELF-SUFFICIENCY

Mary V. Alfred
Texas A&M University

During the production of this book, I have been engaged in self-reflection about my early beginnings in a small farming and fishing village on the tiny island of St. Lucia in the Eastern Caribbean. Reading these chapters on low-income and low-literate adults' struggle to live, to learn, and to earn a living reminded me of my own community's struggle for economic well-being. You see, at the time (mid 1950s to mid 1970s), we did not conceptualize our lives as one of struggles; it was the life we knew and the one we lived. I grew up in a home where my father, who was very intelligent in terms of his oratory skills, his conceptual skills, and his ability to run a successful small meat business, was functionally illiterate—he could not read and write the English language. My mother, although literate, did not complete compulsory education (which at the time was through the age of 15). That was the case of the majority of the members in my rural village, whose livelihood depended on fishing, subsistence farming, share cropping, and craft work.

To understand the context of the narrative, one has to understand a brief history of the island. St. Lucia, first inhabited by Carib and Arawak Indians,

Learning for Economic Self-Sufficiency, pages 213–228

was later discovered by Christopher Columbus in 1502 (although some historians dispute this claim). Many attempts were made by European settlers during the 1600s to settle the island, with the French claiming the first successful attempt in 1746. During the French colonization, the British sought to establish their claim over the island as well. It is noted that both Britain and France saw St. Lucia as a strategic fort from which to launch their exploitation and settlement of the other Caribbean islands. Therefore, for over one hundred years Britain and France were engaged in bitter battles for the possession of the island, and as a result, it changed hands 14 times between the two European nations. The British won the final battle in 1803, and the island was finally ceded to Britain in 1814. In 1842 English became the official language, but a variation of the French language known as Creole Patois, together with French customs, behaviors, and cultures persisted. Moreover, from 1600 to 1870, about four million slaves from West Africa were imported to the Caribbean to work on the sugar plantations. Upon abolition of slavery in St. Lucia in 1838, indentured servants and field laborers were recruited from Southeast Asia, making St. Lucia a multicultural, multiethnic, and multilingual society. This conglomerate of races, ethnicities, languages (West African, English, French Patois, Indian), and cultures made it difficult for the population, particularly those in rural communities, to prosper in what had became an English society. Nevertheless, they found ways to manage the living conditions they had been dealt.

One of the ways that people managed was through a form of networking and exchange of labor and other services. For example, it was a common practice for the rural farmers to help one another in preparing the land for planting. This is how it worked: On Monday, for example, about ten men would gather to help one farmer plough a plot of land. The wife of the farmer who was receiving the service would prepare breakfast and lunch to feed the workers. On another scheduled day, the same farmers, including the one who was helped on Monday, would gather to help one other farmer plough the land, and so the rotation continued until all the farmers in the network had received help from each other. The same practice of self-help happened when one was building a basic home. The community members with various skills gathered to help the home owner. While the men did the physical work, the women did the cooking to feed the workers and other support services. Over a weekend, the basic structures of the home would be built, an event similar to that practiced by today's Habitat for Humanity. However, the process practiced during my early beginnings in the Caribbean was informal, guided by a set of unwritten rules and common understanding. This practice of accumulating and reallocating labor was a form of economic cooperation and the development of economic sustenance in an era when financial capital was not readily available.

At the age of 18, I left my small rural community to attend Teachers' College in the capital city. There I lived with my aunt and her family in what was considered at the time a middle class community, with employment stemming from government, retail, service, and tourism industries. While living with my aunt, I learned of another effort at accumulating financial capital trough networking and collaboration among community groups. Groups of women would come together to form small clubs for the purpose of pooling together small amounts of financial resources. It was a financial networking scheme whereby on a predetermined schedule (monthly, biweekly, etc.), a group of women would contribute a certain amount of money to a pool, which would be allocated to one of the women in the group. For example, if the group consisted of ten women and each contributed $100 a month, each member would receive $1,000 at some point in time. One member of the group is elected to collect and distribute the funds to the predetermined member. The group was kept small, often among close friends, families, and co-workers. This form of community-based savings is referred to in some Caribbean islands as *su-su* and as *partner* in others. According to Seibel (2001), this practice of rotating savings is an ancient one, dating back to at least the 16th century, when Yoruba slaves carried it to the Caribbean. It is a form of micro-economy that has persisted to this day, and according to Siebel, can be found in many parts of the world. Caribbean immigrants, for example, have brought this microfinance system with them to the new country and it has become viable economic systems in the U.S. and UK, despite the proliferation of modern opportunities for building human and economic capital.

The question, then, is, *What was the fundamental core that made these micro-economic systems and rotating physical capital arrangements effective and allowed to persist over long periods of time?* As one examines more closely these informal arrangements and relationships, it becomes clear that *trust* was the underlying factor upon which these relationships were built. There were no written policies, rules, and regulations, but a clear understanding of the commitments each member had made to the group. The members trusted each other, and individuals felt accountable for the success of the group. There was also the element of individual and group pride, a sense of integrity, and the desire to not disappoint self and others. They understood the concept of "give and take" and of community uplift through networking, collaboration, and exchange of resources. Today, this concept of collaboration, networking, and sharing of resources within an element of trust for the improvement and well being of individuals and groups is referred to as social capital (Bourdieu, 1986; Coleman, 1998; Putnam, 2000). The purpose of this chapter is to examine the role of social capital in the development of economic self-sufficiency. It begins with a brief overview of the theoretical literature on social capital theory and then explores how tenets of social capital can be used to enhance opportunities for economically disadvantaged adults, despite its limitations. The chapter concludes with a discussion of the role of education programs and workplace organizations in building social capital among their members.

UNDERSTANDING SOCIAL CAPITAL THEORY

Many have credited Bourdieu (1977, 1986), Coleman (1988, 1998), and Putnam (2000) for their pioneering work on social capital theory. Bourdieu became interested in the ways that members of the middle and upper class were able to capitalize on material and human resource inherent in networks and social groups to advance their own interests (Alfred, 2009). According to Alfred, Bourdieu's conception of social capital emphasizes the resources that people use to secure their own positional advantage. His argument is that social capital is part of the wider structural relations and subjective beliefs that are associated with inequalities of resources and power. He further argues that inequality is caused by the unequal access to and interaction of various kinds of capitals—namely symbolic, cultural, and social. His significant contribution to our understanding of the theory is the interconnection of social capital and social inequalities and the importance of social capital as a source of power to advance one's interest and leverage one's position within a given context.

Unlike Bourdieu, Coleman (1988, 1998) employed the concept of social capital in educational research among young children. Comparing school success among students in public and private schools, Coleman concluded that students in private schools performed better than those in public schools because there was a stronger sense of community and community norms which the parents, teachers, and students embraced (Alfred, 2009). Coleman also examined the educational attainment in poor urban communities and found that social capital could have significant benefits to poor and marginalized communities. He therefore theorized that communities were a source of social capital that could offset some of the impact of socioeconomic disadvantages. As Field (2005) explains, "Social capital, according to Coleman, represents a resource because it involves the expectation of reciprocity, and goes beyond any given individual to involve wider networks whose relationships are governed by a high degree of trust and shared values" (p. 23).

Another major contributor to the theory of social capital is Putnam (2000), who applied Coleman's conceptualization of social capital in his landmark work on the role of trustworthiness and obligation in civil society. Situating his work within the realm of political science, Putnam contends that participation in civic associations can rekindle social solidarity and help to revitalize a decaying community. His basic argument is that in order to build civil society, there must be an element of trust and reciprocity among community members, which could be accomplished through participation in community organizations. Putnam posits that social capital serves both a bonding and a bridging function. As a bonding function, it tends to reinforce community values, cultures, and group homogeneity. As a bridging function, Putnam suggests that social capital can provide linkages to networks and acquaintances that are external to one's immediate community. It is not unusual for ethnic minorities, for example, to have good bonding relations with members of their racioethnic group, but they often have weak bridging ties that link them beyond their ethnocultural communities.

BENEFITS OF SOCIAL CAPITAL: ROLE OF NETWORKS AND COMMUNITIES

The concept of social capital is based on the understanding that informal and formal structures form around certain basic human needs. Some networks are heterogeneous and open to a diversity of participants, while other networks are homogeneous and accept people who share the same characteristics. The basic idea of social capital is that one's family, friends, and associates represent an important asset that can be called upon during periods of crises, enjoyed for its own sake, or leveraged for material gain (Woolcock, 2001). Woolcock therefore concluded that communities were a source of social capital that could offset some of the impact of socioeconomic disadvantages. Similarly, some argue that communities that have a rich array of social networks and civic associations will be in a stronger position to confront poverty and vulnerability or take advantage of new opportunities (Moser, 1996; Woolcock, 1998; Woolcock & Narayan, 2000). Conversely, the absence of significant social networks and ties can hinder access to opportunities and other resources.

According to Lin (2001), individuals engage in interactions and networking in order to produce profits. This assertion suggests social capital is an investment in social relations with an expectation of a beneficial return to those who invest in the relationship. Lin provides the following explanations on the benefits of social networking: (1) it facilitates the flow of information from those with access to those with a need to know; (2) social ties may influence those in power positions to behave favorably towards those who are in less desirable positions who rely on them for help in improving their conditions; (3) those in power positions may serve as social credentials for those seeking entry in employing organizations and other institutions (for example, colleges and universities); (4) the expectation is that social relations will reinforce an individual's identity and visibility within a social group or community.

Social Capital and Information Flow

In an economic downturn with unstable workplace conditions, social networks located in strategic locations or certain hierarchical positions are often better informed about the market and work opportunities. Therefore, individuals in these networks are in a better position to obtain useful information about career and educational opportunities that might not ordinarily be available to them. Similarly, these network ties can help bridge organizational needs with the talents and interests of those invisible to the organization. According to Lin, "Such information would reduce the transaction cost for the organization to recruit 'better' (be it skilled, or technical, or cultural knowledge) individuals and for individuals to find 'better' organizations that can use their capital and provide appropriate rewards" (2001, p. 7). As Alfred (2009) noted, social networks become an information broker between leaders of work organizations and the lay individuals who seek entry into the culture of these organizations.

Social Networks as Agents of Influence

Members of social capital networks may exert influence on decisions about who is included and excluded from organizational life. Some social ties, due to their strategic locations and positions within the hierarchy, carry valued resources and exercise greater power, which can influence organizational decisions in favor of network members. As Lin (2001) noted, "Putting in a word carries a certain weight in the decision-making process regarding an individual" (p. 7). This viewpoint suggests that those who are fortunate to make entry into networks of influence stand to benefit from the power inherent in such social interactions. However, Sandefur and Laumann (2000) remind us that influence and control can be characterized by the ability to influence and control others and the ability to be free of the influence and control of others. Therefore, network members in power positions should use their power to create access rather than deny access to those in less powerful social positions.

Promoting Social Credentials Through Social Networks

According to Lin, putting in a word for a network member carries a certain weight and represents a form of credentialing:

> Standing behind the individual by these ties reassures the organization and its agents that the individual has resources that would be meaningful to the well-

> being of the organization. It makes visible an individual's assets that may not be apparent to those who do not hold membership in that person's networks and social relations. (Lin, 2001, p. 7)

Moreover, Cote and Levine (2002) observe that this social support and social credentialing, when it is made available to individuals, promotes positive identity and a "can do" attitude.

Social Networking and Identity Capital Reinforcement

Advocates of social capital theory (Cote & Levine, 2002; Field, 2005; Lin, 2001) hold the view that building relations and participating in the right networks increase one's sense of personal identity. According to Lin, being assured of one's worthiness as an individual and as a member of a social group provides emotional support and an acknowledgement of one's claim to certain resources. The rewards one garners as a result of participating in network relations reinforces self-identity, and that identity capital has been found to be essential for maintaining mental health and negotiating essential resources. Cote and Levine (2002) define identity capital as "investment individuals make and have in who they are" (p. 147). Therefore, developing an ego identity allows one to maintain positive interactions with community members in order to reap the benefits of social capital resources inherent in communities of support.

The four elements of social capital described above—information, influence, social credentials, and identity reinforcement—may explain why social capital appears to work in instrumental and expressive actions (for example, finding better jobs) not accounted for by forms of personal capital such as economic capital and human capital (Lin, 2001). The assertion here is that whom you know may exert greater power than what you know and that education and training may be less of a negotiating chip than whom you know. However, Wilson (1996) reminds us that poor people do not form or participate in the same kinds of networks as the non-poor and are often denied access to networks of power and information that are critical to their development.

THE DOWNSIDES OF SOCIAL CAPITAL

Despite the impressive and positive outcomes associated with social capital, some have brought attention to its downsides (Bordieu, 1986; Lin, 2001; Portes & Landolt, 1996). For example, Bourdieu, whose work focuses on the roots of social inequality, argues that social capital is distributed unevenly among people who possess different economic and cultural capitals. In other words, what he argues is that one's access to social capital resources and the nature of the social capital are structurally determined by the social position one occupies. As a result, groups in the top hierarchal positions can use their social capital to exclude others and deny them opportunities that limit their social mobility, thus contributing to intergenerational inequalities (Alfred, 2009).

Similarly, Portes and Landolt (1996) caution that we should not overlook the downside of the social capital that assumes that community members are homogenous, and everyone equally benefits from social capital resources. Portes (1998) identified four negative consequences of social capital: (1) the exclusion of outsiders, (2) excess claims on group members; (3) restriction on individual freedom, and (4) downward leveling of norms. In speaking of social capital as an exclusionary resource, Portes notes, "the strong ties that bring benefits to members of a group commonly enable it to bar others from access" (1988, p. 15). These negative consequences can occur among ethnic, gender, religious, or professional groups, to name a few, where any of these constructs is the glue that brings and keeps people together, thus making the network inaccessible to those who do not meet the criteria for belonging. In discussing the downward level of norms, Portes and Landolt use the case of Latinos in Florida to speak to the negative social capital found in certain networks (for example, inner city youth gangs and mafia families) that lead to a downward economic and sociocultural spiral among individuals, families, and communities.

There is a dilemma when the trust of social capital is extended only to immediate family members, blood relatives, and members of an exclusive ethnic group. Woolcock (1998) sees this form of social capital as an "excess of community" built on such fierce ethnic loyalties and familial attachment that discourages members from advancing economically, moving geographically, or engaging in amicable dispute resolution with outsiders. Referred to as "amoral familism" (Woolcock, 1998), this form of social capital network is characterized by the presence of social integration but the absence of social linkages, often found in poor communities. In such communities, there is strong integration and bonding among community members, but linkages to more powerful networks with information and other resources that can help improve the economic outcomes of individuals and groups are often lacking. Thus, Woolcock and Narayan (2000) suggest that for better economic prospects for economically disadvantaged individuals, linkage needs to be combined with integration. Strong intra-community ties, or high levels of integration, can be highly beneficial to the extent that they are complimented by some form of linking networks with those of influence, knowledge, and power.

Moreover, for more than a couple of decades, researchers have shown that in order for those in poverty to turn the odds around in favor of economic self-sufficiency, there need to be effective and creative approaches in training and education programs designed for that segment of the population. In the late 1980s, for instance, Kerka (1989) argued that poor, single mothers with low literacy skills face barriers that are so overwhelming that literacy and job training programs can no longer maintain focus on literacy as an isolated goal. Many have advocated for networks of support in workplaces and communities to bolster an individual's efforts to overcome challenges to economic well-being.

IS EDUCATION AND TRAINING ENOUGH TO ALLEVIATE ECONOMIC DISPARITIES?

> This is the story of how some socially disadvantaged people try to become employed and can't, because they fall for the policy line. It is the story of their struggles and failure to meet society's expectations of what it is to be literate, confident, and employed. These long-term unemployed people try to gain an education and qualifications that will act as the ticket to a job. They repeatedly follow the 'right' procedures, they access and attempt to access courses that show them how to get jobs, and how to acquire the skills for those jobs, only to have the doors shut, the courses gone or inaccessible, the jobs not there, the promises broken, and then have the threat of their allowance being cut for 'being illiterate'. When they hear of networks that include employed people, they find that those people did not, in recent times at least, get their jobs by joining the employment agency queues. Society and the government blame these unemployed people. It's their own fault—who else's fault could it be? These long term unemployed believe 'the policy line'—that training—even lifelong learning—is likely to result in employment. (Falk, 2000, p. 1)

Falk has poignantly captured the realities of low-wage workers, who because they are rendered dispensable, frequently find themselves in unemployment lines and at the mercy of various social service agencies in search of physical and financial resources to meet basic needs. Many believe in the value of education and training or human capital development and, therefore, participate in these activities with the belief that such efforts will be rewarded with sustainable employment that pays at least a living wage. Moreover, discussions of human capital accumulation occurs frequently in recent literature of human resource development (Garavan, Morley, Gunnigle, & Collins, 2001; Kerka, 2000). Bullock, Stallybrass, and Trombley (1988) define human capital as the ability, skills, and knowledge of individuals used to produce goods and services. Therefore, human resource development

(HRD) can be a major vehicle for increasing human capital by providing training and other learning activities to organizational members. Moreover, human capital theory suggests that lifelong learning is inevitable in an ever-changing and global economy. Accordingly, a number of training models of HRD practice demonstrate that an investment in human resources is necessary to build the resources of the future and to retain the resources of the present (Garavan et al., 2001). There is the assumption, then, that an investment in education and training enhances individual competencies, develops organizational competencies, and promotes individual employability (Falk, 2001). This argument suggests that investing in the human capital of low-income and low-literate adults benefits the individuals, the employing organization, and the nation at large and thus increases the individual's ability to negotiate his or her worth in the labor market. However, as much of the current literature suggests, efforts at literacy education and job skills training are not enough to move individuals out of poverty, and it will take an additional investment of social capital to help low-income and low-literate individuals improve their economic positions.

As Balatti and Falk (2001) also argue, "The skills and knowledge of 'human capital' are only able to be brought into socio-economic circulation through social means" (p. 3). What they are suggesting is that, along with education and training that promotes human capital, there must be networks of social support or social capital resources to help transform these acquired skills and knowledge into marketable commodities. Consequently, there must be an emphasis on investments in social capital resources.

To demonstrate the value of social capital, Falk (2000) reported on a study conducted to determine the ways in which unemployed adults were experiencing the phenomenon of unemployment in an era when training for the unemployed was changing rapidly in Australia. His study supported the well-established notion that low-literate, low-income workers perceive that increasing their basic literacy skills of reading, writing, and numeracy as well as developing some form of employment skills are at the core of improving their life's chances. They also believe that the more education and training one has, the better their chances of getting a job that pays a living wage. However, Falk's study revealed that the participants also realized the limitations of education and training in their attempts to develop themselves economically. While they had access to training, not all realized the promise of the job that they anticipated upon completion of the training program. This dilemma is highlighted in the comments of one of his participants, a 20-year-old unemployed worker who said,

> There is work in building areas, but that's only if you are 'in the know.' You've got to know somebody in the business or something like that. Or there is work in hospitality, because it's quite a big market. But a lot of those jobs

> are already taken by family members and stuff like that. This is a big part of employment as a whole, that you have to be in the know before you can get a job, no matter how much training you've had, or what education you've done. (cited in Falk, 2000, p. 10)

The perceptions of this young unemployed worker support the thesis that education and training or the building of human capital is not enough to move one to a position of economic self-sufficiency. Therefore, despite the downside of social capital, when complemented with human capital, it can serve as a catalyst for helping low-income adults find employment and develop their economic potential. The challenge, then, is how to promote social capital among low-literate and low-income adults. Since many low-income workers choose voluntarily or are mandated to participate in education and training programs and to find employment, educational institutions and workplace organizations are ideal sites for the development of social capital.

Adult Education, Adult Learning, and Social Capital

Falk and Kilpatrick (2000) suggest that social capital results from learning interactions that take place in a social, political, and cultural context. Fundamental characteristics of these interactions are reciprocity, trust, and shared norms and values. The more frequent the learning interactions, they theorize, the greater the capacity to accumulate social capital resources. Accordingly, Falk and Kilpatrick suggest that a precondition to building social capital is the existence of a sufficient quantity and quality of learning interactions. Therefore, Alfred (2009) suggests that in designing adult learning programs, instructors can plan to maximize learning interactions, thus helping learners build social capital resources within and outside the immediate learning community.

According to Field (2005), social capital theory calls for a constructivist view of learning and brings attention to the ways in which people learn and construct knowledge as a result of their interactions with homogeneous and heterogeneous network communities. He distinguishes between learning from everyday social interactions and formal education. He writes, "The concept of learning is very different from the concept of education, and people's active engagement in the wider social context is an extremely important aspect of the distinction between the two" (Field, 2005, p. 3). Therefore, the concept of learning should be broadened to include not only formal learning but also to include learning that takes place in networks and communities.

Community education is a well-accepted context for adult learning, and the concept of lifelong learning has taken education beyond the formal institution and into other less formal settings. What remains unexplored is the way in which social networks influence access to and participation in adult learning programs. For example, Field (2005) asks,

> How do social networks help us create and exchange skills, knowledge and attitudes that in turn allow us to tap in to other benefits? If we have more social capital—stronger and more extensive network ties—then are we more likely to learn new things than people with less social capital? And is our learning affected by the types of network that people have—are they qualitatively different in nature? (para. 2)

We often speak of learning communities and communities of practice; therefore, these questions are central to the discourse on learning communities consisting of social networks and the dynamics of interactions. They beg us to consider whether some social arrangements are better than others in promoting learning and, also, what kinds of arrangements are more suitable for different learners and contexts. Despite the unanswered questions, there is the general agreement that adult education can serve as an avenue or the development of social capital (Alfred, 2009).

Building Social Capital in Adult Education

According to Balatti and Falk (2001), using and building social capital are both outcomes of learning as well as the processes by which learning occurs. For learners to develop social capital in the classroom, the authors note, learners must be able and willing to interact in new ways, in new contexts, and with new people. The argument being made is that an individual's knowledge and skills are not enough to develop social capital relationships; the norms of the group within which the resources circulate play a crucial role.

Alfred (2009) maintains that building a classroom community that emphasizes shared norms, mutual respect, and collaboration that fosters bridging across differences holds promise for the building of social networks that can benefit learner participants in both psychosocial and instrumental ways. For example, group learning is a common feature of adult education pedagogy. What often begins as a learning activity at times extends into supportive networks in and out of the classroom. Important information beyond curricular content is often exchanged among group members. For example, how one can access community resources like childcare, housing, and transportation is often information shared among low-income workers in a classroom setting. Moreover, many career opportunities have resulted from relationships that begin as a result of collaborative learning arrangements. For example, in a study of social capital among women learners in ten adult education programs in Australia, Balatti and Falk (2001) found the programs, consisting of faculty, staff, and students, became fertile ground for social capital development. The programs were deliberately designed to create the conditions that encouraged participants to develop trust, norms, and relationships—the building blocks necessary for social capital to develop.

Adult education can also help learners develop linking ties with other networks and capitalize on the resources of these external networks. As an example, instructors can invite professionals from community and workplace organizations to serve as guest teachers, facilitators, or presenters, thus providing opportunities for students to learn and interact with professionals beyond their immediate circles. These interactions can provide instrumental benefits in terms of career and other learning opportunities and can provide immediate access to jobs through the help of organizational members. In summary, while there are inherent risks with social capital networks, with deliberate intent, the classroom and the adult leaning program can foster social capital development whereby learners can capitalize on the resources to improve their living conditions and those of partner members.

Building Social Capital in the Workplace: The Role of Mentoring

One strategy that has been found critical to employment sustainability is that of workplace socialization through mentoring and coaching (Alfred & Martin, 2007; D'Amico, 1999; Ragins, 1995). As D'Amico (1999) notes, "Part of the difference in training and career paths lies in social networks that are accessible to individuals of different race and class status" (p. 7). Also, Schneider (1997) found a lack of socialization and network affiliations to contribute to the dramatic differences in career and training paths across race, nationality, and gender. Her study looked at the experiences of men and women with different racial, ethnic, educational backgrounds and career paths in the city of Philadelphia labor market. Using a social network survey, the study focused on the relationship between work experience, training, and the people and organizations welfare recipients use as resources in order to find jobs and educational programs (Schneider, 1997). Her study found that 83% of the 338 respondents had attended a prior training program and had returned for retraining as a result of being out of work or were looking for better employment opportunities. The participants included low-skilled and low-literate adults who, despite the trainings, had difficulty moving out of low-wage work. The study found that enriching social networks through mentoring or buddy programs helps some people improve their economic situation (Schneider, 1997). This report supports findings from a study on welfare reform and employment retention and advancement in Wisconsin by Alfred and Martin (2007) that revealed that employers and employment counselors at welfare reform agencies have a high level of confidence in mentoring programs, especially worksite mentoring programs. Respondents from the two groups rated this program to be quite effective in employment placement, retention, and promotion, but only 22% of employers sampled had mentoring programs in the workplace (Alfred & Martin, 2007). Given the high level of confidence expressed in these programs, employers could make them an important strategy to assist low-income workers in forming networking relationships with employees who are in more powerful positions within the organization. Such bridging relationships (Putnam, 2000) have been found to significantly increase employment and other opportunities for economically disadvantged individuals. As a result, employers should seriously consider making them a strategy for workplace socialization and, hence, individual, group, and organizational performance improvement.

In addition, since many low-literate workers, particulary former welfare recipients, lack consistent job experience, and some have expressed an initial fear of entering the workplace (Alfred, 2007), mentoring and other socialization programs could assist this group of workers in attaching themselves to the workplace with greater ease. Ragins (1995) notes that mentoring relatonships can help meet both career development and psychosocial needs. From a career development perspective, mentoring can involve coaching, sponsoring advancement, protecting proteges from adverse forces, providing challenging assignments, and fostering visibility. From a psychosocial perspective, she notes, mentoring can provide personal support, friendship, acceptance, counseling, and role modeling. Mentoring in and out of the workplace provides an important avenue for low-income workers to form relationships with other individuals who are outside of their familial networks (Woolcock, 1998), as these have been found to limit opportunities for career advancement and social mobility among socially disadvantaged groups.

In summary, while education and training are important steps in buiding economic independence, the research has shown that these alone are inadequate for building economic capital among low-income, low-literate, and low-skilled adults. Social capital, when combined with human capital, has been found to produce better results in job access, retention, and promotion. Thefore, educators, human resource developers, and policy makers need to move beyond the ideology that basic education and short-term job training will move low-literate and low-income workers into a position of economic self-sufficiency.

REFERENCES

Alfred, M. (2007). Welfare reform and black women's economic development. *Adult Education Quarterly, 57*(4), 293–311.

Alfred, M. V. (2009). Social capital theory: Implications for women's networking and learning. In C. R. Nanton & M. V. Alfred (Eds.), *Social capital and women's support systems: Networking, learning, and surviving* (pp. 3–12). San Francisco, CA: Jossey-Bass.

Alfred, M., & Martin. L. G. (2007). The development of economic self-sufficiency among

former welfare recipients: Lesson from Wisconsin's welfare to work program. *International Journal of Training and Development, 11*(1), 2–19.

Ballati, J., & Falk, I. (2001). *Economic contributions of adult learning to community: A social capital perspective.* CLRA Discussion Paper. Tasmania University, Launceston, Australia: Center for Research and Learning in Regional Australia.

Bourdieu, P. (1986). The forms of capital. In J. G. Richardson (Ed.), *The handbook of theory and research for sociology of education* (pp. 241–258). New York: Greenwood Press.

Bourdieu, P. (1977). Cultural reproduction and social reproduction. In J. Karabel & A. H. Halsey (Eds.), *Power and ideology in education* (pp. 487–511). New York: Oxford University Press.

Bullock, A., Stallybrass, O., & Trombley, S. (Eds.). (1988). *The Fontana dictionary of modern thought* (2nd ed.). London: Fontana.

Coleman, J. S. (1988). Social capital in the creation of human capital. *American Journal of Sociology, 94,* 95–120.

Coleman, J. S. (1998). *Foundations of social theory.* Cambridge, MA: Belknap Press.

Cote , J. E., & Levine, C. (2002). *Identity formation, agency, and culture.* Mahwah, NJ: Erlbaum.

D'Amico, D. (1999). *Politics, policy, practice, and personal responsibility: Adult education in an era of welfare reform.* NCSALL Report #10. (ERIC Document Reproduction Service, No. ED 440254)

Falk, I. (2000, February). Slight of hand: Literacy, social capital and social disadvantage. Paper presented at the Adult Literacy and Numeracy Australian Research Consortium. Melbourne, Australia.

Falk, I. (2001). *Slight of hand: Job myths, literacy and social capital.* Discussion Paper No. D14/2001. Tasmania University, Launceston, Australia: Center for Research and Learning in Regional Australia.

Falk, I., & Kilpatrick, S. (2000). What is social capital? A study of rural communities. *Sociologia Rurlis, 40*(1), 87–110.

Field, J. (2005). *Social capital and lifelong learning.* Bristol, UK: The Policy Press.

Garavan, T. N., Morley, M., Gunnigle, P., & Collins, E. (2001). Human capital accumulation: The role of human resource development. *Journal of European Industrial Training, 25*(2/3/4), 48–68.

Kerka, S. (2000). *Lifelong learning: Myths and realities No. 9.* (ERIC Document Reproduction Service No. 441180). Columbus, OH: ERIC Clearinghouse on Adult, Career, and Vocational Education.

Kerka, S. (1989). *Women, work, and literacy.* (ERIC Document Reproduction Service No. ED 312456). Columbus, OH: ERIC Clearinghouse on Adult, Career, and Vocational Education, Center and Training for Empowerment.

Lin, N. (2001). Building a network theory of social capital. In N. Lin, K. Cook, & R. S. Burt (Eds.), *Social capital: Theory and research* (pp. 3–29). New Brunswick, NJ: Transaction Publishers.

Moser, C. (1996). Development focus: How the urban poor manage in an economic crisis. *Finance and Development, 33*(4), 42–44.

Portes, A. (1998). Social capital: Its origins and applications to modern sociology. *Annual Review of Sociology, 24,* 1–24.

Portes, A., & Landolt, P. (1996). The downside of social capital. *The American Prospect, 26,* 18–24.

Putnam, R. D. (2000). *Bowling alone: The collapse and revival of American community.* New York: Simon and Schuster.

Ragins, B. R. (1995). Diversity, power, and mentorship in organizations: A cultural, structural, and behavioral perspective. In M. M. Chemers, S. Oskamp, & M. A. Costanzo (Eds.), *Diversity in organizations: New perspectives for a changing workplace* (pp. 91–132). Thousand Oaks, CA: Sage Publications.

Sandefur, R. L., & Laumann, E. O. (2000). A paradigm for social capital. In E. L. Lesser (Ed.), *Knowledge and social capital* (pp. 69–86). London: Butterworth-Heinemann.

Seibel, H. D. (2001). Rural finance: Mainstreaming informal financial institutions. *Journal of Development Entrepreneurship, 6*(1), 83–95.

Schneider, A. A. (1997). *Social networks, career and training paths for participants in education and training programs: Technical report.* ERIC Document Reproduction Service (No. ED 449296). Retrieved March 6, 2010, from http://www.eric.ed.gov/ERICDocs/data/ericdocs2sql/content_storage_01/0000019b/80/16/ce/08.pdf

Wilson, W. J. (1996). W*hen work disappears: The world of the new urban poor.* New York: Knopf.

Woolcock, M. (1998). Social capital and economic development: Towards a theoretical synthesis and policy framework. *Theory and Society, 27,* 151–208.

Woolcock, M. (2001). The place of social capital in understanding social and economic outcomes. *ESUMA: Canadian Journal of Policy and Research* 2(1), 1–17.

Woolcock, M., & Narayan, D. (2000). Social capital: Implications for development theory, research, and policy. *The World Bank Research Observer, 15*(2), 225–249.

ABOUT THE CONTRIBUTORS

Mary V. Alfred is associate professor of adult education and associate dean for faculty affairs in the College of Education and Human Development at Texas A&M University. Her research interests include learning and development among women of the African Diaspora, sociocultural contexts of learning, welfare reform and economic disparities among low-income adults, and issues of equity and social justice in higher education and in the workplace. Her most recent book (edited with Carmela Nanton) is *Social Capital and Women's Support Systems: Networking, Learning, and Surviving,* (San Francisco: Jossey-Bass, 2009). Other recent work appeared in *Adult Education Quarterly, International Journal of Training and Development,* and *The Western Journal of Black Studies.*

Irene C. Baird, Affiliate Professor of Education, is director of the Penn State Harrisburg Women's Enrichment Center. She is the author of *Unlocking the Cell,* an AAACE-published monograph of her model of a humanities-oriented/Freirian-inspired program she uses in her prison groups. Her research interests focus on the education of prisoners, abusive relationships and social justice issues.

Laura L. Bierema is professor, University of Georgia, College of Education, Department of Lifelong Education, Administration and Policy, Programs in Adult Education and Human Resource & Organization Development. Her research interests include workplace learning, career development, women's development, organization development, and critical human resource development. She is the editor of *Women's Career Development across the Lifespan: Insights and Strategies for Women, Organizations, and Adult Educators;*

Learning for Economic Self-Sufficiency, pages 229–233

co-author of *Philosophy and Practice of Organizational Learning, Performance and Change;* co-editor of *Critical Issues in Human Resource Development;* and author of the forthcoming, *Implementing a Critical Approach to Organization Development.*

Dominique T. Chlup is an Assistant Professor of Adult Education at Texas A&M University. She's a graduate of Harvard University where her research focused on the history of corrections education for women. Her research interests include women and prison, gender and education, and adult literacies.

Deryl Davis Fulmer is Associate Vice President for Learner Success at Madison Area Technical College. She works closely with workforce efforts including efforts addressing dislocated workers and other adult returning students, continuing education, curriculum and innovation initiatives. She received her Ph.D. in Urban Education/Administrative Leadership and Supervision with an emphasis in Adult and Continuing Education from the University of Wisconsin-Milwaukee. She has been in the Wisconsin Technical College System since 2000 and has served in numerous capacities, including teaching throughout her tenure at two-year institutions. She has been an adjunct faculty member at the University of Wisconsin-Milwaukee, School of Education since 1995. Dr. Davis Fulmer was an ACE Fellow during 2005–2006 and spent her fellowship year at North Carolina A&T State University, Greensboro, NC.

Noelle R. Eason, M.A., is a doctoral candidate in Educational Psychology: Hispanic Bilingual Education at Texas A&M University. She has 9 years of foreign language instruction experience at the university level. Her research interests include measurement and assessment within Hispanic Bilingual Education programs with specific interest in school finance. In addition to finishing writing her dissertation, which examines the funding equity of Bilingual Education programs in Texas, and she currently works as a research assistant for the Dean's Office in the College of Education and Human Resource Development at Texas A&M University.

Janet Groen is an Associate Professor in Workplace and Adult Learning. Her research focuses on transformational learning and learning opportunities for marginalized non-traditional adult learners. Her other area of research explores the link between spirituality and adult learning within various contexts such as the workplace and the university.

Shibao Guo is an associate professor in the Faculty of Education, University of Calgary. He is an affiliated researcher with the Prairie Metropolis Centre of Excellence for Research on Immigration, Integration, and Diversity

(MPC). His research interests include comparative and international education, citizenship and immigration, social justice and equity in education, adult education and community development. His recent works appeared in the *International Journal of Lifelong Education*, *Canadian Journal for the Study of Adult Education*, *Diaspora, Indigenous, and Minority Education*, and *Frontiers of Education in China*.

Catherine A. Hansman is professor of Adult Learning and Development at Cleveland State University. As a Cyril O. Houle Kellogg Research Scholar, she has received a Cleveland State University Distinguished Faculty Award for Research; she chaired the Commission of Professors of Adult Education from 2004–2006, and she is currently the President of the American Association for Adult and Continuing Education (AAACE).

Lilian H. Hill is currently Associate Professor of Adult Education and Program Coordinator for the Adult and Higher Education programs at the University of Southern Mississippi. In recent years, her publications have revolved around the intersection between adult learning and health. Translating discussions in the healthcare world regarding health literacy, cultural competence, and healthcare disparities to education prepares a path for adult educators wishing to form partnerships between the healthcare and adult education sectors to address low health literacy and health disparities.

Tara Hyland-Russell is Associate Professor of English at St. Mary's University College, Calgary AB. Her work focuses on gender and genre as she explores how people "re-story" their lives. She has published articles on contemporary art books; transforming grief and loss through an autobiography of healing; and transformative adult education.

E. Paulette Isaac is an associate professor of Adult Education at the University of Missouri-St. Louis. She currently serves as chair of the Division of Educational Leadership and Policy Studies in the College of Education. Her research interests include adult education in the African American church, African American adult education, adult learning, and educational gerontology. She is a past editor of *Adult Learning*, a publication of the American Association for Adult and Continuing Education, and currently serves as a reviewer for *Education and Urban Society*. Currently, she is conducting research examining the health promotion behaviors of African American non-custodial fathers.

Kathleen P. King, Ed.D. is professor of higher education at University of South Florida's College of Education in Tampa Florida. As an award winning author, popular keynote and conference speaker, mentor, her major areas of research and expertise include transformative learning, adult development and learning, professional development, distance learning, and instructional technology. Visit her website for contact and detailed information www.facultyspeaker.com.

Larry G. Martin is a Professor and the Director of the Urban Education Doctoral Program at the University of Wisconsin-Milwaukee. For over 25 years he has conducted research investigations and published papers concerning the development, implementation and evaluation of workforce development programs, especially as these apply to low-literate employees; curriculum development for literacy programs; and the development and assessment of diversity training programs. In 2004 he coauthored a text, "Adult Education in an Urban Context: Problems, Practices, and Programming for Inner-City Communities, New Directions for Adult and Continuing Education." He earned a Ph.D. at UW-Madison.

Liliana Mina is an assistant professor of higher education administration at the University of Wisconsin – Milwaukee. Her research examines underrepresented groups in postsecondary education, online teaching and learning, and issues affecting adult learners. Mina received her Ph.D. from Michigan State University's Higher, Adult, and Lifelong Education program.

Aida A. Nevárez-La Torre obtained her Bachelor's of Arts in English as a Second Language Education, Magna Cum Laude, from the University of Puerto Rico. She received her Master's of Science in Bilingual Education from the State University of New York at Albany. Her Doctoral Degree is in Reading from Harvard Graduate School of Education. She worked as an ESL and bilingual education teacher in Puerto Rico and the United States. She is currently an associate professor of TESOL and heads the Office of Multilingual Education at Fordham University in New York City. She is also the senior editor of the Journal of Multilingual Education Research, affiliated with the New York State Association for Bilingual Education.

Jennifer A. Sandlin is an Assistant professor in the School of Social Transformation at Arizona State University in Tempe, where she teaches courses focused on consumption and education, cultural studies, and curriculum studies. Her research interests include adult education, public pedagogy, popular culture, informal learning, and various sites of ideological education for children, youth, and adults. Her recent work investigates consumer education, broadly defined, and she is especially interested in sites of public pedagogy, informal learning, and anti-consumption social activism that question the norms of consumption, create resistance to consumer culture, and focus on "unlearning" consumerism. She recently co-edited, with Peter McLaren, *Critical Pedagogies of Consumption: Living and Learning in the*

Shadow of the Shopocalypse (2010, Routledge); and, with Brian Schultz and Jake Burdick, the *Handbook of Public Pedagogy: Education and Learning Beyond Schooling* (2010, Routledge).

Regina O. Smith is an Assistant Professor in the Department of Administrative Leadership in the School of Education at the University of Wisconsin-Milwaukee. She teaches courses in adult education, including adult and organizational learning, adult and organizational development, program planning, administration of adult education programs, education of older adults, teaching multiculture and special needs adults, and courses related to the Technical College System. Her research interests are students' experiences in online collaborative groups, workforce development and other learning for work issues.

CPSIA information can be obtained at www.ICGtesting.com
Printed in the USA
LVOW090812040512

280267LV00002B/4/P

9 781617 351105